Bartolomeo Platina:
Lives of the Popes
Paul II

An Intermediate Reader of Renaissance Latin

Latin Text with Running Vocabulary and Commentary

Thomas G. Hendrickson
Alexandra B. Berman
Pascal Croak
Daniel Gridley
Sebastian Herrera
Jin Lee
Graham Rigby
John Robinson
Gabriela C. Sommer
Kent Ueno
James Whittemore

Bartolomeo Platina: Lives of the Popes, Paul II: An Intermediate Reader of Renaissance Latin: Latin Text with Running Vocabulary and Commentary

First Edition

ISBN-10: 1940997968

ISBN-13: 9781940997964

Published by Faenum Publishing, Ltd.

Cover Design: Evan Hayes

Fonts: Garamond

editor@faenumpublishing.com

TABLE OF CONTENTS

Acknowledgments

We would like to thank Dartmouth College and its Classics Department, which provided the opportunity for the authors to come together on this project under the auspices of a Renaissance Latin seminar organized by Hendrickson. The Whiting Foundation furnished support for Hendrickson to undertake preparatory work at the Ludwig Boltzmann Institute for Neo-Latin Studies, and we are grateful for the generosity of both institutions. We also owe a debt of thanks to the Renaissance Society of America, whose Paul Oskar Kristeller grant afforded Hendrickson the chance to examine the manuscripts in Italy.

Introduction

1. The need for a student edition of Platina's *Paul II*

Renaissance Latin has become a burgeoning field. The historical importance and literary quality of Renaissance Latin (or Neo-Latin, as it is also called) is more apparent than ever. As the field has grown, its scholarly resources have grown as well. The I Tatti series has been publishing facing Latin/English editions (similar to Loebs), and many scholars have been making critical editions of the texts that have never been edited. Four major handbooks have appeared in the last four years: *Brill's Encyclopaedia of the Neo-Latin World*, the *Oxford Handbook of Neo-Latin*, the *Geschichte der neulateinischen Literatur*, and the *Guide to Neo-Latin Literature*. Pedagogical resources have not kept pace.

There is an almost shocking lack of tools for intermediate Latinists and those who teach them. The bilingual I Tatti volumes represent a big step forward in making Renaissance Latin texts available, but they lack grammatical and lexical explanations. Moreover, many teachers (and students) find it counter-productive to be looking constantly at a translation as they try to read the Latin. As for texts geared specifically toward intermediate readers of Latin, they can be counted on one hand.[1] Given the abundance and variety of Latin works from the Renaissance, these few (excellent) editions seem a small party. Many students would enjoy reading Latin from the Renaissance, and many teachers would enjoy bringing it into the classroom. Such Latinists form the primary audience for this text. There may also be some scholars and students of the Renaissance who have only a basic level of Latin, and it is hoped that they too might find it to be of some use.

For the Latinist interested in expanding her base of knowledge to include humanism and the Renaissance, there are few better texts than Platina's *Life of Paul II*. The *Paul II* is part of Platina's larger *Lives of the Popes*, which was a kind of "national history" (to abuse the term) for the Renaissance Papacy.[2] Platina's *Paul*

---

1 A few notable examples: the *Bryn Mawr Latin Commentaries* series has editions of Petrarch's *Selected Letters* (2002, ed. C. Kallendorf) and Erasmus's *Praise of Folly* (1991, ed. J. Collins); Bolchazy-Carducci has a *Latin of New Spain* reader (2016, ed. R. Williams) and the *Introduction to Latin Prose Composition, from Antiquity to the Renaissance* (2004, ed. Minkova and Tunberg) and Sophron has The Neo-Latin Reader (2016, M. Riley).

2 Anthony D'Elia is producing a version of the *Lives of the Popes* (in three volumes) for I Tatti (see bibliography), whose completion we eagerly await. We felt that an intermediate reader, with grammatical aids and without a translation, would still have its own value.

II introduces readers to key institutions like the Papal Curia and the Roman Academy. The text is animated by the controversies stemming from the rediscovery of classical literature. These controversies involve such issues as homoeroticism, republicanism, and disputes about the immortality of the soul.

In Platina's telling, the defining controversy of Paul's pontificate was his conflict with the humanists of Rome. Paul imprisoned and tortured the members of the Roman Academy, accusing them of treason and heresy. The humanists were eventually freed, and among them was Platina himself, Paul's future biographer. A remarkable aspect of Platina's *Paul II* is that the author himself is a character in the story. Indeed, the biographer's conflicts with his subject frame the narrative. The story begins with Paul's dismissal of Platina and the other *abbreviatores* (many of them humanists) from the Papal Curia; the climax of the *Life* is the confrontation between the biographer and his subject over the meaning and value of humanism, and over its compatibility with Christianity.

2. Bartolomeo Platina and his clash with Paul II[3]

Bartolomeo Sacchi (1421-1481) took the name "Platina" from his hometown of Piadena. He spent four years as a mercenary, serving under the *condottieri* Francesco Sforza and Niccolò Piccinino.[4] Platina subsequently studied and taught in Mantua at the school that Vittorino da Feltre had started a generation earlier. There he developed a relationship with the ruling Gonzaga family, whose members would act as his patrons throughout his life. Platina next went to Florence in order to improve his Greek by studying under John Argyropoulos. In 1462 he came to Rome where he bought a position as an abbreviator.

It was Platina's work as an abbreviator that first brought him into conflict with Paul II. The abbreviators worked in the chancery (*Cancellaria Apostolica*), where they had a role in the drafting of papal bulls (*litterae apostolicae*).[5] The practice of buying and selling (non-spiritual) positions had been steadily becoming more prevalent in the Papal Curia, as it had in secular courts as well. Platina had been hired by Pope Pius II (born Enea Silvio Piccolomini), who was himself a humanist and who, in taking the name Pius, became *Pius Aeneas* (Enea). Paul II (Pietro Barbo), who succeeded Pius II in 1464, dismissed the abbreviators whom Pius had hired. They would be reimbursed what they had paid for the office, but they

---

3   This treatment owes much to Bauer (2006: 1-88), who provides a thorough study of Platina's life and works, and to D'Elia (2009), who focuses more specifically on Platina's clash with Paul II.

4   *Condottieri* were mercenary generals, many of whom were feudal lords in their own right.

5   For a more thorough background on the Papal Curia and the positions taken by humanists, see D'Amico 1983: 19-37.

were stripped of their jobs. Platina was furious. He tried to bring Paul to trial and, failing that, threatened to call a Church council.[6] The Council of Constance (1414-1418) had deposed three popes, ending the Western Schism, which some saw as a precedent for the superiority of councils over popes (a position called "conciliarism"). Paul responded by imprisoning Platina in Castel Sant'Angelo, though Platina was released four months later through the intercession of Cardinal Francesco Gonzaga, who had been his student in Mantua.

Platina's second, and more serious, clash with Paul came four years later. This clash was bound up with his involvement in the Roman Academy. Platina was one of the leading members of the Roman Academy, which was an informal group of men who shared an interest in ancient Rome, its language, and its material remains. The Academy had been started by Pomponio Leto, who had come to Rome to study under Lorenzo Valla. Valla was the humanist who had used his philological skill to expose the Donation of Constantine as a forgery. Leto himself later became a professor at the University of Rome. Another major figure in the Roman Academy was Filippo Buonaccorsi, also known as Callimachus. Academy members met in Leto's home to discuss ancient literature and philosophy, as well as their own literary compositions.

Not all observers would have seen the activities of this Academy as unobjectionable. Among the poems composed, several expressed homoerotic desire, and Pomponio Leto was later arrested for sodomy in Venice. Leto also encouraged members to take on ancient Roman names, which some critics argued was a rejection of Christianity on the grounds that it was a rejection of the names of saints.[7] Certain members of the Academy had been known to voice anti-clerical sentiments—especially Callimachus, and especially when he had been drinking.

Humanism itself, it should be stressed, was not anti-Christian in nature. Indeed, it was a thoroughly Christian phenomenon. Petrarch, who was among the earliest and most famous humanists, was a monk who took seriously his identity as a Christian. Moreover, the Papal Curia had employed many of the most prominent humanists, like Leonardo Bruni, Poggio Bracciolini, and Lorenzo Valla—all of whom served as apostolic secretaries. Humanism was a reawakening of interest in ancient Rome, especially its language and literature. A central preoccupation of humanism was the recovery of Classical Latin, which had been lost over the course of the Middle Ages. Indeed, the very idea that there is such a thing as "Classical Latin" is a notion that we owe to humanism.

---

6   Platina narrates these events in chapters 12-18 of his *Paul II*.

7   Leto's birth name was Giulio Sanseverino, and he himself took the name Julius Pomponius Laetus, although he is commonly referred to by the Italianized version of that name: (Giulio) Pomponio Leto. Platina recounts the accusation that using ancient names was a rejection of Christianity in chapters 56 and 66 of *Paul II*.

A passion for Latin was not incompatible with Christianity, yet humanists also showed a pronounced enthusiasm for other aspects of Ancient Rome, some of which were contrary to the values of fifteenth-century Christianity. Aside from the different sexual *mores* and the traditional Roman religion(s), there was also the matter of philosophy. The rediscovery of Lucretius, who presented a compelling and alluring case for ignoring the gods, was especially problematic. In addition, there was the republicanism of ancient authors. The works of Livy, Sallust, and Cicero all celebrated Rome as a republic. These sentiments would have been unwelcome to the theocratic monarchy of the Papal Curia.

In 1468, Paul received word that the members of the Roman Academy had formed a conspiracy with his enemies and were plotting his violent overthrow. It was said that they had conspired with Luca Tozzoli, an exile living in Naples, who was at that very moment hiding outside the city with armed men. Callimachus fled, and Pomponio Leto was already on trial in Venice, though he was later extradited. Platina was immediately arrested, along with other members of the Roman Academy.

Rumors of a conspiracy were not to be dismissed lightly. Paul's uncle, Pope Eugene IV, had to flee Rome after an uprising in 1434 and was not able to return for almost ten years. The year 1452 saw another revolt against papal rule, this time with one rebel, Stefano Porcari, explicitly articulating his motivation as a desire to return to the republican values and government of Antiquity. In 1460, just four years before Paul's pontificate, a group of young Romans under a man named Tiburzio took control of the city while Pope Pius II was out of town.

Conspirators often relied on help from outside powers who would benefit from the pope's downfall. In the rebellion of 1434, Francesco Sforza of Milan briefly aided the rebels, as did the *condottieri* Niccolò Fortebraccio and Niccolò Piccinino. The young rebel Tiburzio was aided by Niccolò Piccinino's son Jacopo. Pope Paul had uneasy relationships with Naples, Venice, and France. In addition, Sultan Mehmet II had taken Constantinople in 1453, and there was a constant fear that he would go farther into Europe.

In the event, the accusation of conspiracy became less convincing when a crucial tenet proved unfounded: the exiled Luca Tozzoli had never left Naples, and he was certainly not lurking outside Rome with armed men. It may be the case that the conspiracy was real, as many scholars believe. After all, Platina certainly was not above colluding with outside powers against the pope—he had called for a council when Paul had dismissed him from his job. On the other hand, it may also be the case that the humanists' treason had not extended beyond some complaints over drinks.[8] Paul, in any case, ultimately dropped the accusation of

---

8   For the narration of Platina's arrest and his defense against the charge of conspiracy, see chapters 45-54.

treason. He did not, however, release the humanists; instead, he charged them with heresy.

Platina claims that Paul charged Academy members with heresy only to keep himself from looking foolish.[9] The reports of conspiracy had stirred a panic in the city, and the Academy members had been tortured as part of the investigation. Paul risked looking both cruel and easily frightened. Despite Platina's protestations, the humanists did have some unconventional beliefs. In Platina's telling, Paul charged them with being followers of Plato, whom (Platina points out) many Christian thinkers had found acceptable. One suspects that the charge might rather have been following Epicurus. Ultimately, Paul relented on the charge of heresy as well.

3. *The Lives of the Popes*

After Paul's death in 1471, Platina enjoyed more favor with his successor, Sixtus IV. It was to Sixtus that Platina dedicated his *Lives of the Popes*, which he wrote in the years from 1472 to 1474. The authority that Jesus bestowed on the apostle Peter (Matthew 16:18-19) was the ideological cornerstone for the papacy, since the popes saw themselves as Peter's successors. Platina takes an even more expansive view of papal succession, beginning his *Lives of the Popes* not with Peter but with Jesus himself.

The *Lives* took their inspiration most obviously from Suetonius's *Lives of the Caesars*, and the choice of genre was not a coincidence. When Leonardo Bruni, the humanist from the republic of Florence, had written the *History of the Florentine People*, he followed the model of Livy, who had recounted the history and growth of the Roman republic. Platina, instead, followed Suetonius's succession of imperial leaders, even going so far as to refer to Jesus as "the emperor of the Christians" (*Vita Christi* 13).

Platina's *Lives* was not the first collection of papal biographies. The *Liber Pontificalis*, which was written intermittently over hundreds of years, contained brief sketches of the popes up to Martin V (r. 1417-1431). Platina's preface to his *Lives* suggests that the decision to take on the project was partly due to the unpleasant (to a humanist's eyes) Medieval Latin in which the *Liber Pontificalis* was written. But Platina did not merely revise the language of the *Liber Pontificalis*, he wrote an entirely new work, different in scope and drawing on a range of ancient and contemporary sources.

In the first print edition, from 1479, the last *Life* treated was that of Paul II, to which we now turn.

---

9   Platina narrates the accusations of heresy and defends himself in chapters 55-67.

4. Structure and content of *Paul II*

Platina's *Paul II* is a remarkable piece of literature. It is a biography in which the main conflict in the story takes place between the protagonist and the author himself. (And Platina is nothing if not antagonistic.) Sometimes Platina's hostility comes out in his unflattering portrayal of Paul, whom he portrays as manipulative (ch. 6-9), greedy (80), vain (71-72), and above all ignorant (2, 61-62, 65, 86). At other times, Platina becomes an actual character in the story (*Platyna*), who confronts the pope at crucial points. In one instance the two merge, and it is unclear whether the long defense against the charge of heresy (ch. 60-61) is supposed to represent the words of *Platyna* the character to Pope Paul, or the words of Platina the author to his readers.

The *Paul II* can be divided into five main sections. The first (ch. 1-11) deals with the early career of Paul II (then Pietro Barbo), and in particular his rivalry with Alovisius Patavinus. The second section (ch. 12-18) narrates Paul's dismissal of the abbreviators and Platina's response. The third section (ch. 19-41) treats a variety of events in Paul's pontificate, from navigating external wars to mediating internal feuds. Section four (ch. 42-70) recounts Paul's reaction to the alleged conspiracy. Finally (ch. 71-88), Platina sums up by commenting on Paul's appearance and habits.

Since we assume that most readers will not already be intimately familiar with the story, we provide a detailed breakdown of the chapters:

Outline of Platina's *Paul II*

I. Early Career of Pietro Barbo (Paul II)

1. Born in Venice, Pietro Barbo planned to become a merchant, until his uncle was elected pope

2. Pietro Barbo abandons his plan to be a merchant in order to prepare for an ecclesiastical career

3. Pietro quickly rises in the Church hierarchy with the help of his brother, Paolo, and of his uncle, Pope Eugene IV

4. Pietro becomes a cardinal and a rival of Alovisius Patavinus

5. Pietro and Alovisius have a bitter feud

6. When Eugene IV dies, Pietro Barbo uses charm and manipulation to insinuate himself into the good graces of the new pope, Nicholas V

73. Paul also favored extravagant dress for the cardinals; some believed this splendor did not serve Christianity

74. Paul had even promised summer palaces for all the cardinals, although he did not actually provide them

75. Paul attempted to increase papal glory through influence and arms. The first example of the former is his mediation of a dispute between the Duke of Burgundy and the People of Liège

76. The second example of an attempt to increase papal power through influence: Paul deposed the Hussite King of Bohemia; he unsuccessfully tried to replace him with Mathias Corvinus

77. First example of an attempt to increase papal power through arms: Paul unsuccessfully besieged Tolfa before buying its loyalty

78. Second example of an attempt to increase papal power through arms: Paul besieged Rimini but failed to take it due to his stinginess in paying soldiers and his indecisiveness

79. Paul had a hesitant nature, which he himself valued but which ultimately proved harmful

80. Paul was aggressive in collecting money, and his actions sometimes verged on simony

81. Paul used his money liberally, caring for those in need and assuring necessary supplies for Rome

82. Paul also used his money for building projects and popular entertainments

83. Paul was nocturnal and difficult to deal with

84. Paul had peculiar tastes in food, which might have contributed to his death

85. Paul was considered to be just and merciful

86. Paul discouraged humanistic education, favoring only practical literacy

87. Paul could be unkind to those asking favors, but he ultimately delivered more than he had promised

88. Paul kept his underlings in check, which was appreciated by the Romans and the court

5. Editorial principles I: The constitution of the text

We will be following the text of the *editio princeps* (that is, the first print edition), which was published in Venice in 1479. This approach might seem strange to an audience of classicists, and so we provide a few words of explanation.

Classical texts are usually published as critical editions that draw from multiple manuscripts. Since no autographs survive, editors make a composite text from bits and pieces of various manuscripts in an attempt to reconstruct what the author might have written. For texts from the Renaissance, however, we often have an autograph (sometimes more than one), or an *editio princeps* supervised by the author. It is possible to create a single composite text, but there is some question as to the purpose and benefits of doing so. Approaches to textual criticism are hotly debated in the Neo-Latin world, but one method would be to choose a single text and note how the others differ. Such an approach recognizes each iteration as its own coherent whole.

Platina's *Lives of the Popes* is especially unsuited to a composite critical edition. There are three manuscripts that bear corrections in Platina's hand, as well as an *editio princeps* that he himself oversaw; these four sources are not different witnesses to any single, original text, but instead show different versions that Platina composed over the course of his lifetime. In the following paragraphs, we outline the manuscript and print history of the *Lives of the Popes*, as well as the decisions that we made in establishing the text of the present edition.

Ludwig Pastor, the famous scholar of the papacy, discovered one of the manuscripts with Platina's autograph corrections in 1888. This manuscript, which is housed at the Vatican Library (Vat. Lat. 2044, referred to as V), was the dedication copy that Platina gave to Pope Sixtus IV. Pastor reports (1890) that Platina's changes to the text were concentrated in the *Life of Paul II*. Pastor observed that in these changes Platina generally walked back or lightened his criticisms of Paul, although Platina did occasionally sharpen criticisms of other figures.

Another manuscript bearing Platina's autograph corrections can be found in Rome's Angelica Library (ms. 222, referred to as A). These corrections are nearly the same as those found in V. When Giacinto Gaida made his critical edition of the *Lives of the Popes* for the *Rerum Italicarum Scriptores* series, he made use of three sources: V, A, and the *editio princeps* (referred to as E).[10]

Not long ago, there was a spectacular discovery in the Biblioteca Nazionale Centrale of Florence: the manuscript on which E was based (Conv. soppr.

---

10 Gaida (pp. lxxxv-c) describes V, A, and E, as well as later print editions and translations.

C.4.797, referred to as F).[11] F also bears autograph corrections by Platina, and its main text evidently has an earlier version of the Life than the others, since it contains a number of comments (marked for deletion) missing from the other manuscripts and left out of the *editio princeps*. Like the other marginal corrections, these changes involved a number of hostile comments that Platina had apparently decided went a step too far.

These manuscripts, and their corrections, were not all made at the same time. It is clear that the main text of F was written first, that some marginal corrections and revisions were made to F before the main texts of V and A were copied, that further marginal corrections and revisions were then made to all three manuscripts, and that F was then used to make the *editio princeps* (E).

This reader is not the place to offer a critical edition, but a new one would be welcome. Obviously, it would be good to have a text that accounts for the readings of the Florence manuscript. Beyond that, there are some serious problems with Gaida's critical edition. His edition is excellent in many respects, but there is a fundamental flaw in that his method of choosing between variants was simply to take the reading of any two of his sources over the third.[12] (Again, these sources are V, A, and E.) This method obscures the stages of change, which are distinct and important. A second problem is the presence of errors in the apparatus criticus. Any work of scholarship will have errors, but Gaida's apparatus criticus has enough to warrant a new look at the manuscripts.[13]

We had no plans to make a new critical edition, but we thought that rather than printing Gaida's mixed version of the text, we would follow one single exemplar as a coherent whole. The manuscripts show a clear editorial progression, of which the *editio princeps* is the final product. The *editio princeps*, while conveniently digitized, also had the virtue of being the version of the text that Platina decided to have widely distributed. The added and deleted comments in the manuscripts were too interesting to pass up, so we occasionally included these in our commentary, although we did not aim to be comprehensive.

---

11   The manuscript was discovered by Piero Scapecchi (1999).

12   Gaida explains his method at pp. xcviii-c of his edition.

13   We note many of these errors below in our corrections to the *editio princeps* text, notes 15-20. In addition to those noted below, the following are a few more examples: in ch. 5, Gaida (p. 366) gives *iuratur* as the reading of A, when the manuscript actually reads *inuratur*; in ch. 9, Gaida (p. 367) gives *non sine urbanitate* as the reading of both V and A, although A in fact reads *cum urbanitate*; in ch. 64, Gaida (p. 389) gives *surdafer* as the reading of A, when it appears to be *surdaster* just like V. In ch. 63, Gaida (p. 388) notes that the sentence about Leonardo of Perugia is marked for expunction in V, and that the expunction is missing in A and E. In fact, the sentence exists and has no marks for expunction in A, but is entirely left out of E. Finally, in ch. 79, Gaida gives *perposterus* as the reading of E, though it is actually *praeposterus*.

The *editio princeps* lacks chapter divisions, which we have added. The *editio princeps* also lacks printed page numbers, although hand-written folio numbers can be faintly seen on the copy digitized by Google. For folio numbers, the side of a page that a reader first encounters is numbered and referred to as the "recto"; after turning that page, the number is not usually re-written, but the page is referred as the "verso" of that number. So (e.g.) the first page of Platina's *Paul II* is on the recto of folio 231 (that is, on 231r), and the second page is then 231v. We have added the folio numbers in {curly brackets} for those who would like to make use of the digitized *editio princeps*. We have added Gaida's page numbers in [square brackets], in order to make it easier to make use of his historical notes.

We corrected several mistakes in the text of the *editio princeps*. Most of these were simple printing errors caused by a letter being left out or confused for a similar letter, and they produce a reading that is obviously wrong.[14] There are also some words that, while not obvious printer's errors, do seem to be mistakes rather than revisions. In twelve of these cases we followed the reading of the manuscripts. These include: *immiti* for an *editio princeps* reading of *inimici* (ch. 14), *ullo suo dispendio* for *ullo dispendio* (ch. 19), *vir quidem ditissimus* for *vir ditissimus quidem* (ch. 23), *fore* for *foret* (ch. 31), *diceret eum* for *diceret* (ch. 41), *tantum tumultus* for *tantum tumultum* (ch. 60), *inusta* for *iunsta* (ch. 65),[15] *negocium* for *negocii* (ch. 78), *procurante* for *procurantem* (ch. 78), *fatigatus* for *fugatus* (ch.79), *id sibi* for *ut sibi* (ch. 79), and *nepote* for *nepotes* (ch. 82).

In five places we took corrections from the important early editions of Eucharius Cervicorn (1540) and Onofrio Panvinio (1562): *mentis opinione* for a reading of *mente opinionis* in the *editio princeps* and the manuscripts (ch. 37),[16] *incitarent* for a reading of *incitaret* (ch. 56),[17] *confesso* for *confosso* (ch. 58),[18]

---

14   E.g. *ia* for *iam* (ch. 2) and *tevocas* for *revocas* (ch. 13); the most common such error is the result of putting in letters <u> and <n> upside-down, yielding such readings as *prodennte* for *prodeunte* (ch. 25) and *iucohata* for *incohata* (ch. 77). There are a dozen total of these printer's errors, which did not seem worth listing, with the exception of *iunsta* for *inusta* (see n. 15.)

15   The reading *iunsta* in E must be a typographical error for *inusta*, which is the reading of F and V. This difficult reading gave rise to several mistaken corrections. Manuscript A gives this word as *iniusta*, and the editions of Cervicorn (p. 305) and Panvino (f. 256r) read *iusta*. Gaida (p. 389) mistakenly reports *iusta* as the reading of A and V, and *iniuncta* as the reading of E.

16   The reading *mentis opinione* is found in Cervicorn (p. 301) and Panvinio (f. 253r). In this case, Gaida (p. 378) mistakenly ascribed the reading *mentis opinione* to V.

17   The reading *incitarent* is found in Cervicorn (p. 304) and Panvinio (f. 255r).

18   The reading *confesso* is found in Cervicorn (p. 304) and Panvinio (f. 255v).

Macedonianos for *Macedonios* (ch. 61),[19] and *contemnebatque* for *contemnebat* (ch. 66).[20] We also corrected *nisi* to *non nisi* (ch. 79) on the basis of sense.

6. Editorial principles II: Orthography[21]

We have largely preserved spelling conventions of the *editio princeps* rather than standardizing everything to Classical Latin.[22] Unusual spellings can be an obstacle for the intermediate reader, but the on-page running glossary should keep any confusion to a minimum. Moreover, these spelling conventions allow access to a defining feature of Renaissance Latin: the attempt (not always successful) to recover the Latinity of ancient Rome. Some non-Classical spellings are the result of changes that had happened over the course of the Middle Ages. Others are the result of hyper-correction as humanist scholars tried to restore Classical orthography. In this section, we briefly outline a few of the most commonly encountered differences between the spelling of words found in this edition and the spelling of Latin as most students will have learned it.

A. Variability between –ti and –ci

> The hard <t> in Classical Latin was palatalized in any sequence of <ti> followed by another vowel, i.e. *negotium*, resulting in a "ts" sound similar to the "zz" in "pizza" (so *negotium* was pronounced as neg-oats-ee-um). The <c> of Classical Latin had also been palatalized before <i> and <e>, with the result that <ti> and <ci> could be interchangeable, and so Platina often writes things like *negocium* (CL *negotium*) and *precium* (CL *pretium*).

---

19   The reading *Macedonianos* is found in Panvinio (f. 256r), while Cervicorn (p. 304) reads *macedonios*, as do V, A, and E. Gaida (p. 388) mistakenly attributes the reading *Macedonianos* to V.

20   The reading *contemnebatque* is found in Cervicorn (p. 305) and Panvinio (f. 256r). Gaida (p. 389) mistakenly suggests that only A had a reading of *contemnebat*, which was in fact shared by V and E. As we now know from F, Palatina had originally added more to the sentence.

21   On the orthography of Renaissance Latin more generally, see "Orthography of Neo-Latin" (Minkova) in *Brill's Encyclopaedia of the Neo-Latin World*.

22   We did alter Platina's punctuation and capitalization, since these seemed likely to present a major obstacle to intermediate readers. Platina is not entirely consistent in his approach to spelling, but we did not attempt to standardize it. We did expand most abbreviations and ligatures.

B. Diphthongs

In post-Classical Latin, the diphthongs <ae> ("y" in "sky") and <oe> ("oy" in "boy") changed in their pronunciation to the point where they became indistinguishable from the long vowel <e> ("ay" in "bay"). Humanist scholars like Platina, as part of the process of rediscovering Classical Latin, attempted to undo these changes and determine the original Latin pronunciation. Sometimes, they missed places that should have diphthongs, like when Platina wrote *Ecclesie* instead of *Ecclesiae* as the dative singular (ch. 26). Other times, they made hypercorrections, substituting an <ae> or <oe> for an <e>. Renaissance authors, for instance, tended to write the word *ceterus* ("the other") as *caeterus* because they believed it came from the Greek καὶ ἕτερος (*kai heteros*). We have chosen to preserve these false diphthongs, but we express them with the symbol <ę>, known as *e caudata*, "e with a tail" (so, *cęterus*). It should be noted though, that the *editio princeps* used the *e caudata* to indicate all instances, both proper and erroneous, of the diphthong <ae>.

C. Confusion between double and single consonants

Classical Latin distinguished between a single consonant and doubled consonants, i.e. the "k" sound in *ecce* was longer than the similar sound in *locum*. In post-Classical Latin, changes in pronunciation led to some spelling confusion among the humanists, and so we see in the *editio princeps* the word *legitima* as *legittima*, and the name *Callistus* as *Calistus*.

D. Confusion between <u> and <o>, <i> and <e>

In unstressed syllables, <o> and <e> ceased to be distinguished from <u> and <i>, respectively—a process that was already beginning in the Classical period. In the *editio princeps*, we find such words as *adolescens* (CL *adulescens*) and *scrineum* (CL *scrinium*).

E. Confusion between <i> and <y>

The letter <y> originally entered the Roman alphabet to transcribe words that used the Greek upsilon <υ>, which was pronounced like the German <ü>. The sound soon merged with the sound of the letter <i>, and the two are largely interchangeable in Medieval Latin. Renaissance scholars were still working out the proper usage of <y>, and in the *editio princeps* one occasionally sees spellings like *hyems* (CL *hiems*).

F. Assimilation of nasals to the following consonant

Throughout all periods of Latin, nasal sounds sometimes assimilated to their following consonant, so *in* + *pensa* might be written *impensa*, with the nasal sound assimilating to the following labial consonant. It was also possible for a labial nasal to assimilate to a following dental consonant,

so *eum* + *-dem* is usually written *eundem*. In the orthography of the *editio princeps*, this process applies more widely, and includes both dental and palatal consonants, so one finds *aliquandiu* (CL *aliquamdiu*) and *quanquam* (CL *quamquam*).

We have not attempted to reproduce the abbreviations from the *editio princeps*, which would likely prove a substantial obstacle to the intermediate reader. Yet since these abbreviations would have been a major element of the contemporary reading experience, we do provide a small sample from the *editio princeps* (figure 1) along with brief explanations. Abbreviations originally arose in manuscripts, which had to be laboriously copied by hand and took countless hours of painstaking work. Generally, these abbreviations were employed to save time and space by shortening words in an understandable way. Even after the invention of the printing press, abbreviations were still used to save on space. The first few sentences of Platina's *Life of Paul II*, shown here in figure 1, exhibit many of these abbreviations.

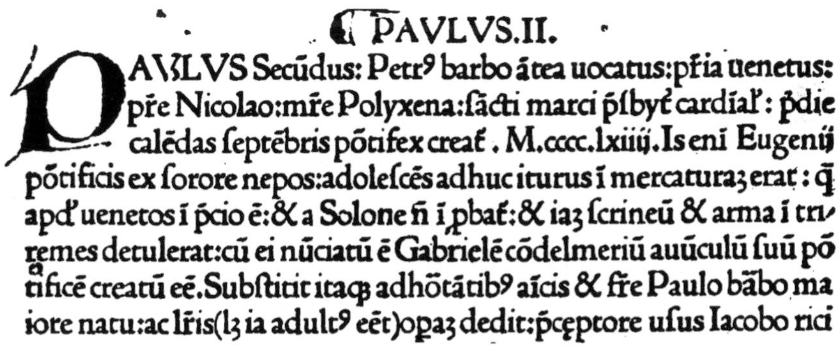
PAVLVS.II.
PAVLVS Secūdus: Petr9 barbo ātea uocatus:pr̄ia uenetus:
pr̄e Nicolao:mr̄e Polyxena:ſācti marci p̄ſbyt̄ cardial̄: p̄die
calēdas ſeptēbris pōtifex creat̄. M.cccc.lxiiij.Is eni Eugenij
pōtificis ex ſorore nepos:adoleſcēs adhuc iturus ī mercaturaȝ erat: q̄
apd̄ uenetos ī p̄cio ē:& a Solone fi ī p̄bat̄:& iaȝ ſcrineū & arma ī triremes detulerat:cū ei nūciatū ē Gabrielē cōdelmeriū auūculū ſuū pō
tificē creatū eē.Subſtitit itaq; adhōtātib9 aīcis & fr̄e Paulo bābo ma
iore natu:ac lr̄is(lȝ ia adult9 eēt)opaȝ dedit:p̄ceptore uſus Iacobo rici

FIGURE 1: The first lines of the *Life of Paul II* in the 1479 *Editio Princeps* (digitized by Google)

ū A bar over a vowel replaces a following (or sometimes preceding) <n> or <m>, seen here for example in *Secu(n)dus* in the first line and *a(m)icis* in the seventh

9 A raised <9> symbol at the end of a word replaces an <-us> ending, cf. *Petr(us)* in the first line

ō A barbell shape over a vowel replaces a following <r>, cf. *adho(r)ta(n) tib(us)* and *ba(r)bo* in line seven

r̄ A bar over a mid-word consonant can replace any number of letters in common words, cf. *p(at)ria* in the first line or *l(ac)r(im)is* in the eighth

t̄ A curl added to the top of the letter <t> represents an <-ur> or <-er> ending, cf. *p(re)sbyt(er)* in the second line and *creat(ur)* in the third

ꝉ A curl added near the top of the letter <l> replaces an <-is> ending, cf. *cardi(n)al(is)* in the second line

Ȝ A <3> symbol appearing at the end of a word usually replaces a final <-m>, cf. *ia(m)* in the fifth line

ꝗꝫ A small <3> symbol after the letter <q> replaces the letters <-ue>, cf. *itaq(ue)* in the seventh line

q̄ A <q> with a bar on top stands for *q(uod)*, cf. line four

& The <&>, which was originally a ligature of *et*, is used frequently, cf. line five

ē An <e> with a bar above it (<ē>) stands for *est*, cf. line five

eē An double <e> with a bar over the second (<eē>) stands for *esse*, cf. line seven

ñ An <n> with a bar above it stands for *non*, cf. line five

ꝓ A <p> with a tail proceeding down and backwards from the loop stands in for *pro*, cf. *i(m)p(ro)bat(ur)* in line five

ꝑ A <p> with a bar across the descender stands in for *per*, cf. *op(er)a(m)* in line eight

p̄ A <p> with a bar above it stands in for *pre* or *prae*, cf. *p(re)sbyt(er)* in the second line and *p(rae)ceptore* in the eighth

7. Grammatical and Stylistic Notes on Platina and Renaissance Latin[23]

Perhaps the defining feature of humanism was the quest to restore Latin as it existed in the age of Cicero.[24] A humanist like Platina, then, would be dismayed to see his own Latin treated as a discrete phenomenon with rules different from Classical Latin. The gradual progress and ultimate triumph of humanism can be seen in the Latin of the humanists themselves, which came closer and closer to the Classical standard with every generation. Petrarch wrote in a Latin that was largely still medieval, although it had some classicizing features. A hundred years after his death, Platina wrote in a Latin that very closely approximates

---

23 On the differences between Medieval Latin and Renaissance Latin, see "From Medieval Latin to Neo-Latin" (Pade) in *Brill's Encyclopaedia of the Neo-Latin World*.

24 On this quest see "Neo-Latin: Character and Development" (Ramminger) in *Brill's Encyclopaedia of the Neo-Latin World*.

what one would find in Cicero. Yet there are differences, and we sketch out a few of the most pronounced ones here:

A. Ablative of Extent of Time

> Because the ablative can denote time within which, it sometimes overlaps with the concept of duration. When the fired abbreviators sat vigil persistently outside of Paul's door, Platina describes the situation with these words (ch. 14): *Hac autem diligentia **viginti continuis noctibus** usi sumus,* "We employed this diligence for **twenty straight nights**." Even Classical writers such as Cicero and Livy had occasionally used this construction, but it is encountered very commonly in Platina's *Paul II*.

B. *Ad* + Accusative Replacing the Dative

> One feature of later Latin is that many uses of the cases (especially the genitive and dative) came to be expressed with prepositions. The humanists did much to restore the case usage of Classical Latin, but Platina still frequently uses *ad* + acc. instead of the dative. Platina depicts Pomponio Leto (ch. 56), for instance, as replying to his interrogators with a sharp *Quid **ad vos**?* ("What's it **to you**?") where we would normally expect a dative of reference: *Quid vobis?*

C. *Dum* + Imperfect Subjunctive for "While/When"

> When *dum* takes the subjunctive, it normally means "until" or "provided that." The word *dum* means "while" when it begins a clause with a verb in the indicative (usually in the present). However, *dum* and *cum* came to blend together in a number of usages. In particular, the circumstantial use of *cum* + imperf. subjunctive ("while/when") influenced the use of *dum*, so that one also encounters *dum* + imperf. subjunctive to mean "while/when." Platina describes his torture in Castel Sant'Angelo as follows (ch. 51): ***dum penderem** miser … rogabat* ("**While I was hanging** miserably … he was asking"). This usage begins in the Classical period, but increases dramatically in the Middle Ages.

D. Pluperfect Passive as Perfect Passive Participle + Pluperfect of *sum*

> In Classical Latin, the pluperfect passive was normally formed by combining the perfect passive participle with a form of *sum* in the imperfect, e.g. *Laudatus eram* ("I had been praised"). Already in the Classical period, authors sometimes formed the pluperfect passive as if it were a combination of the passive participle (*laudatus*) and the pluperfect (*fueram*): *Laudatus fueram* ("I had been praised"). Platina regularly uses this construction.

E. *Homo, Hominis* as a Third Person Pronoun

> Platina very often uses a form of *homo, hominis* where one would expect *is, eius*. So, for example, when Pope Paul first hears that there is a plot against him, Platina describes his vice-chamberlain's action as follows (ch. 44): *Augebat **hominis** timorem Vianesius* ("Vianesio was stoking **his** fear"). It would not be unreasonable to translate this as "Vianesio was stoking the man's fear," but the sense is more generally that of a third person pronoun than a reference to a "person" or "man."

F. Classical Words with Non-Classical Meanings

> There are a number of words that had gained new meanings after the Classical era. The word *dux*, for instance, could mean "duke" as well as "leader." In these cases, our glossary includes both the Classical and the post-Classical meanings, e.g. "**dux, ducis** *m.*: leader; duke."

8. A note on the running glossary and commentary

The running glossary provides translations for all the words in the text, excepting the ones students are most likely to know already, like *mater* and *video* (these can be found in the Common Vocabulary List in the back). We do continue to gloss words that occur frequently in the text, so one still finds (e.g.) **pontifex, -ficis** in the final chapters. Our assumption is that not all students will be reading the work from cover to cover. Given the limited space for Renaissance Latin in the typical curriculum, one might well only be able to read a few chapters.

We gloss words as they appear in the text; in cases where the form is post-Classical, we provide the Classical orthography in parentheses: "**negocium, -i** (CL *negotium*)."[25] We gloss all words (no matter how common) when they differ in meaning or orthography from Classical Latin.

The commentary provides grammatical and historical assistance. Given that many classicists will have a limited familiarity with fifteenth-century Italian politics, there are more historical notes than one might expect in an intermediate reader. In making these notes we have had constant recourse to D'Elia 2009, Bauer 2006, D'Amico 1983, Pastor 1902, and the notes in Gaida's critical edition. The grammatical help in our commentary will usually consist of parsing a potentially confusing form (e.g. *manus* as gen. sing.) or identifying a syntactic usage (e.g. "rel. clause of characteristic"). We generally do not gloss phrases, except those that are especially difficult, on the grounds that excessive glossing (much like working with a translation) can be counter-productive.

---

25 It should be noted that Platina is not consistent in his spelling choices, using, e.g., sometimes *negocium* and others *negotium*.

BIBLIOGRAPHY

Manuscripts and print editions

F   =   Conventi Soppressi C.4.797 in the Biblioteca Nazionale Centrale di Firenze (Florence)

V   =   Vaticanus Latinus 2044 in the Bibliotheca Apostolica Vaticana (Rome)

A   =   codex 222 in the Bibliotheca Angelica (Rome)

E   =   *editio princeps*. 1479. *Excellentissimi historici Platinae in vitas summorum pontificum ad Sixtum IIII. pontificem maximum praeclarum opus.* Venice: Johannes de Colonia Agripinensi and Johannes Manthen.

Cervicorn   =   1540. *Bap. Platinae Cremonensis, De vitis ac gestis summorum pontificum, ad sua usque tempora, Liber Vnus. Huic additæ sunt Vitæ ac res gestae eorum qui interim fuere pontificum, a Paulo uidelicet II. ad Paulum huius nominis III.* Cologne: Eucharius Cervicorn and Gottfried Hittorp.

Panvinio   =   1562. *B. Platinae Historia, De Vitis Pontificum Romanorum, À D. N. Iesv Christo usque ad Paulum Papam II. Longè quàm antea emendatior; cvi Onvphrii Panvinii Veronensis Fratris Eremitæ Augustiniani opera, reliquorum quoque pontificum uitæ usque ad Pium IIII. pontificem maximum adiunctæ sunt.* Venice: Michael Tramezinus.

Gaida   =   Gaida, Giacinto, ed. 1913-1923. *Liber de vita Christi ac omnium pontificum.* Rerum Italicarum Scriptores 3.1. Città di Castello: Lapi, and Bologna: Zanichelli.

I Tatti Latin/English edition (so far only the first volume of three has been published):

D'Elia, Anthony F. 2008. *Bartolomeo Platina. Lives of the Popes. Volume I: Antiquity.* Cambridge, MA: Harvard University Press.

Articles announcing the discovery of new codices:

Pastor, Ludwig. 1890. "Die Originalhandschrift von Platina's Geschichte der Päpste." *Deutsche Zeitschrift für Geschichtswissen.*

Scapecchi, Piero. 1999. "Un nuovo codice del Liber de vita Christi ac omnium pontificum di Bartolomeo Platina usato come esemplare di tipo per le edizioni veneziane del 1479 e del 1504." *Roma nel Rinascimento* 247-52.

English translation:

Rycaut, Paul, trans. 1685. *The Lives of the Popes, from the time of our Saviour Jesus Christ, to the Reign of Sixtus IV.* London: Christopher Wilkinson.

Two contemporary (Latin) biographies Paul II:

Zippel, Giuseppe, ed. 1904. *Le vite di Paolo II di Gaspare da Verona e Michele Canensi.* Rerum Italicarum Scriptores 3.16. Città di Castello: Lapi.

Andrews, Avery. 1970. "The 'Lost' Fifth Book of the Life of Pope Paul II by Gaspar of Verona." *Studies in the Renaissance* 17: 7-45.

Historical background on Platina, Paul II, and Rome in the Renaissance:

Bauer, Stefan. 2006. *The Censorship and Fortuna of Platina's Lives of the Popes in the Sixteenth Century.* Turnhout: Brepols.

D'Amico, John. 1983. *Renaissance Humanism in Papal Rome: Humanists and Churchmen on the Eve of the Reformation.* Baltimore: Johns Hopkins University Press.

D'Elia, Anthony. 2009. *A Sudden Terror: The Plot to Murder the Pope in Renaissance Rome.* Cambridge, MA: Harvard University Press.

Pastor, Ludwig. 1902. *A History of the Popes. Volume IV: Paul II and Sixtus IV.* Trans. Frederick Antrobus. St. Louis: Herder.

Stinger, Charles. 1985. *The Renaissance in Rome.* Bloomington: Indiana University Press.

Walsh, Michael. 2015. *A Dictionary of Popes, 3rd Edition.* Oxford: Oxford University Press.

<u>Latin in the Renaissance</u>:

New handbooks on Neo-Latin:

> Ford, Philip, Jan Bloemendal and Charles Fantazzi, eds. 2014. *Brill's Encyclopaedia of the Neo-Latin World*. 2 vols. Leiden: Brill.

> Knight, Sarah and Stefan Tilg, eds. 2015. *The Oxford Handbook of Neo-Latin*. Oxford: Oxford University Press.

> Korenjak, Martin. 2016. *Geschichte der neulateinischen Literatur: Vom Humanismus bis zur Gegenwart*. Munich: C. H. Beck.

> Moul, Victoria, ed. 2017. *A Guide to Neo-Latin Literature*. Cambridge: Cambridge University Press.

Dictionaries: given the attempts of humanists to write in a Classical idiom, the *Oxford Latin Dictionary* and *Lewis and Short* work well for most words.

For words that have changed more substantially, one of the best dictionaries is free online (though in German): Johann Ramminger's *Neulateinische Wortliste*: www.neulatein.de

Another good dictionary is:

> Hoven, René. 2006. *Dictionary of Renaissance Latin from Prose Sources*. Leiden: Brill.

FIGURE 2:   Map of Italy, c. 1450 (credit: E. Hayes)

Timeline of Events

1458	Callistus III dies; Enea Silvio Piccolomini succeeds him as Pope Pius II
1459	Pietro Barbo made Bishop of Padua
1460	Tiburzio and the Roman youth revolt against Pius II, briefly hold city
1462	Platina travels to Rome with Cardinal Francesco Gonzaga
1464, Mar.	Platina becomes an Abbreviator in the Papal Chancery
1464, Aug.	Pius II dies; Pietro Barbo succeeds him as Pope Paul II
1464, Oct.	Paul II dissolves the College of Abbreviators; Platina protests, threatens a council, and is arrested and imprisoned in Castel Sant'Angelo
1465, Jan.	Platina is released from Castel Sant'Angelo
1465	Jacopo Piccinino dies in the custody of King Ferdinand of Naples
1466	Francesco Sforza, Duke of Milan, dies
1467	Battle of Molinella
1468, Feb.	Paul II arrests Platina and other members of the Roman Academy
1469, Summer	Platina is released from prison
1471, July	Paul II dies; Francesco della Rovere succeeds him as Pope Sixtus IV
1472-1474	Platina writes the *Lives of the Popes*, dedicates it to Sixtus IV
1475	Sixtus IV makes Platina the first head of his new Vatican Library
1481, Sept.	Platina dies

ABBREVIATIONS

abl.	ablative	indic.	indicative
abl. abs.	ablative absolute	inf.	infinitive
acc.	accusative	m.	masculine
adj.	adjective	neg.	negative
adv.	adverb	n.	neuter
alt.	alternate	nom.	nominative
CL	Classical Latin	obj.	object(ive)
compar.	comparative	pass.	passive
cond.	condition(al)	perf.	perfect
dat.	dative	pl.	plural
f.	feminine	pluperf.	pluperfect
fut.	future	pres.	present
gen.	genitive	refl.	reflexive
imperf.	imperfect	rel.	relative
impers.	impersonal	sing.	singular
ind.	indirect	subj.	subject
indecl.	indeclinable	superl.	superlative

Bartolomeo Platina
Life of Paul II

Paulus II

Born in Venice, Pietro Barbo planned to become a merchant, until his uncle was elected pope

1 Paulus Secundus, Petrus Barbo antea vocatus, patria Venetus, patre Nicolao, matre Polyxena, Sancti Marci presbyter cardinalis, pridie Calendas Septembris pontifex creatur [364] MCCCCLXIIII. Is enim Eugenii Pontificis ex sorore nepos, adolescens adhuc iturus

---

adhuc (*adv.*): till now, still
adolescens, -entis (CL *adulescens*) *m./f.*: young person
antea (*adv.*): formerly
Calendae, -arum *f.*: Kalends, first day of the month
cardinalis, -is *m.*: cardinal
creo, -are, -avi, -atus: create; elect
nepos, -otis *m./f.*: nephew

patria, -ae *f.*: native land, home
pontifex, -ficis *m.*: pontiff, pope
presbyter, presbyteri *m.*: priest
pridie (*adv.*): day before
sanctus, -i *m.*: saint
secundus, -a, -um: second
September, -bris *m.*: September
Venetus, -a, -um: Venetian
voco, -are, -avi, -atus: to call, name

Petrus Barbo: Pietro Barbo (*Barbo* is indeclinable)
patria: abl. of respect
patre Nicolao, matre Polyxena: abls. of origin in asyndeton; Niccolò Barbo was a Venetian nobleman; Polyxena Condulmaro, his wife, was the sister of Pope Eugene IV
Sancti Marci: St. Mark's in Rome was dedicated to St. Mark the Evangelist and built in 336 by Pope Mark. Pietro Barbo served as cardinal priest of the church from 1451-1464. See figure 3 (p. 72)
presbyter cardinalis: a cardinal who directed one of the titular basilicas in Rome
pridie Calendas Septembris: *Calendas* is regularly acc. after *pridie*; "the day before the Kalends of September," or August 31
MCCCCLXIIII: 1464
Eugenii Pontificis: Pope Eugene IV (r. 1431-1447), born Gabriele Condulmaro, Pietro Barbo's uncle
ex sorore: abl. of origin "from his sister (i.e on his mother's side)," referring to Polyxena
iturus: fut. act. participle of *eo* "to go"

3

in mercaturam erat, quae apud Venetos in precio est, et a Solone non improbatur; et iam scrineum et arma in triremes detulerat, cum ei nunciatum est Gabrielem Condelmerium avunculum suum pontificem creatum esse.

Pietro Barbo abandons his plan to be a merchant in order to prepare for an ecclesiastical career

2 Substitit itaque adhortantibus amicis et fratre Paulo Barbo maiore natu ac litteris, licet iam adultus esset, operam dedit,

---

adhortor, -ari, -atus sum: encourage
adultus, -a, -um: grown, adult
arma, -orum *n.*: arms
avunculus, -i *m.*: maternal uncle
creo, -are, -avi, -atus: create; elect
defero, deferre, detuli, delatus: bring down
iam (*adv.*): already, by now
improbo, -are, -avi, -atus: disapprove of
licet: although (+ *subjunctive*)
litterae, -arum *f.*: letters, literature

mercatura, -ae *f.*: trade, commerce
natus, -us *m.*: birth
nuncio, -are, -avi, -atus (CL *nuntio*): announce
opera, -ae *f.*: work; effort
precium, -i (CL *pretium*) *n.*: price, value
scrineum, -i (CL *scrinium*) *n.*: box, case
subsisto, -sistere, -stiti, - : halt, stand
triremis, -is *f.*: trireme, ship
Venetus, -a, -um: Venetian

---

mercaturam ... Venetos: Venice was one of the wealthiest trading cities in the Renaissance world with a long seafaring tradition. At its height, Venice was the most powerful trading empire in the Eastern Mediterranean

quae apud ... non improbatur: in the manuscripts, Platina added this phrase in the margin

in precio: idiom, "of value"

Solone: a reference to the start of Plutarch's *Life of Solon* (ch. 2), in which Solon, an Athenian statesman, was said to have spent time as a merchant

triremes: a warship with three banks of oars

cum ... nunciatum est: temporal *cum* clause; impers., "when it was announced"

Gabrielem ... creatum esse: ind. statement introduced by *nunciatum est*

Gabrielem Condelmerium: Gabriele Condulmaro, Pietro Barbo's uncle, who became Pope Eugene IV (r. 1431-47)

adhortantibus amicis et fratre: abl. abs.

Paulo Barbo: Paolo Barbo, Pietro Barbo's older brother, an educated humanist, and a member of Venice's governing body, the Council of Ten

maiore: compar. of *magnus*, agreeing with *fratre Paulo Barbo*

natu: abl. of respect, greater in respect to age, so "older"

litteris: dat. of ind. obj. with *operam dedit*

operam dedit: idiom, "put effort into"

praecęptore usus Iacobo Ricionio, qui [365] diligentiam hominis ea in re* laudare consueverat. Habuit et alios praecęptores, nec tamen ob aetatem admodum profecit; quos omnes praeter Ricionem, dum pontifex esset, dignitate et facultatibus honestiores reddidit, ostendens per eos non stetisse quominus doctior evaderet.

---

admodum (*adv.*): very much, exceedingly
aetas, -tatis *f.*: age
consueo, -suere, -suevi, -suetus: be accustomed
dignitas, -tatis *f.*: honor, rank
diligentia, -ae *f.*: diligence
doctus, -a, -um: learned
evado, -ere, evasi, evasus: emerge; turn out
facultas, -tatis *f.*: capability; means, resources (*pl.*)
honestus, -a, -um: distinguished
laudo, -are, -avi, -atus: praise
ostendo, -ere, ostendi, ostensus: show; make clear

per: through; on account of (+ *acc.*)
pontifex, -ficis *m.*: pontiff, pope
praecęptor, -oris (CL *praeceptor*) *m.*: teacher
praeter: besides, except (+ *acc.*)
proficio, -ficere, -feci, -fectus: accomplish, make progress
quominus (*conj.*): that not
reddo, -ere, reddidi, redditus: pay back, render
sto, -are, steti, status: stand; remain
utor, uti, usus sum: use, make use of, enjoy (+ *abl.*)

---

praecęptore: appositive with *Iacobo Ricionio*
Iacobo Ricionio: one of Pietro Barbo's tutors; the last name is 2nd declension (or indecl.) here and 3rd declension in the next sentence.
ea: agreeing with *re*
in re*: Platina originally wrote and then later crossed out before printing: ... *in re, etsi eius rude ingenium esset* ("although his intellect was coarse")
quos: connecting rel., "and all these" referring to the *praecęptores*
dum ... esset: *dum* + imperf. subjunctive, "while he was pontifex" (see Introduction 7.C)
dignitate ... facultatibus: abls. of respect
honestiores: compar. of *honestus*; predicate acc. after *quos*, "whom he rendered more distinguished"
stetisse: impers. inf. in ind. statement introduced by *ostendens*
quominus ... evaderet: prevention clause, "showing that it did not stand on account of them *that he did not turn out more learned*"
doctior: nom. sing. masc.; compar. of *doctus*

Pietro quickly rises in the Church hierarchy with the help of his brother, Paolo, and of his uncle, Pope Eugene IV

3 Paulus autem Barbo magni animi ac prudentiae vir, cognita fratris natura, quae potius quietem quam negocia appetebat, Eugenium rogat (nam Florentiam videndi hominis causa venerat) ut Petrum ad se vocet, initiatumque sacris in aliquo dignitatis gradu collocet. Vocatus itaque Petrus, archidiaconatum Bononiensem {231v} ac non ita multo post episcopatum Cerviae commendatione

---

aliqui, -qua, -quod: some
animus, -i *m.*: mind; intellect
appeto, -ere, -ivi, -itus: desire; long for
archidiaconatus, -us *m.*: office of archdeacon
Bononiensis, -e: of Bologna
Cervia, -ae *f.*: Cervia, a town in Italy
cognosco, -noscere, -novi, -nitus: become acquainted with, aware of
colloco, -are, -avi, -atus: place; establish
commendatio, -onis *f.*: recommendation
dignitas, -tatis *f.*: rank; office
episcopatus, -us *m.*: bishopric; bishop's office

Florentia, -ae *f.*: Florence
gradus, -us *m.*: position
initio, -are, -avi, -atus: initiate into (+ *dat.*)
multo (*adv.*): much; long (before/after)
negocium, -i (CL *negotium*) *n.*: work, business
potius (*adv.*): rather, more
prudentia, -ae *f.*: good sense, wisdom
quies, -etis *f.*: quiet, rest, peace
sacrum, -i *n.*: religious rites (*pl.*)
voco, -are, -avi, -atus: to call; summon

Paulus ... Barbo: Paolo Barbo (*Barbo* is indeclinable), Pietro's older brother
animi ... prudentiae: genitives of description
cognita ... natura: abl. abs.
potius ... quam: "rather ... than"
Florentiam: acc. of place to which; Florence was a powerful republic in Tuscany. Eugene's papal court was long located in Florence because of civil unrest in Rome
videndi ... causa: *causa* + gen. gerundive to express purpose "for the sake of the man to be seen (i.e. to see the man)"
ut ... vocet ... collocet: ind. command dependent on *rogat*
Petrum: Pietro Barbo
initiatumque: agrees with *Petrum*, "and when he had been initiated"
commendatione: abl. of means

6

adeptus, protonotarius ab avunculo creatur, ex his potissimum qui emolumentorum participes sunt.

Pietro becomes a cardinal and a rival of Alovisius Patavinus

4 His autem facultatibus aliquot annis vitam ducens, tandem [366] una cum Alovisio Patavino medico, quem postea patriarcham et camerarium appellarunt, cardinalis ab Eugenio creatur, instantibus quibusdam Eugenii familiaribus, ut haberent quem Alovisii

---

adipiscor, adipisci, adeptus sum: obtain; come into
aliquot (*indecl.*): some, several
annus, -i *m.*: year
appello, -are, -avi, -atus: call; address
avunculus, -i *m.*: maternal uncle
camerarius, -i *m.*: chamberlain
cardinalis, -is *m.*: cardinal
creo, -are, -avi, -atus: create; elect, appoint
emolumentum, -i *n.*: profit; benefit
facultas, -tatis *f.*: capability; means, resources (*pl.*)
familiaris, -is *m./f.*: friend; household member

insto, -are, institi, - : urge; press hard
medicus, -i *m.*: doctor
particeps, -cipis *m./f.*: sharer, partaker
patriarcha, -ae *m.*: patriarch (ecclesiastical office)
postea (*adv.*): afterwards
potissimum (*adv.*): especially
protonotarius, -i *m.*: protonotary
quidam, quaedam, quoddam: a certain one/ thing
tandem (*adv.*): finally; after some time
una (*adv.*): at the same time, together
vita, -ae *f.*: life, career

---

protonotarius: a chief clerk, one of twelve directly serving under the vice-chancellor, the cardinal in charge of the *Cancellaria Apostolica* ("chancery"), the Curia's general administrative department

ex his: assume *officiis*

emolumentorum: obj. gen.

His ... facultatibus: abl. of means

aliquot annis: abl. of extent of time (post-Classical, see Introduction 7.A)

Alovisio Patavino: Alovisius of Padua, also called Ludovico Trevisan, cardinal priest of San Lorenzo in Rome, patriarch and Cardinal of Aquileia, a military leader, and rival of Pietro Barbo

quem postea: refers to Alovisius

camerarium: "Chamberlain," the title of the cardinal in charge of the *Camera Apostolica*, which administered papal revenues and properties

appellarunt: syncopated from *appella(ve)runt*

Eugenio: Pope Eugene IV (r. 1431-47)

instantibus ... familiaribus: abl. abs.

ut haberent: purpose clause

quem ... obiicerent: rel. clause of characteristic, "(to have someone) whom they might put in the way of"

potentiae interdum obiicerent; inter quos postea tanta simultas fuit, ut nusquam maiore odio certatum sit, his etiam discordias alentibus, qui seditionibus ali et augeri consueverant. Dolebat enim Petrus primum locum sibi apud Eugenium subripi, cum nepos esset, cumque etiam patricius Venetus.

Pietro and Alovisius have a bitter feud

5 Hanc ob rem inimicitias non vulgares exercuit cum Francisco Condelmerio vicecancellario ex amita Eugenii nato; quo deinceps

---

alo, -ere, -ui, -itus: feed

amita, -ae *f.*: paternal aunt

augeo, -ere, auxi, auctus: augment

certor, -ari, -atus sum: contend

consueo, -suere, -suevi, -suetus: accustom; be accustomed

deinceps (*adv.*): thereafter

discordia, -ae *f.*: disagreement, discord

doleo, -ere, -ui, -itus: hurt; grieve

exerceo, -ere, -ui, -itus: exercise

inimicitia, -ae *f.*: enmity

interdum (*adv.*): sometimes

locus, -i *n.*: rank, position

natus, -a, -um: born, arisen (from)

nepos, -otis *m./f.*: nephew

nusquam (*adv.*): never

obiicio, -ere, obieci, obiectus: throw before; put in the way of

odium, -i *n.*: hatred

patricius, -i *m.*: patrician, noble

postea (*adv.*): afterwards

potentia, -ae *f.*: power

primus, -a, -um: first

seditio, -onis *f.*: sedition; rivalry

simultas, -tatis *f.*: rivalry

subripio, -ripere, -ripui, -reptus: snatch away, steal

Venetus, -a, - um *m.*: Venetian

vicecancellarius, -i *m.*: vice-chancellor

vulgaris, -e: common

---

potentiae: dat. with a compound verb, *obiicerent*

inter quos: connective rel., "and between them"

ut … certatum sit: impers. pass. in result clause, "there was so great a rivalry *that there was never a contention with greater hatred*"

maiore odio: abl. of manner; *maiore* is compar. of *magnus*

his … alentibus: abl. abs. with causal force; *his* looks forward to following *qui*

discordias: acc. obj. of *alentibus*

ali et augeri: two pres. pass. infinitives, complementary with *consueverant*

Petrus: Pietro Barbo

primum locum … subripi: ind. statement initiated by *dolebant*

cum nepos esset: concessive *cum* clause, "although he was his nephew"

cumque … Venetus (esset): concessive *cum* clause

vicecancellario: cardinal in charge of the *Cancellaria Apostolica* ("chancery")

ex amita: abl. of origin with *nato*

nato: in apposition with *Francisco etc.*

quo … mortuo: abl. abs., connective rel.; "and when he died"

mortuo, totum se in patriarcham vertit, licet saepius intercedentibus amicis in gratiam rediissent simulato animo. Hanc ob rem
sub diversis pontificibus ita inter se mutuis odiis certarunt, ut alter
alteri non pepercerit, sive facultates sive dignitatem inspicias. Iactata
et inter eos varia probra sunt, quae consulto praetereo, ne maledicis
fidem praestitisse videar.

---

alter, altera, alterum: one, another
animus, -i *m.*: mind; feelings
certo, -are, -avi, -atus: vie (with)
consulto (*adv.*): deliberately
dignitas, -tatis *f.*: rank, status
diversus, -a, -um: different
facultas, -tatis *f.*: capability; estate, resources
(*pl.*)
fides, fidei *f.*: faith; credibility
gratia, -ae *f.*: goodwill
iacto, -are, -avi, -atus: throw, hurl
inspicio, -ere, inspexi, inspectus: observe,
consider
intercedo, -cedere, -cessi, -cessus: intervene;
intercede
licet: although (+ *subjunctive*)

maledicus, -i *m.*: a slanderer
mutuus, -a, -um: mutual
odium, -i *n.*: hate, hatred
parco, -ere, peperci, parsus: spare
patriarcha, -ae *m.*: patriarch (ecclesiastical
office)
pontifex, -ficis *m.*: pontiff, pope
praesto, -stare, -stiti, -stitus: offer, present
praetereo, -ire, -ivi(ii), -itus: omit, pass over
probrum, -i *n.*: abuse, insult
redeo, -ire, -ivi(ii), -itus: return
simulo, -are, -avi, -atus: simulate; counterfeit
sive (*conj.*): whether … or
totus, -a, -um: whole
varius, -a, -um: different; various
verto, -ere, verti, versus: turn

---

saepius: compar. of *saepe*
intercedentibus amicis: abl. abs.
simulato animo: abl. abs.
certarunt: syncopated from *certa(ve)runt*
ut … pepercerit: result clause, perf. subjunctive
alter alteri non pepercerit: "one did not spare the other, and vice versa": with two
forms of *alter* in different cases, this often implies a comparison where both antecedents of the *alter* fit both roles
inspicias: potential subjunctive, "(whether) you should consider"
ne … videar: neg. purpose clause, "lest I seem"; Palatina originally wrote *ne vitae
utriusque aliqua nota inuratur* ("lest a mark of censure be branded upon the life of
either")
praestitisse: perf. inf., complementary with *videar*

When Eugene IV dies, Pietro Barbo uses charm and manipulation to insinuate himself into the good graces of the new pope, Nicholas V

6 Mortuo autem Eugenio, cum in eius locum Nicolaus Quintus suffectus esset, tantum apud hominem gratia et blanditiis valuit ut et primum ipse locum e natione sua apud eum tenuerit, fratre Nicolai hominem adiuvante, et ita Nicolaum animaverit ut camerarii dignitatem Alovisio diminueret.

Erat enim Petrus Barbo natura blandus, arte humanus*, ubi opus erat. Praeterea vero eo indignitatis plerunque deveniebat, cum

---

adiuvo, -are, adiuvi, adiutus: help
animo, -are, -avi, -atus: animate, rouse
ars, artis *f.*: skill; craft
blanditia, -ae *f.*: flattery
blandus, -a, -um: charming, pleasant
camerarius, -i *m.*: chamberlain
devenio, -ire, deveni, deventus: descend to
dignitas, -tatis *f.*: rank, status
diminuo, -ere, -ui, -utus: lessen, diminish
eo (*adv.*): there, to such a point
gratia, -ae *f.*: grace; charm
humanus, -a, -um: refined; kind
indignitas, -tatis *f.*: vileness, baseness
locus, -i *m.*: position; rank

natio, -onis *f.*: nation, people
opus, operis *n.*: work; need
plerunque (CL *plerumque*) (*adv.*): generally, very often
praeterea (*adv.*): in addition
primus, -a, -um: first
sufficio, -ficere, -feci, -fectus: put in place, vote in
tantum (*adv.*): so greatly
teneo, -ere, tenui, tentus: hold, possess
ubi (*adv.*): when
valeo, -ere, -ui, -itus: prevail (upon)
vero (*adv.*): truly, in fact

Mortuo ... Eugenio: abl. abs.; Pope Eugene IV (r. 1431-1447)
cum ... suffectus esset: circumstantial *cum* clause
Nicolaus Quintus: Pope Nicholas V (r. 1447-1455), born Tommaso Parentucelli; a major patron of humanism, he established a library at the Vatican and encouraged scholars to work there
ut ... tenuerit ... animaverit: result clause, perf. subjunctives
e natione sua: "out of his countrymen"
fratre ... adiuvante: abl. abs.
ut ... diminueret: result clause
camerarii: Chamberlain, the cardinal in charge of the *Camera Apostolica*, which handled financial matters
Alovisio: dat. of disadvantage; Alovisius of Padua, rival of Pietro Barbo
natura: abl. of respect
humanus*: Platina originally wrote but later crossed out before printing: ... *humanus, simulator ac dissimulator* ("a pretender and a dissembler")
eo indignitatis: "to such a degree of indignity"
cum ... posset: circumstantial *cum* clause

pręcando, rogando, obtestando quod vellet consequi non posset, ut ad faciendam fidem precibus lachrymas adderet. Hanc ob rem Pius pontifex hominem "Mariam pientissimam" appellare interdum per iocum solebat.

Pietro uses the same tactics on the next pope, Callistus III, and convinces him to send Alovisius away to fight the Turks

7 His quoque artibus [367] apud Calistum usus, eo perpulit hominem ut Alovisium cum triremibus in Thurcos mitteret, ostendens hominis amplitudinem huic tantae rei maxime convenire,

---

addo, -ere, addidi, additus: add
amplitudo, -dinis *f.*: greatness
appello, -are, -avi, -atus: call
ars, artis *f.*: skill, trick
consequor, -sequi, -secutus sum: acquire, achieve
convenio, -venire, -veni, -ventus: be appropriate to, fit (+ *dat.*)
eo (*adv.*): to such an extent
fides, fidei *f.*: faith, credibility
interdum (*adv.*): sometimes
iocus, -i *m.*: joke
lachryma, -ae (CL *lacrima*) *f.*: tear
obtestor, -ari, -atus sum: implore

ostendo, -ere, ostendi, ostensus: show; suggest
per: through (+ *acc.*)
perpello, -pellere, -puli, -pulsus: compel; prevail upon
piens, pientis: pious, holy
pontifex, -ficis *m.*: pontiff, pope
prex, precis *f.*: prayer, request
pręcor, -ari, -atus sum (CL *precor*): entreat, pray
soleo, -ere, -itus sum: be accustomed (to)
Thurcus, -a, -um: Turkish, (*pl.*) the Turks
triremis, -is *f.*: trireme, ship
utor, uti, usus sum: use, make use of (+ *abl.*)
volo, velle, volui, - : wish, want

---

pręcando ... obtestando: gerunds, abls. of means

quod vellet: rel. clause of characteristic, antecedent is an assumed obj. of *consequi*

ut ... adderet: result clause

ad faciendam fidem: *ad* + acc. gerundive to express purpose, "for credibility to be made (i.e. to establish credibility)"

Pius pontifex: Pope Pius II (r. 1458-1464), born Enea Silvio Piccolomini, predecessor of Pope Paul II

pientissimam: superl. of *piens*

per iocum: "as a joke," this phrase is not found in A, but Platina added it in the margin of V and F

Calistum: Pope Callistus III (r. 1455-1458), born Alfonso de Borgia

ut ... mitteret: result clause

Alovisium: Alovisius of Padua, rival of Pietro Barbo

triremibus in Thurcos: in August 1457, Callistus ordered Alovisius to make a naval assault against the Turks at Mytilene; Alovisius won and received praise from the pope

ostendens: referring to Pietro Barbo, begins an ind. statement

11

cum alias et exercitus ductasset et ditionem Ecclesiae ab hostibus constanter tutatus fuisset. Hac demum molestia liberatus Petrus, Calistum deinceps ita in sententiam suam semper traxit ut donec vixerit nullius magis quam huius consilio sit usus. Facile praeterea quicquid volebat a pontifice impetrabat, sua vel amicorum causa.

Pietro helps his friends and takes special care of the sick, but perhaps with ulterior motives

8 Erat enim propensior in amicos; et quos in clientelam susceperat quibuscumque rebus poterat iuvabat, ac constantissime tuebatur, cum apud unum quenque magistratum, tum vel maxime apud

---

alias (*adv.*): at another time
clientela, -ae *f.*: clientship
consilium, -i *n.*: advice, counsel
constanter (*adv.*): constantly, loyally
deinceps (*adv.*) thereafter
demum (*adv.*): finally
ditio, -onis (CL *dicio*) *f.*: power, authority
donec (*conj.*): as long as
ducto, -are, -avi, -atus: lead (repeatedly)
Ecclesia, -ae *f.*: the Church
exercitus, -us *m.*: army
facile (*adv.*): easily
hostis, -is *m./f.*: enemy
impetro, -are, -avi, -atus: obtain
iuvo, -are, iuvi, iutus: help, assist
libero, -are, -avi, -atus: free (from)
magistratus, -us *m.*: magistrate

molestia, -ae *f.*: trouble
nullus, -a, -um: no one, not any
pontifex, -ficis *m.*: pontiff, pope
praeterea (*adv.*): thereafter
propensus, -a, -um: well disposed, favorable
quique, quaeque, quodque (CL acc. *quemque*): each
quisquis, quicquid: whoever, whatever
sententia, -ae *f.*: opinion, thought
suscipio, -cipere, -cepi (CL *suscepi*), **-ceptus**: accept, take up
traho, -ere, traxi, tractus: draw (on)
tueor, -eri, tutus sum: protect, watch (over)
tutor, -ari, -atus sum: guard, defend
utor, uti, usus sum: use, make use of (+ *abl.*)
vivo, -ere, vixi, victus: live
volo, velle, volui, - : wish, want

---

cum ... ductasset ... fuisset: causal *cum* clause; *ducta(vi)sset* the syncopated form
Hac ... molestia: abl. of separation, referring to Pietro Barbo's rival Alovisius
ut ... sit usus: result clause, subject is Callistus
vixerit: subjunctive by attraction, "so long as he lived"
nullius: gen. sing., "the advice of *no one* more than this man"
sua ... causa: *sua* agrees with *causa*, "for his own sake or that of his friends"
propensior: compar. of *propensus*
quibuscumque rebus poterat: "by means of whatever things he was able"
cum ... tum: "not only ... but also"

pontificem. Tantae praeterea humanitatis fuit* ut in aegritudinibus curiales ipsos, qui aliquo in precio erant, inviseret, et quibusdam remediis adhibitis eos ad valitudinem adhortaretur. Semper enim domi habebat unguenta Venetiis avecta: oleum, tyriacam, et cętera id genus, quae ad curandam valitudinem faciunt. Ex his aliquod ad aegrotos mittebat. Curabat item ut uni sibi magis quam alteri aegrotantium testamenta committerentur, quae postea ex arbitrio

---

adhibeo, -ere, -ui, -itus: use, apply
adhortor, -ari, -atus sum: encourage, rally
aegritudo, -dinis *f.*: sickness, disease
aegroto, -are, -avi, -atus: be sick
aegrotus, -a, -um: sick, diseased
aliqui, -qua, -quod: someone, something
arbitrium, -i *n.*: choice, judgment
aveho, -ere, avexi, avectus: carry away; export
committo, -mittere, -misi, -missus: entrust
curialis, -is *m.*: member of the curia
curo, -are, -avi, -atus: take care of; provide for
cęterus, -a, -um (CL *ceterus*): the remaining, rest, other
domus, -i *f.*: house, home
genus, generis *n.*: kind, sort

humanitas, -tatis *f.* kindness
inviso, -ere, invisi, invisus: go to see, visit
item (*adv.*): likewise, also
oleum, -i *n.*: oil, olive oil
pontifex, -ficis *m.*: pontiff, pope
postea (*adv.*): afterwards
praeterea (*adv.*): besides, in addition
precium, -i *n.* (CL *pretium*): price, worth
quidam, quaedam, quoddam: certain one/thing
remedium, -i *n.*: remedy, medicine
testamentum, -i *n.*: will
tyriaca, -ae *f.*: antidote
unguentum, -i *n.*: perfume, ointment
valitudo, -dinis *f.*: good health
Venetiae, -arum *f.*: Venice

Tantae ... humanitatis: gen. of description
fuit*: Platina originally added and later crossed out before printing: ... *fuit sive illa vera fuerit sive ficta* ("whether it might have been true or fabricated")
ut ... inviseret ... adhortaretur: result clause
aliquo in precio: "of some worth"
quibusdam remediis adhibitis: abl. of means
domi: locative
Venetiis: abl. of place from which; in the manuscripts, Platina added the words *Venetiis avecta* in the margin
oleum, tyriacam, et cętera: appositives to *unguenta avecta*
id genus: idiom, "of that sort"
ad curandam valitudinem: *ad* + acc. gerundive expressing purpose, "for health to be taken care of (i.e. to take care of health)"
Curabat item ut: Platina originally wrote, then crossed out, *subornatis servis* ("having bribed the servants")
ut ... committerentur: noun clause, obj. of *curabat*
ex arbitrio suo: "in accordance with his judgement"

13

suo partiebatur: et si quid inerat quod ad rem suam pertineret, facto tamen sub hasta precio, id sibi pecunia vindicabat.

Pietro's charm makes him popular in Rome and in the Papal Curia

9 Romanorum vero quorundam amicitia delectatus est, quos saepe in convivium adhibebat, tum ad iocum, tum ad risum: quem et Priabisius suus et Franciscus Malacaro salibus, mimis, dicteriis, scommatibus {232R} frequenter non sine urbanitate excitabant. His quidem artibus effecerat ut tum civibus Romanis tum aulicis ipsis carus esse putaretur.

---

adhibeo, -ere, -ui, -itus: invite
aliquis, aliquid: someone, something
amicitia, -ae *f.*: friendship
ars, artis *f.*: craft, trick
aulicus, -i *m.*: courtier
carus, -a, -um: dear, beloved
civis, -is *m./f.*: citizen
convivium, -i *n.*: banquet, dinner party
delector, -ari, -atus sum: be delighted, take pleasure
dicterium, -i *n.*: witticism
efficio, -ere, effeci, effectus: bring about
excito, -are, -avi, -atus: stir up, excite
frequenter (*adv.*): frequently
hasta, -ae *f.*: spear
insum, -esse, -fui, -futurus: be there; be in

iocus, -i *m.*: joke
mimus, -i *m.*: farce
partior, -iri, -itus sum: divide up, distribute
pertineo, -tinere, -tinui, -tentus: relate to, pertain to
precium, -i (CL *pretium*) *n.*: price
quidam, quaedam, quoddam: certain one/thing
risus, -us *m.*: laughter
sal, salis *m.*: salt; wit
scomma, -atis *n.*: joke, taunt
sine: without (+ *abl.*)
urbanitas, -tatis *f.*: sophistication, wit
vero (*adv.*): truly, in fact
vindico, -are, -avi, -atus: claim

---

si quid: "if anything" (after *si, nisi, num* and *ne*, "*ali*" takes a holiday)
quod ... pertineret: rel. clause of characteristic
facto ... precio: abl. abs., "when the value had been determined"
sub hasta: a spear was placed in the ground to mark the location of a public auction
amicitia: abl. with *delectatus est*
tum ... tum: "now ... now"
quem: connecting rel., referring to Pietro Barbo
Priabisius ... Franciscus Malacaro: identities not certain
salibus, mimis, dicteriis, scommatibus: abls. of means
non sine urbanitate: in the manuscripts, Platina added this phrase in the margin (and in A it appears in the slightly different form *cum urbanitate*)
His ... artibus: abl. of means
ut ... putaretur: noun clause, obj. of *effecerat*
tum ... tum: "both ... and," followed by dats. of reference
carus esse: ind. statement introduced by *putaretur*; *carus* nom. agreeing with the subject

14

Pietro also has success outside of Rome, although it makes him an enemy of Count Everso

10 Praeterea autem ne domi tantum posse videretur, foris etiam auctoritatem sibi comparare annixus est. Nam et in Hernicos, quam nunc Campaniam Romanam vocant, profectus est ad populos quosdam sędandos, qui [368] de finibus contendebant; et litem componere inter comitem Aversae et Neapolionem Ursinum conatus, paulum abfuit quin turpiter captus in vincula coniiceretur; adeo in

---

absum, -esse, -fui, -futurus: be away
adeo (*adv.*): to such a degree
annitor, anniti, annixus sum: strive, try
auctoritas, -tatis *f.*: power, authority
capio, -ere, cepi, captus: take hold, capture
comes, comitis *m.*: companion; count
comparo, -are, -avi, -atus: provide, procure
compono, -ponere, -posui, -positus: settle
coniicio, -iicere, -ieci, -iectus: throw
conor, -ari, -atus sum: attempt, try
contendo, -tendere, -tendi, -tentus: contend, dispute
domus, -i *f.*: house, home
finis, -is *m./f.*: limit, boundary
foris (*adv.*): abroad
Hernicus, -a, um: Hernician, a people in Latium
lis, litis *f.*: lawsuit, quarrel
nunc (*adv.*): now
paulum (*adv.*): by a little; barely
populus, -i *m.*: people
praeterea (*adv.*): in addition
proficiscor, -ficisci, -fectus sum: set out; proceed
quidam, quaedam, quoddam: certain one/thing
quin: so that not, that not
sędo, -are, -avi, -atus (CL *sedo*): settle; pacify
tantum (*adv.*): only
turpiter (*adv.*): disgracefully
vinculum, -i *n.*: chain
voco, -are, -avi, -atus: to call, name

ne ... videretur: neg. purpose clause; *video* in pass. is "seem"
domi: locative; here "at home" has the sense of "in domestic matters," in contrast with *foris*
posse: complementary inf. with *videretur*; here, "to be powerful"
sibi: dat. of advantage
in Hernicos: substantive assuming *fines*, "into the Hernician (territory)"
Campaniam Romanam: Roman Campania, the countryside surrounding Rome; different from the southern "Campania" region around Naples
ad ... sędandos: *ad* + acc. gerundive expressing purpose, "for certain peoples to be pacified (i.e. to pacify certain peoples)"
comitem Aversae: the Count Everso degli Anguillara (d. 1464), whom Platina seemingly mistakenly calls "the Count of Aversa"
Neapolionem Ursinum: Napoleone Orsini, an Italian *condottiero* (mercenary leader) from Naples and a rival of Count Everso
quin ... coniiceretur: prevention clause, "(it was barely absent) that he, having been disgracefully captured, be thrown into chains"

eum comes Aversus ob quandam verborum licentiam male animatus erat. Re itaque infecta abiens, homini semper adversatus est.

When Callistus III dies, Pietro finds his ambitions thwarted by the new pope, Pius II

11 Mortuo deinde Calisto, in eiusque locum Pio suffecto, cum permutare episcopatum Vincetinum in Patavinum instando acerbe nimium rogandoque anniteretur, et Pii pontificis et Venetorum iram adeo incurrit ut et Paulum fratrem senatorio munere amoverint

---

abeo, -ire, -ivi(ii), -itus: depart, go away
acerbe (*adv.*): stridently, harshly
adeo (*adv.*): to such an extent
adversor, -ari, -atus sum: be against, oppose (+ *dat.*)
amoveo, -ere, amovi, amotus: remove
animo, -are, -avi, -atus: rouse, animate
annitor, anniti, annixus sum: strive, try
comes, comitis *m.*: companion; count
deinde (*adv.*): then
episcopatus, -us *m.*: bishopric, bishop's office
incurro, -ere, incucurri, incursus: meet (with); incur
infectus, -a, -um: unfinished, incomplete
insto, -are, institi, - : pursue; insist
ira, -ae *f.*: anger; resentment
licentia, -ae *f.*: freedom

locus, -i *m.*: rank, position
male (*adv.*): badly, terribly
munus, muneris *n.*: office
nimium (*adv.*): too, very
Patavinus, -a, -um: Paduan, of Padua
permuto, -are, -avi, -atus: exchange (for); swap
pontifex, -ficis *m.*: pontiff, pope
quidam, quaedam, quoddam (CL *quamdam*): certain
senatorius, -a, -um: of a senator, senatorial
sufficio, -ficere, -feci, -fectus: put in place, vote in
Venetus, -a, -um *m.*: Venetian
verbum, -i *n.*: word
Vi(n)cetinus, -a, -um: of Vicenza (a town near Venice)

---

quandam verborum licentiam: "a certain freedom of words," that is, Pietro Barbo was free with his speech, angering Everso

Re ... infecta: abl. abs.

Mortuo ... Calisto: abl. abs.; Pope Callistus III (r. 1455-1458)

Pio suffecto: abl. abs.; Pope Pius II (r. 1458-1464), born Enea Silvio Piccolomini

in Patavinum: Platina originally wrote, then crossed out, *melioris proventus causa* ("for the sake of greater profit")

cum ... anniteretur: causal *cum* clause

instando, rogandoque: gerunds, abls. of means

et ... et: "both ... and," coordinating Pius and the Venetians, not *anniteretur* and *incurrit*

incurrit: main verb

ut ... amoverint ... interdixerint: result clause

Paulum fratrem: Pietro's older brother, Paolo Barbo

senatorio munere: abl. of separation

et ei interdixerint quominus aliorum beneficiorum proventibus potiretur, nisi sententiam mutaret. Hanc ob rem indignatus homo, ulciscendi tempus observans, interim acerbe nimium in eos invehebatur per quos stetisset quominus voto potiretur.

When Pius II dies, Pietro gets elected pope, becoming Paul II; he quickly disbands the College of Abbreviators

12 Mortuo autem Pio, in eius locum ipse suffectus, statim ubi magistratum iniit, sive quod ita pollicitus erat, sive quod Pii decreta

---

acerbe (*adv.*): stridently, harshly
beneficium, -i *n.*: benefice, a Church-owned fief
decretum, -i *n.*: decree, decision
indignor, -ari, -atus sum: be indignant
ineo, -ire, -ivi(ii), -itus: enter
interdico, -dicere, -dixi, -dictus: forbid
interim (*adv.*): meanwhile, at the same time
inveho, -ere, invexi, invectus: drive; (*pass.*) inveigh against
locus, -i *m.*: occupation, position
magistratus, -us *m.*: office, magistracy
muto, -are, -avi, -atus: change
nimium (*adv.*): too, excessively
observo, -are, -avi, -atus: watch (for)

per: by, by means of (+ *acc.*)
polliceor, -eri, -itus sum: promise
potior, -iri, -itus sum: obtain, acquire, possess (+ *abl.*)
proventus, -us *m.*: income; produce
sententia, -ae *f.*: opinion
sive ... sive: whether ... or
statim (*adv.*): immediately
sto, -are, steti, status: stand, remain
sufficio, -ficere, -feci, -fectus: put in place, vote in
tempus, temporis *n.*: time, occasion
ubi (*adv.*): when
ulciscor, ulcisci, ultus sum: avenge
votum, -i *n.*: vote

---

ei: dat. with a compound verb, *interdixerint*
quominus ... potiretur: prevention clause, "(they forbid) that he obtain the incomes of other benefices"
ulciscendi: gerund, obj. gen.; "for avenging"
stetisset: subjunctive of alleged reason
quominus ... potiretur: prevention clause dependent on *per quos stetisset*, "that he not have a vote"
Mortuo ... Pio: abl. abs.; Pope Pius II (r. 1458-1464)
ipse: Pietro Barbo, now Pope Paul II; he also considered the names Formosus (rejected as too immodest) and Mark (too Venetian)
quod ... pollicitus erat ... quod ... oderat: *quod* causal clauses, "because he had promised ... because he hated;" the former is an insinuation that Paul had gotten the support of Rodrigo Borgia, the vice-chancellor, by promising to disband the abbreviators, which would give Borgia more control over the chancery

et acta oderat, abbreviatores omnes, quos Pius in ordinem redęgerat, tanquam inutiles et indoctos, ut ipse dicebat, exauctoravit. Eos enim bonis et dignitate indicta causa spoliavit: quos etiam propter eruditionem et doctrinam ex toto orbe terrarum conquisitos, magnis pollicitationibus et praemiis vocare ad se debuerat. Erat quidem illud collegium refertum bonis ac doctis viris. Inerant divini atque humani iuris viri peritissimi. Inerant poetae et oratores plerique, qui

---

abbreviator, -oris *m.*: clerk
actum, -i *n.*: act, deed
bona, -orum *n.*: goods; wealth, estate (*pl.*)
collegium, -i *n.*: college, corporate body
conquiro, -quirere, -quisivi, -quisitus: seek out
debeo, -ere, -ui, -itus: ought, should
dignitas, -tatis *f.*: status; position
divinus, -a, -um: divine
doctrina, -ae *f.*: teaching
doctus, -a, -um: learned, wise
eruditio, -onis *f.*: instruction, education
exauctoro, -are, -avi, -atus: release, dismiss
humanus, -a, -um: human
indictus, -a, -um: not mentioned; unheard
indoctus, -a, -um: ignorant
insum, -esse, -fui, -futurus: be there; belong
inutilis, -e: useless
ius, iuris *n.*: law

odi, odisse: hate
orator, -oris *m.*: speaker, orator
orbis, -is *m.*: circle
ordo, ordinis *m.*: rank
peritus,-a, -um: skilled, experienced (+ *gen.*)
plerusque, -aque, -umque: very many
poeta, -ae *m.*: poet
pollicitatio, -onis *f.*: promise
praemium, -i *n.*: reward, gift
propter: on account of; because of (+ *acc.*)
redigo, -ere, redęgi (CL *redegi*), **redactus**: render; gather
refercio, -ire, refersi, refertus: fill up
spolio, -are, -avi, -atus: rob, strip
tanquam (CL *tamquam*): just as if
terra, -ae *f.*: earth, land
totus, -a, -um: whole, all, entire
voco, -are, -avi, -atus: to call

---

abbreviatores: abbreviators worked in the chancery drafting papal bulls; Platina himself was among the abbreviators who lost their positions
bonis et dignitate: abls. of separation
indicta causa: abl. abs. with concessive sense
quos: antecedent is *eos* at the beginning of the sentence
orbe terrarum: "the whole world"
magnis pollicitationibus et praemiis: abls. of means
Erat ... refertum: perf. pass., subject is *illud collegium*
peritissimi: superl. of *peritus*
poetae et oratores: these words are often used to describe humanists

certe non minus ornamenti ipsi curiae afferebant, quam ab eadem acciperent, quos omnes Paulus tanquam inquilinos et advenas possessione pepulit, licet emptoribus cautum esset litteris apostolicis, cautum etiam fisci pontificii auctoritate ne qui bona fide emissent e possessione honesta ac legitima deiicerentur.

Platina and the Abbreviators try to take Paul to trial, provoking his anger

[369] **13** Tentarunt tamen ii, ad quos res ipsa pertinebat, hominem e sententia dimovere. Atque ego certe, qui horum de numero

---

accipio, -ere, accepi, acceptus: receive
advena, -ae *m./f.*: foreigner
affero, afferre, attuli, allatus: bring to
apostolicus, -a, -um: apostolic
auctoritas, -tatis *f.* decree, order; authority
caveo, -ere, cavi, cautus: beware; stipulate
certe (*adv.*): surely, certainly
curia, -ae *f.*: papal court
deicio, -ere, deieci, deiectus: drive/throw out
dimoveo, -ere, dimovi, dimotus (CL *demoveo*): move (away)
emo, -ere, emi, emptus: buy; gain, acquire, obtain
emptor, -oris *m.*: buyer, purchaser
fides, fidei *f.*: faith, credit
fiscus, -i *m.*: treasury

honestus, -a, -um: honest
inquilinus, -i *m.*: traveler; lodger
legitimus, -a, -um: lawful; legitimate
licet: although (+ *subjunctive*)
litterae, -arum *f.*: a letter (epistle)
numerus, -i *m.*: number, rank
ornamentum, -i *n.*: ornament; distinction
pello, -ere, pepuli, pulsus: drive out
pertineo, -tinere, -tinui, -tentus: concerns, pertain to
pontificius, -a, -um: pontifical
possessio, -onis *f.*: possession, property
sententia, -ae *f.*: opinion; decision
tanquam (CL *tamquam*): as, just as, just as if
tento, -are, -avi, -atus: attempt, try

---

minus ornamenti: *minus* is compar. of *parvus* (in neut. sing. acc.); *ornamenti* partitive gen., "less (of) distinction"
quam … acciperent: compar. clause set up by *non minus*, "than they might receive"
possessione: abl. of separation
emptoribus: dat. of reference, the abbreviators had purchased their office
cautum esset … cautum (esset): 3rd person pass. subjunctive with *licet*
litteris apostolicis: abl. of means; an apostolic letter is a papal bull
ne … deiicerentur: neg. ind. command
qui … emissent: rel. clause of characteristic with an elided antecedent *ii* serving as the subject of *deiicerentur*, "those who had bought with good faith"
possessione: abl. of separation modified by *honesta* and *legitima*
Tentarunt: syncopated from *tenta(ve)runt*
ii: the dismissed abbreviators
e sententia: abl. of separation, "from his decision"
ego: Platina intrudes into the narrative for the first time
horum: partitive gen.

eram, rogando etiam ut causa ipsa iudicibus publicis, quos rotae auditores vocant, committeretur—tum ille torvis oculis me aspiciens, "Ita nos," inquit, "ad iudices revocas? Ac si nescires omnia iura in scrineo pectoris nostri collocata esse? Sic stat sententia," inquit, "loco cedant omnes, eant quo volunt, nihil eos moror, pontifex sum, mihique licet pro arbitrio animi aliorum acta et rescindere et approbare."

---

actum, -i *n.*: act, deed

animus, -i *m.*: mind

approbo, -are, -avi, -atus: approve, endorse, allow

arbitrium, -i *n.*: judgment; will

aspicio, -ere, aspexi, aspectus: look on/at

cedo, -ere, cessi, cessus: withdraw, leave

colloco, -are, -avi, -atus: put together, locate

committo, -mittere, -misi, -missus: commit, entrust

inquam, -, -, - : say

iudex, iudicis *m.*: judge; juror

ius, iuris *n.*: law

licet, -ere, -uit, -itus est (*impers.*): it is permitted

locus, -i *m.*: place, position

moror, -ari, -atus sum: delay

nescio, -ire, -ivi, -itus: not know, be unaware

oculus, -i *m.*: eye

pectus, pectoris *n.*: breast, heart; feeling, soul, mind

pontifex, -ficis *m.*: pontiff, pope

pro: according to (+ *abl.*)

publicus, -a, -um: public; common, of the people/state; official

quo (*adv.*): to where

rescindo, -ere, rescidi, rescissus: annul; rescind

revoco, -are, -avi, -atus: refer

scrineum, -i (CL *scrinium*) *n.*: box, case

sententia, -ae *f.*: opinion

sic (*adv.*): thus

sto, -are, steti, status: stand; remain

torvus, -a, -um: pitiless, stern

voco, -are, -avi, -atus: to call, name

volo, velle, volui, - : wish, want

---

rogando: abl. gerund, exact sense unclear since main verb is lacking

ut ... committeretur: ind. command dependent on *rogando*

rotae auditores: the Rota was a judicial body in the Curia; *auditores* here is the predicate of *quos*, "whom they call the auditors"

Tum: this cuts off the previous sentence, which lacks a main verb, creating an anacolouthon that gives a sense of Paul interrupting Platina

Ac si: "as if"

Ac si ... nescires: protasis of a pres. contrafactual cond. with an elided apodosis

omnia iura ... collocata esse: ind. statement

loco: abl. of separation

cedant ... eant: jussive subjunctives

nihil: adverbial, "in no way"

mihique: dat. of reference with *licet*

pro arbitrio animi: "by the judgment of my mind"

rescindere et approbare: subject infinitives of *licet*

The Abbreviators try to change Paul's mind, but can no longer gain an audience

14 Hac vero tam immiti sententia accępta, ut lapidem immobilem volveremus, {232v} obversabamur et frustra quidem die ac noctu in foribus aulae, vilissimum etiam quenque servum rogantes ut nobis alloqui pontificem liceret. Reiiciebamur non sine contumelia tanquam aqua et igni interdicti ac prophani. Hac autem diligentia viginti continuis noctibus usi sumus; nil enim fere nisi noctu agebat.

---

accipio, -ere, accepi, accęptus (CL *acceptus*): receive, accept
ago, -ere, egi, actus: do
alloquor, alloqui, allocutus sum: speak to, address
aqua, -ae *f.*: water
aula, -ae *f.*: court
continuus, -a, -um: continuous
contumelia, -ae *f.*: insult
dies, diei *m./f.*: day
diligentia, -ae *f.*: diligence
fere (*adv.*): almost; nearly
foris, -is *f.*: door, gate
frustra (*adv.*): in vain
ignis, -is *m.*: fire
immitis, -e: cruel, harsh, stern
immobilis, -e: immovable
interdico, -dicere, -dixi, -dictus: forbid, prohibit
lapis, -idis *m.*: stone
licet, -ere, -uit, -itus est (*impers.*): it is permitted

nil (*indecl.*): nothing
noctu (*adv.*): by night
nox, noctis *f.*: night
obversor, -ari, -atus sum: appear before, take a position outside
pontifex, -ficis *m.*: pontiff, pope
prophanus, -a, -um (CL *profanus*): profane, impious
quisque, quaeque, quodque (CL acc. *quemque*): each
reiicio, -ere, reieci, reiectus: repel; reject
sententia, -ae *f.*: opinion, sentence
servus, -i *m.*: slave; servant
sine: without (+ *abl.*)
tam (*adv.*): so, to such an extent/degree
tanquam (CL *tamquam*): just as if
utor, uti, usus sum: use, make use of, practice (+ *abl.*)
vero: but, however
viginti (*indecl.*): twenty
vilis, -e: common
volvo, -ere, volvi, volutus: turn over

Hac … immiti sententia accępta: abl. abs.
ut … volveremus: "as if," contrafactual comparison
et: "even"
die: abl. of time when
vilissimum … quenque: "each (of the) vilest"
ut … liceret: ind. command dependent on *rogantes*
alloqui: subject inf. of *liceret*
aqua et igni: abls. of separation, "forbidden from water and fire," a reference to a punishment in Ancient Rome under which it was forbidden for someone to receive any aid
interdicti ac prophani: nom. pl. masc., agreeing with the subject of *reiiciebamur*
viginti continuis noctibus: abl. of extent of time (post-Classical, see Introduction 7.A)
nil … nisi noctu: Platina also comments on Paul's nocturnal habits in ch. 83

Platina, infuriated, writes a letter decrying the injustice of the dismissal and calling for a Church Council to overrule Paul's decision

15 Ego vero tanta ignominia excitus, quod mihi ac sociis meis coram non licebat, id agere per litteras institui. Scripsi itaque epistolam his ferme verbis: "Si tibi licuit indicta causa spoliare nos emptione nostra iusta ac legittima, debet et nobis licere conqueri illatam iniuriam iniustamque ignominiam. Reiecti a te, ac tam insigni contumelia affecti, dilabemur passim ad reges, ad principes,

---

afficio, -ere, affeci, affectus: afflict
ago, -ere, egi, actus: do; handle, manage
conqueror, -queri, -questus sum: complain of
contumelia, -ae *f.*: abuse, insult
coram (*adv.*): in person, face-to-face
debeo, -ere, -ui, -itus: ought
dilabor, dilabi, dilapsus sum: flee, escape, disperse
emptio, -onis *f.*: acquisition
epistola, -ae *f.*: letter
excio, -ire, -ivi, -itus: summon; rouse
ferme (*adv.*): almost, precisely
ignominia, -ae *f.*: disgrace, ignominy, dishonor
indictus, -a, -um: not said; unheard
infero, inferre, intuli, illatus: inflict
iniuria, -ae *f.*: injury; injustice
iniustus, -a, -um: unequal

insignis, -e: remarkable, extraordinary
instituo, -ere, -ui, -utus: decide
iustus, -a, -um: just; lawful
legittimus, -a, -um (CL *legitimus*): legitimate
licet, -ere, -uit, -itus est (*impers.*): it is permitted
litterae, -arum *f.*: a letter (epistle)
passim (*adv.*): here and there; everywhere
per : through; by means of (+ *acc.*)
princeps, -cipis *m.*: leader; prince
reicio, -ere, reieci, reiectus (CL *reiectus*): reject, scorn
scribo, -ere, scripsi, scriptus: write; compose
socius, -i *m.*: associate, companion
spolio, -are, -avi, -atus: rob, deprive (+ *abl.*)
tam (*adv.*): so, so much
verbum, -i *n.*: word
vero (*adv.*): truly, in fact

---

tanta ignominia: abl. of means
quod: "that which," antecedent is the following *id*
id: referring to the act of communicating with Paul II
agere: obj. inf. of *institui*
his ... verbis: abl. of description
indicta causa: abl. abs. with concessive sense
spoliare: subject inf. of *licuit*
debet: impers., "it ought"
licere: complementary inf. with *debet*
conqueri: subject inf. of *licere*
insigni contumelia: abl. of means

eosque adhortabimur ut tibi concilium indicant, in quo potissimum rationem reddere cogaris, cur nos legitima possessione spoliaveris."

Paul jails Platina for treason, on charges of libel and summoning a council; Platina counters that libel is anonymous, whereas Platina signed his name on the letter

16 Lectis litteris, Platynam [370] reum maiestatis accersit, in carcerem trahit, compedibus revincit, mittit Theodorum Tarvisinum episcopum, qui questionem habeat. Is statim me reum facit, quod et libellos famosos in Paulum sparsissem, et concilii mentionem

---

accersio, -ire, - , - : summon
adhortor, -ari, -atus sum: encourage, rally
carcer, -eris *m.*: prison
cogo, -ere, coegi, coactus: force, compel
compes, -edis *f.*: shackles
concilium, -i *n.*: council
cur (*adv.*): why; for what reason/purpose
episcopus, -i *m.*: bishop
famosus, -a, -um: slanderous
indico, -ere, indixi, indictus: declare
legitimus, -a, -um: lawful; legitimate
lego, -ere, legi, lectus: read
libellus, -i *m.*: pamphlet
litterae, -arum *f.*: letter (epistle)

maiestas, -tatis *f.*: greatness; high treason
mentio, -onis *f.*: mention
possessio, -onis *f.*: property
potens, potentis: strong; capable
questio, -onis (CL *quaestio*) *f.*: inquiry
ratio, -onis *f.*: account
reddo, -ere, reddidi, redditus: deliver
reus, -i *m.*: accused, defendant; guilty, culprit
revincio, -ire, revinxi, revinctus: bind fast
spargo, -ere, sparsi, sparsus: disseminate
spolio, -are, -avi, -atus: rob, strip (+ *abl.*)
statim (*adv.*): immediately
traho, -ere, traxi, tractus: drag

---

ut ... indicant: ind. command
tibi: dat. of disadvantage
concilium: some argued that Church Councils could overrule popes, a position called "conciliarism"; this was a major threat, since the councils of Constance (1414-1418) and Basel (1431-1449) had deposed (or attempted to depose) several popes
quo ... cogaris: rel. clause of characteristic; *cogaris* is a pres. pass. subjunctive
potissimum: superl. adv. of *potens,* here "most of all"
cur ... spoliaveris: ind. question; *spoliaveris* is a perf. subjunctive
possessione: abl. of separation
Platynam: Platina now refers to himself in third person
reum maiestatis: defendant on a charge of high treason; *maiestas* here means "(diminishing the) greatness (of the state)"
Theodorum Tarvisinum episcopum: Teodoro Lelli, Bishop of Treviso, was one of Paul II's chief advisers
qui ... habeat: rel. clause of purpose, "in order that he may hold an inquiry"
me (esse) reum facit: "he found me guilty"
quod ... sparsissem ... fecissem: clause of alleged reason, "on the grounds that I had..."

fecissem. Primum crimen ita confutavi: eos quidem dici libellos famosos, in quibus scribentis nomen reticetur, at meum nomen in calce litterarum extare; non igitur libelli famosi sunt.

Platina counters the second accusation by pointing out the authority of the ancient Ecumenical Councils

17 Quod vero de concilio mentionem fecerim, me non adeo grave crimen id putasse, cum in synodis a sanctis patribus stabilita sint fundamenta orthodoxae fidei, prius sparsim iacta a Salvatore nostro

---

adeo (*adv.*): to such a degree
calx, calcis *m./f.*: heel; bottom
concilium, -i *n.*: council
confuto, -are, -avi, -atus: disprove
crimen, criminis *n.*: accusation, charge; crime
exto, -are, extiti, - : stand forth; be visible
famosus, -a, -um: slanderous
fides, fidei *f.*: faith
fundamentum, -i *n.*: foundation
gravis, -e: serious
iacio, -ere, ieci, iactus: throw; spread
igitur: therefore
libellus, -i *m.*: pamphlet

litterae, -arum *f.*: letter, epistle
mentio, -onis *f.*: mention
orthodoxus, -a, -um: orthodox
primus, -a, -um: first
prius (*adv.*): previously
reticeo, -ere, -ui, - : leave unsaid
salvator, -oris *m.*: savior
sanctus, -a, -um: sacred, holy
scribo, -ere, scripsi, scriptus: write
sparsim (*adv.*): in a scattered way
stabilio, -ire, -ivi, -itus: make firm, establish
synodus, -i *m.*: synod, general council
vero: but, however

---

libellos famosos: a reference to the letter quoted above (ch. 15), criticizing Paul for disbanding the Abbreviators

concilii: a Church Council might remove (or attempt to remove) a pope, meaning that the call for a council could be interpreted as a threat to overthrow Paul

eos ... dici, meum ... extare: ind. statements recounting Platina's defense

quibus: *eos ... libellos* is the antecedent

scribentis: possessive gen. dependent on *nomen*

meum nomen: Platina originally tried to circulate the letter anonymously, which undercuts his (already somewhat specious) argument

Quod ... fecerim: noun clause, "the fact that I made mention of a council"

me ... putasse: ind. statement still giving Platina's rebuttal, more easily understood in the following order: *me non putasse id (esse) adeo grave crimen*

id: referring to the above noun clause *Quod ... fecerim*

putasse: syncopated from *puta(vi)sse*

cum ... stabilita sint: causal *cum* clause, subject is *fundamenta*

sanctis patribus: the early Church fathers who had set out the principles of Christianity in the ecumenical councils

iacta: agrees with *fundamenta*

Salvatore ... discipulis: Jesus and the apostles

eiusque discipulis, ut maiores cum minoribus aequo iure viverent, ne cuiquam fieret iniuria. Unde etiam apud Romanos instituta est censura, qua, et qui privati et qui in magistratu fuerunt, rationem habiti magistratus et vitae ante actae reddere cogebantur.

Platina's pleas are unsuccessful, but he is ultimately freed through the help of his patron, Cardinal Francesco Gonzaga

18 Cum vero his rationibus nihil profecissem, revinctus compedibus, et quidem gravissimis, media hyeme sine foco celsa in turri ac

---

aequus, -a, -um: fair, equal
ago, -ere, egi, actus: conduct, spend (time)
celsus, -a, -um: high
censura, -ae *f.*: office of censor, censorship
cogo, -ere, coegi, coactus: force, compel
compes, -edis *f.*: chains (*pl.*)
discipulus, -i *m.*: disciple, student
fio, fieri, factus sum: happen; take place
focus, -i *m.*: hearth
gravis, -e: heavy, serious
hyems, hyemis (CL *hiems*) *f.*: winter
iniuria, -ae *f.*: injustice, wrong
instituo, -ere, -ui, -utus: establish, found
ius, iuris *n.*: law; legal system
magistratus, -us *m.*: magistracy, civil office

medius, -a, -um: middle
privatus, -i *m.*: private citizen
proficio, -ere, profeci, profectus: accomplish; make progress
quisquam, quidquam: anyone, anything
ratio, -onis *f.*: an account, reasoning; rational argument
reddo, -ere, reddidi, redditus: return; render
revincio, -ire, revinxi, revinctus: bind fast, fasten
sine: without (+ *abl.*)
turris, -is *f.*: tower
unde (*adv.*): from where, whence
vero: but, however
vivo, -ere, vixi, victus: live

---

ut … viverent: purpose clause

maiores … minoribus: compar. of *magnus* and *parvus*, used substantively, "the greater men with the lesser men"

aequo iure: abl. of manner, "under equal law (i.e. equally)"

ne … iniuria: neg. purpose clause

censura: office in ancient Rome responsible for the census and the morals of public figures

qua: abl. of means

et qui … et qui: antecedent is an assumed *ii*, subject of *cogebantur*

rationem: acc. obj. of *reddere*

habiti magistratus et vitae … actae: coordinated genitives, dependent on *rationem*

cum … profecissem: causal *cum* clause

gravissimis: agrees with *compedibus*

media hyeme: abl. of time when, "in the middle of winter"

ventis omnibus exposita coherceor mensibus quattuor: tandem vero Paulus, Francisci Gonzagae Cardinalis Mantuani precibus fatigatus, aegre pedibus stantem molestia carceris me liberat; admonet ne ab urbe discedam. "In Indiam," inquit, "si proficiscere, inde te retrahet Paulus." Feci mandata. Triennio in urbe commoratus sum, arbitratus hominem aliquam medelam meis incommodis interim allaturum.

---

admoneo, -ere, -ui, -itus: warn
aegre (*adv.*): painfully, with difficulty
affero, afferre, attuli, allatus: offer; produce
aliqui, -quae, -quod: some
arbitror, -ari, -atus sum: believe; judge
carcer, -eris *m.*: prison
cardinalis, -is *m.*: cardinal
coherceo, -ere, -ui, -itus (CL *coerceo*): enclose, confine
commoror, -ari, -atus sum: abide; remain
discedo, -cedere, -cessi, -cessus: depart
expono,-ere, -ui, -itus: set out; expose
fatigatus, -a, -um: weary
incommodum, -i *n.*: misfortune
inde (*adv.*): from there
India, -ae *f.*: India
inquam, -, -, -: say
interim (*adv.*): meanwhile

libero, -are, -avi, -atus: free
mandatum, -i *n.*: order
Mantuanus, -a, -um: of Mantua
medela, -ae *f.*: cure, remedy
mensis, -is *m.*: month
molestia, -ae *f.*: trouble, hardship
pes, pedis *m.*: foot
prex, precis *f.*: prayer, request
proficiscor, -ficisci, -fectus sum: depart, set off
quattuor: four
retraho, -ere, retraxi, retractus: draw back, bring back
sto, -are, steti, status: stand
tandem (*adv.*): finally
triennium, -i *n.*: three years
ventus, -i *m.*: wind
vero: but, however

---

exposita: agrees with *turri*
coherceor, liberat, admonet, retrahet: historical pres.
mensibus quattuor: abl. of extent of time (post-Classical, see Introduction 7.A)
Francisci ... Mantuani: Francesco Gonzaga, Cardinal of Mantua, Platina's patron
precibus: abl. of means
molestia: abl. of separation with *liberat* or cause with *aegre pedibus stantem*
ne ... discedam: ind. command
inquit: subject is Paul (who refers to himself in third person)
proficiscere: = *proficisceris*, fut. indic. with alternate 2nd sing. ending '-re'
Triennio: abl. of extent of time (post-Classical, see Introduction 7.A)
hominem ... allaturum (esse): ind. statement
meis incommodis: dat. of reference

Paul involves himself with the canons of the Lateran, provoking some ill will

19 Coronatus Paulus de more, memor a Calisto [371] quondam pulsos esse e Sancto Iohanne Laterano canonicos regulares, quos eodem in loco Eugenius pontifex ante collocaverat, eosdem revocavit, ut seorsum a canonicis saecularibus divina officia celebrarent. Praeterea vero canonicorum saecularium eo in loco nomen aboliturus, si quis moriebatur, in demortui locum neminem sufficiebat;

---

aboleo, -ere, -evi, -itus: abolish
canonicus, -i *m.*: clergyman; canon
celebro, -are, -avi, -atus: perform
colloco, -are, -avi, -atus: place in position; post
coronatus, -a, -um: crowned
demorior, demori, demortuus sum: decease, die off
divinus, -a, -um: divine
idem, eadem, idem: the same
locum, -i *n.*: place
locus, -i *m.*: place; position
memor, -oris: remembering; mindful
mos, moris *m.*: custom

nemo, neminis *m./f.*: no one
officium, -i *n.*: office
pello, -ere, pepuli, pulsus: drive out; banish
pontifex, -ficis *m.*: pontiff, pope
praeterea (*adv.*): besides
quondam (*adv.*): formerly
regularis, -e: regular
revoco, -are, -avi, -atus: call back; withdraw
saecularis, -e: secular
seorsum (*adv.*): separately
sufficio, -ficere, -feci, -fectus: put in place, replace
vero (*adv.*): truly, in fact

---

de more: "according to custom"
Calisto: Pope Callistus III (r. 1455-1458), who expelled the canons regular from the Basilica of St. John Lateran
pulsos esse ... canonicos regulares: ind. statement introduced by *memor*
Sancto Iohanne Laterano: St. John Lateran, one of the four major basilicas in Rome
canonicos regulares: "canons regular," clerics who lived under a monastic rule (*regula*) and had renounced their property; antecedent of *quos*
eodem in loco: St. John Lateran
Eugenius: Pope Eugene IV (r. 1431-1447), maternal uncle of Paul II
revocavit: subject is *Paulus*
ut ... celebrarent: purpose clause
canonicis saecularibus: "canons secular," clerics who had not renounced their property
aboliturus: Pope Paul is the subject of *aboliturus*
quis: *aliquis* (after *si, nisi, num* and *ne*, "*ali*" takes a holiday)
in demortui locum: "in the place of the deceased"

aut si quod {233ʀ} beneficium vacabat, coactos se canonicatibus illis abdicare ad alias ecclesias transferebat ut tandem beneficia illa, in unum corpus redacta, canonicis regularibus satisfacerent sine ullo suo dispendio, cum eos tum pascere ob inopiam oporteret. Hanc autem ob rem Paulus multum a se alienavit civium animos, quod dicerent illa beneficia, a maioribus suis instituta, pulsis civibus, inquilinis dari. Neque hoc contentus Paulus, seorsum canonicos

---

abdico, -are, -avi, -atus: resign
alieno, -are, -avi, -atus: alienate
animus, -i *m.*: mind; feelings
beneficium, -i *n.*: benefit; benefice, fiefdom given by the pope
canonicatus, -us *m.*: office of canon
canonicus, -i *m.*: canon; clergyman
civis, -is *m./f.*: citizen
cogo, -ere, coegi, coactus: force, compel
contentus, -a, -um: content, satisfied (+ *abl.*)
corpus, corporis *n.*: body
dispendium, -i *n.*: expense, loss
ecclesia, -ae *f.*: church
inopia, -ae *f.*: poverty
inquilinus, -i *m.*: foreigner
instituo, -ere, -ui, -utus: set up
maiores, maiorum *m.*: ancestors (*pl.*)

multum (*adv.*): greatly
oportet, -ere, -uit, - (*impers.*) : it is necessary
pasco,-ere, pavi, pastus: feed; maintain, support
pello,-ere, pepuli, pulsus: drive out
redigo, -ere, redegi, redactus: reduce
regularis, -e: regular
satisfacio, -facere, -feci, -factus: satisfy (+ *dat.*)
seorsum (*adv.*): separately
sine: without (+ *abl.*)
tandem (*adv.*): eventually
transfero, -ferre, -tuli, -latus: transfer
ullus, -a, -um: any
unus, -a, -um: one
vaco, -are, -avi, -atus: be vacant

---

quod: *aliquod* (after *si, nisi, num* and *ne*, "*ali*" takes a holiday)
se ... abdicare: ind. statement introduced by *coactos*; *se* is the reflexive acc. obj. of *abdicare*, "having been compelled to resign (themselves)"
ut ... satisficerent: purpose clause
cum ... oporteret: causal *cum* clause
eos: acc. obj. of *pascere*; it was necessary to feed them because they had given up their property
Hanc autem ob rem: "but on account of this thing," Paul's preference for the canons regular
quod dicerent: clause of alleged reason
beneficia ... dari: ind. statement
a maioribus suis: abl. of personal agent
instituta: participle agreeing with *beneficia*
pulsis civibus: abl. abs.

28

quosdam allocutus, eos minis etiam adhibitis abdicare se illis canonicatibus impellebat. Nonnulli tamen eius minas contemnentes, tempus
vindicandae libertatis expectabant, quod postea eo mortuo eluxit.

*Paul calls for a crusade against the Turks, but the various Christian powers are
fighting amongst themselves*

20 At vero cum nunciatum esset, Thurcos, capta iam fere tota
Epiro, in Illyricum iter parare, oratores statim ad reges et principes

---

abdico, -are, -avi, -atus: resign
adhibeo, -ere, -ui, -itus: use, employ
alloquor, alloqui, allocutus sum: speak to
canonicatus, -us *m.*: office of canon
capio, -ere, cepi, captus: capture, seize
contemno, -temnere, -tempsi, -temptus:
  despise, disdain
eluceo, -ere, eluxi, - : be manifest; happen
Epirus, -i *f.*: Epirus
expecto, -are, -avi, -atus: await, expect
fere (*adv.*): almost
iam (*adv.*): now, already
Illyricum, -i *n.*: Illyricum
impello, -ere, impuli, impulsus: persuade;
  urge on
iter, itineris *n.*: path; march

libertas, -tatis *f.*: freedom
minae, -arum *f.*: threats
nonnullus, -a, -um: some, several
nuncio, -are, -avi, -atus (CL *nuntio*):
  announce
orator, -oris *m.*: speaker; ambassador
paro, -are, -avi, -atus: prepare
postea (*adv.*): afterwards
princeps, -cipis *m.*: leader; prince
quidam, quaedam, quoddam: a certain one
statim (*adv.*): immediately
tempus,-oris *n.*: time; condition, right time
Thurcus, -a, -um: Turkish
totus, -a, -um: whole, all
vero: but, however
vindico, -are, -avi, -atus: vindicate; win back

---

minis ... adhibitis: abl. of means
abdicare: obj. inf. of *impellebat*; *eos* is the subject acc. of *abdicare* and *se* its obj.; "(he
  was compelling them) to resign (themselves)"
illis canonicatibus: abl. of separation
vindicandae libertatis: gerundive phrase, "of liberty to be won back (i.e. of winning
  back liberty)"
quod: antecedent is *tempus*
eo mortuo: abl. abs.
cum nunciatum esset: circumstantial *cum* clause, impers. construction, "when it had
  been announced"
Thurcos: substantive adj., "the Turks"
capta ... tota Epiro: Epirus, a state on the Adriatic Sea, today located between Greece
  and Albania; note that it is fem. and agrees with *capta* and *tota*
Illyricum: Illyricum, a Roman province up the Adriatic shoreline from Epirus, today
  located roughly in Croatia
parare: ind. statement introduced by *nunciatum esset*; subject acc. is *Thurcos* and obj.
  is *iter*

misit, eos oratum, ut compositis rebus suis de bello Thurcis inferendo ad propulsandam iniuriam cogitarent. Qua de re nil certe actum est, cum inter sese gravissimis bellis decertarent: hinc Germani, hinc Anglici, nunc veterem regem, interdum vero novum expetentes. Hinc Hispani, hinc Galli principes veriti regis potentiam, qui regio nomini

---

ago, -ere, egi, actus: do
Anglicus, -a, -um: English
certe (*adv.*): certainly
cogito, -are, -avi, -atus: think; consider
compono, -ere, -posui, -positum: bring together, put in order
decerto, -are, -avi, -atus: fight it out
expeto, -ere, expeti, expetitus: ask for; desire; seek after
Gallus, -a, -um: Gallic, French
Germanus, -a, -um: German
gravis, -e: serious; grave
hinc (*adv.*): from here
Hispanus, -a, -um: Spanish

infero, inferre, intuli, illatus: bring in; inflict
iniuria, -ae *f.*: injustice, wrong, injury
interdum (*adv.*): sometimes
nil *n.* (*indecl.*): nothing
novus, -a, -um: new
oro, -are, -avi, -atus: advise; beseech, entreat
potentia, -ae *f.*: power
princeps, -cipis *m.*: leader; prince
propulso, -are, -avi, -atus: drive back
regius, -a, -um: royal
vereor, -eri, -itus sum: fear
vero (*adv.*): truly, in fact
vetus, veteris: old

---

eos: the *reges et principes*

oratum: acc. supine expressing purpose

ut ... cogitarent: ind. command

de bello Thurcis inferendo: *de* + abl. gerundive phrase, "about the war that must be waged on the Turks (i.e. about waging war on the Turks)"

ad propulsandam iniuriam: *ad* + acc. gerundive expressing purpose, "for the purpose of injustice to be driven back (i.e. to drive back injustice)"

Qua de re: referring to the Turkish march north up the Adriatic

cum ... decertarent: causal *cum* clause

gravissimis bellis: abl. of means

Germani ... Anglici: substantive adjs., "the Germans ... the English"

Hispani ... Galli: each agrees with *principes*

veriti: nom. pl. masc.

regis: the Spanish and French each feared the power of their own king; antecedent of *qui*

30

omnes obtemperare volebat iactabatque se brevi facturum, ut eos
poeniteret, qui secus fecissent.

*Paul is troubled by heresy in Bohemia, but is hindered from acting because of the
Turkish situation and a succession crisis in Hungary*

21 Praeterea vero Paulum urgebat regis Boemiae perfidia, qui
se paulatim a toto corpore Christiani nominis subtrahebat. In hunc
itaque mittere Ungariae [372] regem cum exercitu instituerat, si ei
per bellum in Thurcos susceptum licuisset, sique rem inter regem

---

Boemia, -ae *f.*: Bohemia
brevi (*adv.*): briefly; soon
Christianus, -a, -um: Christian
corpus, corporis *n.*: body
exercitus, -us *m.*: army
iacto, -are, -avi, -atus: throw out; boast
instituo, -ere, -ui, -utus: decide
licet, -ere, -uit, -itus est (*impers.*): it is
permitted, allowed
obtempero, -are, -avi, -atus: obey (+ *dat.*)
paulatim (*adv.*): little by little, gradually
per: through; in the midst of (+ *acc.*)
perfidia, -ae *f.*: faithlessness; heresy

poenitet, -ere, -uit, - (CL *paenitet*): cause to
regret; make sorry
praeterea (*adv.*): in addition
secus (*adv.*): otherwise
subtraho, -trahere, -traxi, -tractus: withdraw
suscipio, -cipere, -cepi, -ceptus (CL
susceptus): take up, begin
Thurcus, -a, -um: Turkish
totus, -a, um: whole, entire
Ungaria, -ae *f.*: Hungary
urgeo, -ere, ursi, - : vex, burden
vero: but, however
volo, velle, volui, - : wish, want

---

obtemperare: obj. inf. of *volebant*; subject acc. is *omnes*
iactabatque ... fecissent: "he was bragging that he would soon bring it about that
they regret it, those who had done otherwise"
se ... facturum: ind. statement introduced by *iactabatque*
ut eos poeniteret: impers. verb, subjunctive in noun clause, obj. of *facturum*, "that it
cause them to regret (i.e. that they regret it)"
qui ... fecissent: rel. clause of characteristic
Boemiae: a region in what is now the Czech Republic
qui: antecedent is *regis Boemiae*
a toto corpore Christiani nominis: "from the entire body of the Christian name (i.e.
from the whole Christian Church)"
In hunc: "against this man (the King of Bohemia)"
instituerat si ... licuisset ... potuissent: past contrafactual cond.; apodosis can
sometimes be indic. for vividness
bellum ... susceptum: "the war having been undertaken (i.e. the undertaking of
war)"

et imperatorem componere potuisset. Nam mortuo Ladislao rege Ungariae eius nepote, qui hẹrede carebat, imperator ipse regnum illud, quod Matthias Vaiovadae filius occupaverat, sibi deberi praedicabat.

Paul mediates a feud between the Caffarelli and Albertini in Rome

22 Differendam itaque rem Paulus in aliud tempus censens, ad componendas quasdam simultates civium Romanorum inter se

---

careo, -ere, -ui, -itus: be without, lack (+ *abl.*)

censeo, -ere, censui, census: judge; assess

civis, -is *m./f.*: citizen

compono, -ponere, -posui, -positus: make up; settle; put in order

debeo, -ere, -ui, -itus: owe

differo, differre, distuli, dilatus: postpone, delay

hẹres, hẹredis (CL *heres*) *m./f.*: heir/heiress

imperator, -oris *m.*: general; emperor

nepos, -otis *m./f.*: nephew/niece

occupo, -are, -avi, -atus: capture, occupy

praedico, -are, -avi, -atus: proclaim, declare

regnum, -i *n.*: kingdom

simultas, -tatis *f.*: enmity

tempus, temporis *n.*: time

Ungaria, -ae *f.*: Hungary

---

mortuo Ladislao rege ... nepote: abl. abs.

Ladislao: Ladislaus V, King of Hungary, 1440-1457; he was involved in a prolonged civil war, royal murders, and a power struggle that resulted in his poisoning in Prague in 1457

rege ... eius nepote: *rege* and *nepote* agree with *Ladislao*; *eius* refers forward to the *imperator*

qui: antecedent is *Ladislao*

imperator: Frederick III the Peaceful, Holy Roman Emperor, r. 1452-1493. After Ladislaus' death, he claimed Hungary for himself

regnum illud ... deberi: ind. statement introduced by *praedicabat*

quod: antecedent is *regnum illud*

Matthias Vaiovadae: Matthias Corvinus (1443-1490), son of the Voivode (Slavic title for a principal commander of military force); he was elected King of Hungary by the Diet of Hungary in 1457-1458 to avoid civil war

Differendam (esse) ... rem: pass. periphrastic in ind. statement, "that the thing ought to be delayed"

ad componendas quasdam simultates: *ad* + acc. gerundive expressing purpose, "in order for certain enmities to be settled (i.e. to settle certain enmities)"

dissidentium animum adięcit. Orta nanque rixa erat inter Iacobum Ioannis Alberini filium et Foelicem nepotem Antonii Capharelli: hanc ob rem accitis ad se patribus familias, eos aliquandiu renitentes, ad concordiam datis vadibus compulit. Verum non ita multo post Iacobus Alberini filius, nusquam laturus iniuriam patri illatam, Antonium Capharellum interficere conatus, confossum

---

accio, -ire, -ivi, -itus: send for, summon
adicio, -ere, adięci (CL *adieci*), **adiectus**: throw; apply one thing to another
aliquandiu (CL *aliquamdiu*) (*adv.*): for some time
animus, -i *m.*: mind
compello, -pellere, -puli, -pulsus: force, compel
concordia, -ae *f.*: harmony, peace
confodio, -fodere, -fodi, -fossus: stab, wound
conor, -ari, -atus sum: attempt, try
dissideo, -ere, dissedi, - : disagree
familia, -ae *f.*: household; family

fero, ferre, tuli, latus: endure, bear
infero, inferre, intuli, illatus: inflict
iniuria, -ae *f.*: injury; insult
interficio, -ficere, -feci, -fectus: kill
multo (*adv.*): much; long (before/after)
nanque (CL *namque*): for indeed, for truly
nepos, -otis *m./f.*: nephew, niece
nusquam (*adv.*): on no occasion
orior, -iri, ortus sum: arise, emerge, crop up
renitor, reniti, renisus sum: struggle
rixa, -ae *f.*: violent quarrel, feud
vas, vadis *m.*: surety, (financial) guarantee
verum: but yet, however

---

dissidentium: pres. act. participle agreeing with *civium Romanorum*

animum adięcit: "he applied his mind (i.e. he turned his attention to)"

rixa: the feud arose out of a rivalry over the love "of a certain courtesan" (*cuiusdam meretricis*) according to Gaspar of Verona (*De Gestis Pauli II* p. 9 Zippel)

Iacobum Ioannis Alberini filium: Giacomo Alberini, son of the rich Roman merchant Giovanni Alberini

Foelicem: Felice Caffarelli, nephew of Antonio Caffarelli, a consistorial advocate

patribus familias: *familias* is an archaic gen., frozen in the form *pater familias*, "head of household"

datis vadibus: abl. of means; Paul asks for a surety, which would then be taken away if the violence were to continue

Iacobus Alberini filius: Giacomo, son of Giovanni Alberini

laturus: fut. act. participle of *fero*

iniuriam patri illatam: his father Giovanni had just been attacked by Felice's brother Lorenzo

Antonium Capharellum: Antonio Caffarelli

confossum: agrees with *Antonium Capharellum*

aliquot gravibus vulneribus, tanquam mortuum reliquit. Hanc ob rem indignatus Paulus, quod contra atque Alberinus iuraverat filius ęgisset, eversis eorum aedibus, redactisque in fiscum omnibus bonis, eos ab urbe exules demum facit. Hos tamen postea suo iussu ad urbem redeuntes in gratiam recępit, restitutis rebus omnibus, paceque inter dissidentes composita, cum tamen ambo aliquandiu in carcere stetissent.

---

aedes, aedis *f.*: shrine; (*pl.*) house
ago, -ere, ęgi (CL *egi*)**, actus**: act
aliquandiu (CL *aliquamdiu*) (*adv.*): for some time
aliquot: a number (of); more than one
ambo, -ae, -o: both
bona, -orum *n.*: goods; possessions; wealth, estate
carcer, -eris *m.*: prison
compono, -ponere, -posui, -positus: make up; settle
contra (*adv.*): against; contrarily
demum (*adv.*): finally
dissideo, -sidere, -sedi, -sessus: disagree
everto, -ere, everti, eversus: destroy, ruin
exul, -ulis *m./f.*: exile
fiscus, -i *m.*: papal treasury

gratia, -ae *f.*: goodwill, friendship
gravis, -e: serious; grave
indignor, -ari, -atus sum: become angry; scorn
iuro, -are, -avi, -atus: swear; promise
iussus, -us *m.*: order, command
postea (*adv.*): afterwards
recipio, -ere, recępi (CL *recepi*)**, receptus**: take in; take back
redeo, -ire, -ivi(ii), -itus: return, go back
redigo, -ere, redegi, redactus: reduce; bring to
relinquo, -ere, reliqui, relictus: leave behind
restituo, -ere, -ui, -utus: restore
sto, -are, steti, statum: stand; remain
tanquam (CL *tamquam*): just as, as if
vulnus, -eris *n.*: wound

---

gravibus vulneribus: abl. of means
quod ... ęgisset: clause of alleged reason
contra atque: "contrary to," "otherwise than"
Alberinus: Giovanni Alberini, whose son broke the truce by attacking Antonio Caffarelli
eversis ... aedibus, redactisque ... omnibus bonis: abl. abs.
exules: predicate acc. of *eos*, "made them exiles"
suo iussu: "at his own command"
in gratiam recępit: idiom, "received back into his favor"
restitutis rebus omnibus: abl. abs.
paceque ... composita: abl. abs.
cum ... stetissent: circumstantial *cum* clause
ambo: nom. pl.

Alovisius Patavinus dies, leaving his estate to two nephews

23 Anno vero MCCCCLXV Alovisius Patavinus pontificis {233v} camerarius, et tituli Sancti Laurentii in Damaso presbyter cardinalis, vir quidem ditissimus, et in rebus agendis sagax, sed ultimo suae vitae tempore parum prudens; quippe qui ex testamento maxima ex parte heredes reliquerat duos fratres cognomento Scarampos, alioquin bonos et liberalis ingenii, sed nequaquam tantis fortunis et

---

ago, -ere, egi, actus: do; manage
alioquin (*adv.*): otherwise
annus, -i *m.*: year
camerarius, -i *m.*: chamberlain
cardinalis, -is *m.*: cardinal
cognomentum, -i *n.*: surname
dis, ditis: rich, wealthy
duo, -ae, -o: two
fortuna, -ae *f.*: wealth, property
heres, heredis (CL *heres*) *m./f.*: heir/heiress
ingenium, -i *n.*: nature; natural disposition
liberalis, -e: noble
nequaquam (*adv.*): by no means

pars, partis *f.*: part; share
parum (*adv.*): too little, not enough
prudens, -entis: sensible, prudent
presbyter, presbyteri (CL *presbyter*) *m.*: priest
quippe (*adv.*): as you see; obviously
relinquo, -ere, reliqui, relictus: leave
sagax, sagacis: wise; acute
tempus, -oris *n.*: time
testamentum, -i *n.*: will, testament
titulus, -i *m.*: title; titular church
ultimus, -a, -um: last, final
vero: but, however

Anno … MCCCCLXV: abl. of time when (1465); this sentence lacks a main verb, presumably *mortuus est*

Alovisius Patavinus: Alovisius of Padua, also called Ludovico Trevisan, was Paul's former rival (see ch. 4-7)

pontificis camerarius: Chamberlain, the cardinal in charge of the *Camera Apostolica*, which handled papal financial matters

tituli … cardinalis: a cardinal priest was assigned to each "titular church" in Rome, named after their founders; the San Lorenzo in Damaso lies in central Rome

in rebus agendis: "in accomplishing things," a reference to his military successes

ultimo … tempore: abl. of time when; a reference to his lack of sense in making his will

quippe qui: "since he"

maxima ex parte: idiom, heirs "of the largest part"

heredes: pred. acc. with *duos fratres … Scarampos*

cognomento: abl. of respect, "*Scarampos* in respect to their name"; Alovisius Patavinus was also from the Scarampi family

liberalis ingenii: gen. of description

tantis fortunis et proventibus: abls. with *dignos*

proventibus Ecclesiae partis dignos. (Quid homines suspicarentur scimus.)

Paul voids the will of Alovisius Patavinus, redistributing his estate more fairly

24 Has autem facultates Paulus, ei licet testandi facultatem ultro permisisset, sibi vindicavit. Scarampos cępit, et [373] tam diu honesto tamen loco retinuit, quoad quae Florentiam delata fuerant ad se deferrentur. Fugientes Scarampi, dum hac de re ageretur, capti

---

ago, -ere, egi, actus: to do, handle
capio, -ere, cępi (CL *cepi*), **captus**: take, seize, arrest
defero, -ferre, -uli, -latus: carry, bring
dignus, -a, -um: worthy, deserving (+ *abl.*)
diu (*adv.*): for a long time
Ecclesia, -ae *f.*: the Church
facultas, -tatis *f.*: opportunity; capability; resources (*pl.*)
Florentia, -ae *f.*: Florence
fugio, -ere, fugi, fugitus: flee
honestus, -a, -um: respected, honorable
licet: although (+ *subjunctive*)

locus, -i *m.*: place
pario, -ere, peperi, partus: produce; acquire
permitto, -mittere, -misi, -missus: permit, allow
proventus, -us *m.*: income; success
quoad: until (+ *subjunctive*)
retineo, -ere, retinui, retentus: restrain; keep
scio, -ire, -ivi, -itus: know
suspicor, -ari, -atus sum: suspect
tam (*adv.*): so
testor, -ari, -atus sum: make a will
ultro (*adv.*): voluntarily
vindico, -are, -avi, -atus: claim

---

partis: perf. pass. participle of *pario*, agreeing with *fortunis et proventibus*

quid … suspicarentur: ind. question; Platina is explaining that the previous sentence is not his own opinion

ei: referring to the deceased Alovisius Patavinus

testandi: gerund, "of making a will"

permisisset: Paul is subject

sibi: dat. of advantage

cępit … retinuit: Paul is subject

honesto … loco: abl. of place where

quae: antecedent is an assumed *ea*

Florentiam: acc. of place to which

dum … ageretur: *dum* + imperf. subjunctive as "while" (see Introduction 7.C); impers. pass., "while there was a doing concerning this thing (i.e. while the matter was being handled)"

in carcerem coniiciuntur. Verum, cum bona patriarchae Florentia Romam delata fuissent, Scarampos cum bona parte incolumes dimittens, in reliquos patriarchae familiares maiore benignitate usus est quam ipse testator instituisset. Atque hoc modo bona hominis tanta diligentia parta, maiore retenta - cum magna opum iactatione

---

benignitas, -tatis *f.*: liberality, favor

bona, -orum *n.*: goods, possessions; wealth (*pl.*)

carcer, -eris *m.*: prison, jail

coniicio, -iicere, -ieci, -iectus: throw together; put

defero, -ferre, -tuli, -latus: bring; deliver

diligentia, -ae *f.*: diligence; care

dimitto, -ere, dimisi, dimissus: send away; release

familiaris, -is *m./f.*: household member

Florentia, -ae *f.*: Florence

iactatio, -onis *f.*: boasting; showing off

incolumis, -e: unharmed

instituo, -ere, -ui, -utus: set up, establish

modus, -i *m.*: manner, way

ops, opis *f.*: power; resources, wealth (*pl.*)

pario, -ere, peperi, partus: produce; acquire

pars, partis *f.*: part, share; portion

patriarcha, -ae *m.*: patriarch

reliquus, -a, -um: rest of, remaining

retineo, -ere, retinui, retentus: retain

Roma, -ae *f.*: Rome

testator, -oris *m.*: testator; one who makes a will

utor, uti, usus sum: use (+ *abl.*)

verum: but yet, however

---

cum ... delata fuissent: circumstantial *cum* clause

bona patriarchae: the goods of Alovisius Patavinus (Ludovico Trevisan), which he had left to the Scarampi brothers

Florentia: abl. of place from which

Romam: acc. of place to which

Scarampos: relatives of Alovisius Patavinus

bona parte: abl. of accompaniment

patriarchae: possessive gen. of *reliquos ... familiares*, still referring to Alovisius Patavinus

maiore: compar. of *magnus*; abl. sing. f. with *benignitate*

quam: compar., "than"

hoc modo: abl. of manner

bona hominis: referring to the estate or goods of Alovisius Patavinus

tanta diligentia: abl. of means

parta ... retenta: participles agreeing with *bona*

maiore: compar. of *magnus*, abl. sing. f. with an implied *diligentia*, abl. of manner

cum magna ... iactatione: abl. of manner

ac si annos Matusalem victurus esset - ab eo sunt partim possessa, partim destributa, quocum diutius simultatibus, odiis, maledicentia certaverat, cum maluisset ad Thurcos ipsos quam ad Paulum bona sua recidere. Sed neque hoc contenta Divina Providentia voluit quoque eius corpus iam sepultum in praedam dari. Ab ipsis enim,

---

annus, -i *m.*: year

certo, -are, -avi, -atus: dispute; fight

contentus, -a, -um: content, satisfied (+ *abl.*)

corpus, corporis *n.*: body; corpse

destribuo, -ere, -ui, -utus (CL *distribuo*): distribute

diu (*adv.*): (for) a long time

divinus, -a, -um: divine

iam (*adv.*): now, already

maledicentia, -ae *f.*: slander

malo, malle, malui, - : want more, prefer

odium, -i *n.*: hatred

partim (*adv.*): partly

possideo, -sidere, -sedi, -sessus: seize; hold possession of

praeda, -ae *f.*: booty; prey

providentia, -ae *f.*: providence

recido, -ere, recidi, recasus: go to; fall back, happen upon

sepelio, -ire, sepelivi, sepultus: bury, inter

simultas, -tatis *f.*: grudge; enmity

Thurci, -orum *m.*: the Turks

vinco, -ere, vici, victus: to conquer

volo, velle, volui, - : wish, want

---

ac si ... victurus esset: *ac si* "as if"; protasis of a pres. contrafactual cond. with an elided apodosis

annos Matusalem: here *vinco* takes a double acc., "beat Methuselah his years" (Methuselah was said to have lived to 969 years)

ab eo: referring to Paul

possessa (sunt) ... destributa (sunt): subject is *bona hominis*

quocum: abl. of accompaniment, "with whom," antecedent is *eo*

diutius: compar. of *diu*

simultatibus, odiis, maledicentia: abls. of means

certaverat ... maluisset: Alovisius Patavinus is subject

cum maluisset: concessive *cum* clause

ad Thurcos ipsos ... ad Paulam: Platina says that Alovisius Patinavus would prefer that his wealth "go to the Turks themselves rather than to Paul"

quam: compar., "than"

recidere: obj. inf. of *maluisset*; *bona sua* is subject acc. of the inf.

hoc: abl. with *contenta*, neuter "thing" referring to Paul taking charge of Alovisius' goods

Divina Providentia: nom.; "Divine Providence"

corpus ... dari: *dari* is obj. inf. of *voluit*, *corpus* is subject acc. of *dari*

sepultum: perf. pass. participle agreeing with *corpus*

in praedam: idiom, "for the sake of plunder"

ipsis: antecedent of *quibus*, refers to the canons of San Lorenzo in Damaso and a member of the cardinal's household

quibus ipse beneficia Sancti Laurentii in Damaso dederat, noctu aperto sepulchro, annulo et vestibus spoliatus est. In hos autem Paulus, re cognita, graviter animadvertit.

Paul generously hosts Frederick, son of King Ferdinand of Naples, and gives him a golden rose

25 Eodem fere tempore Foedericus adolescens ęgregius Ferdinandi filius, Mediolanum iturus ad ducendam Francisci Sfortiae

---

adolescens, -entis (CL *adulescens*) *m./f.*: young adult
animadverto, -vertere, -verti, -versus: notice; punish (with *in* + acc.)
annulus, -i *m.*: ring
aperio, -ire, aperui, apertus: uncover, open
beneficium, -i *n.*: benefit; benefice
cognosco, -noscere, -novi, -nitus: learn
ęgregius, -a, -um (CL *egregius*): distinguished

fere (*adv.*): about; nearly, generally
graviter (*adv.*): severely
idem, eadem, idem: the same
Mediolanum, -i *m.*: Milan
noctu (*adv.*): at night
sepulchrum, -i *n.*: grave, tomb
spolio, -are, -avi, -atus: rob; deprive (+ *abl.*)
tempus, temporis *n.*: time
vestis, -is *f.*: clothes

---

beneficia: "benefices," the rights to income from an ecclesiastical property, in this case San Lorenzo
Sancti Laurentii: San Lorenzo in Damaso in central Rome
aperto sepulchro: abl. abs.
re cognita: abl. abs.
Eodem ... tempore: abl. of time when
Foedericus: Frederick IV of Naples (1452-1504), son of the Ferdinand I of Naples (1423-1494), from the House of Trastámara
Ferdinandi: Ferdinand I of Naples (1423-1494), son of Alfonso V of Aragon; he used support from the pope and from his allies in Milan to put down a rebellion led by the Orsini and the French John of Anjou in Naples from 1459-1465
Mediolanum: acc. of place to which
iturus: fut. act. participle, "about to go"
ad ducendam ... filiam: *ad* + acc. gerundive to express purpose, "in order for the daughter to be led (i.e. to lead the daughter)"
Francisci Sfortiae: Francesco I Sforza (1401-1466), a *condottiero* (mercenary leader) and the Duke of Milan, was a military and political power-broker who balanced a complicated web of allies and enemies from Genoa to Naples

filiam, fratris uxorem, in regnum, Romam veniens, prodeunte obviam honorato quoque et Rhodorico vicecancellario, perbenigne a Paulo suscipitur, ac Rosa donatur, quam pontifices quotannis donare alicui ex principibus Christianis consuevere.

---

aliquis, aliquid: someone, something
Christianus, -a, -um: Christian
consuesco, -suescere, -suevi, -suetus: be accustomed; tend
dono, -are, -avi, -atus: give; present with (+ *abl.*)
honoratus, -a, -um: honored; noble
obviam (*adv.*): on the way to meet
perbenigne (*adv.*): very kindly
pontifex, -ficis *m.*: pontiff, pope

princeps, -cipis *m.*: leader; prince
prodeo, -ire, -ivi(ii), -itus: go out
quotannis (*adv.*): every year, yearly
regnum, -i *n.*: kingdom (here Naples)
Roma, -ae *f.*: Rome
rosa, -ae *f.*: rose
suscipio, -cipere, -cepi, -ceptus: receive
uxor, -oris *f.*: wife
vicecancellarius, -i *m.*: vice-chancellor

---

filiam: Ippolita Maria Sforza (1446-1484), first wife of Alfonso II, Duke of Calabria
fratris: Alfonso II of Naples (1448-1495), Duke of Calabria in 1465; he was a patron of Renaissance arts
uxorem: in apposition with *filiam*
in regnum: Frederick's purpose for going to Milan is to fetch Francesco Sforza's daughter, his brother's wife, and take her to Naples ("the kingdom")
Romam: acc. of place to which
honorato: substantive adj., "the nobility"
Rhodorico: Rodrigo Borgia (1431-1503), later Pope Alexander VI (r. 1492-1503)
vicecancellario: the vice-chancellor was in charge of the chancery (*Cancellaria Apostolica*)
a Paulo: abl. of personal agent with *suscipitur*
Rosa: abl. with *donatur*, the Golden Rose, presented annually by the pope as a token of reverence from the Church
quam: rel. pronoun, antecedent is *Rosa*
alicui: dat. of ind. obj.
consuevere: alternative form of *consueverunt*

Paul calls on Ferdinand, King of Naples, to help him fight the sons of Count Everso

26 Interim vero cum Ferdinando in animo esset, eos bello persequi, et potissimum in regno suo existentes, qui, dum a Gallis premeretur, a se defecerant, misissetque copias quasdam ea mente, ut ducem Soranum adoriretur, pontifex, divertere id bellum cupiens, archiepiscopum Mediolanensem eo propere misit oratum

---

adorior, -iri, adortus sum: attack
animus, -i *m.*: mind
archiepiscopus, -i *m.*: archbishop
copia, -ae *f.*: abundance; troops (*pl.*)
cupio, -ere, -ivi, -itus: wish
deficio, -ere, defeci, defectus: defect
diverto, -ere, diverti, diversus: divert; derail
dux, ducis *m.*: leader; duke
eo (*adv.*): there, to that place
existo, -ere, existiti, existitus: exist
Gallus, -a, -um: Gallic
interim (*adv.*): meanwhile
Mediolanensis, -e: Milanese

mens, mentis *f.*: mind; intention
oro, -are, -avi, -atum: ask, beg
persequor, -sequi, -secutus sum: pursue; attack; take vengeance on
pontifex, -ficis *m.*: pontiff, pope
potissimum (*adv.*): especially
premo, -ere, pressi, pressus: pursue; harass
propere (*adv.*): quickly
quidam, quaedam, quoddam: certain, some
regnum, -i *n.*: kingdom (here "of Naples")
Soranus, -a , -um: of Sora
vero: but, however

---

cum ... esset ... misissetque: causal *cum* clause

Ferdinando in animo esset: *Ferdinando* is dat. of the possessor, he "had it in mind"; King Ferdinand of Naples (1423-1494)

eos ... existentes ... defecerant: the town of Sora had abandoned Ferdinand when he had counted on it in his wars with John of Anjou and the French; he considered them traitors

eos ... persequi: ind. statement introduced by *in animo esset*

bello: abl. of means

dum ... premeretur: *dum* + imperf. subjunctive "while" (see Introduction 7.C)

Gallis: substantive adj., "by the French." Ferdinand had to defend his kingdom from a claim from the French, led by John of Anjou from 1459-1464

a se defecerant: ind. refl., "they had defected from him(self)"

ea mente: abl. of manner, "with this intent"

ut ... adoriretur: noun clause in apposition to *ea mente*, "with this intent (namely) to attack the Duke of Sora"

ducem Soranum: Pier Paolo Guantelmo; the Duchy of Sora, located between Rome and Naples, was a fief to the Kingdom of Naples before 1463, when Pope Pius II made Sora a papal fief

archiepiscopum Mediolanensem: Stefano Nardini (d. 1484), a cardinal, also Archbishop of Milan; he served as *nuncio* to multiple popes

oratum: acc. supine expressing purpose

ut copias illas - quemadmodum ratione pheudi tenebatur - ad se mitteret, quod [374] diceret sibi in animo esse comitis Aversae filios, Ecclesie nequaquam obtemperantes, e medio tollere.

The sons of Count Everso had long been defying the pope's authority

27 Nam eo fere tempore Aversae comes moritur, quo Paulus pontifex creatur; corpusque eius, Romam delatum, in Basilica Sanctae

---

animus, -i *m.*: mind
comes, comitis *m.*: companion; count
copia, -ae *f.*: abundance; (*pl.*) troops
corpus, -oris *n.*: body
creo, -are, -avi, -atus: create; elect
defero, -ferre, -tuli, -latus: brought down
Ecclesia, -ae *f.*: the Church
fere (*adv.*): about, nearly
medium, -i *n.*: middle; midst
nequaquam (*adv.*): by no means

obtempero, -are, -avi, -atus: obey (+ *dat.*)
pheudum, -i (or *feudum*) *n.*: fief; feudal allegiance
quemadmodum (*adv.*): in as much as
ratio, -onis *f.*: reason; rule
Roma, -ae *f.*: Rome
tempus, -oris *n.*: time
teneo, -ere, tenui, tentus: hold, keep
tollo, -ere, sustuli, sublatus: lift; take away

---

ut ... mitteret: ind. command; Ferdinand is subject of *tenebatur* and *mitteret*

copias illas: referring to the *copias quasdam* with which Ferdinand had intended to fight his betrayers

ratione pheudi: abl. of means, "by reason of his feudal allegiance"

ad se: ind. refl., "to him (the pope)"

quod diceret: clause of alleged reason; Paul is subject of *diceret*

sibi in animo (id) esse: ind. statement introduced by *diceret*; implied *id* refers to *tollere e medio*

sibi: dat. of possession

comitis Aversae: Count Everso degli Anguillara (d. 1464) was a feudal lord who owned great estates in northern Latium; he had disobeyed papal authority since the early 1450s in pursuit of various mercenary activities and backed a rebellion in 1460

filios: acc. obj. of *tollere*; Deifobo and Francesco, sons of Count Everso

Ecclesie: dat. sing. (CL *Ecclesiae*, see Introduction 6.B)

e medio: idiom, "from their midst"

eo ... tempore: abl. of time when, antecedent of *quo*; date is 1464

Aversae comes: Count Everso, whom Platina seemingly mistakenly calls "the Count of Aversa"

Romam: acc. of place to which

delatum: agrees with *corpus*

Basilica Sanctae Mariae Maioris: Basilica di Santa Maria Maggiore, one of the four major Basilicas in Rome

Mariae Maioris sepęlitur. Rex itaque, acerrimus Deiphoebi hostis, quippe qui ab eo superiore bello insidiis, veneno, et armis petitus fuerat, copiarum suarum praefectis mandat ut primo quoque {234R} tempore proficiscantur, quo pontifex ire iusserit. Antea enim Deiphoebum et Franciscum ad se vocatos monuerat ut et iter tutum a latronibus servarent, ne Romam aliunde venientes in ipsis prope urbis Romae portis spoliarentur; utque Securanciae praefecti

---

acer, acris, acre: sharp, vehement
aliunde (*adv.*): from elsewhere
antea (*adv.*): before
arma, -orum *n.*: arms
copia, -ae *f.*: abundance; troops (*pl.*)
hostis, -is *m./f.*: enemy
insidiae, -arum *f.*: plot; treachery; ambush
iter, itineris *n.*: road
iubeo, -ere, iussi, iussus: order
latro, -onis *m.*: thief
mando, -are, -avi, -atus: commission; order, command
moneo, -ere, -ui, -itus: warn, advise
peto, -ere, -ivi, -itus: attack
pontifex, -ficis *m.*: pontiff, pope
porta, -ae *f.*: door, gate
praefectus, -i *m.*: commander; prefect

primus, -a, -um: first
proficiscor, proficisci, profectus sum: depart, set out
prope (*adv.*): near; close by
quippe: of course, naturally
quisque, quaeque, quodque: each
quo (*adv.*): to where
Roma, -ae *f.*: Rome
sepęlio (CL *sepelio*), **-ire, sepelivi, sepultum**: bury
servo, -are, -avi, -atus: guard, preserve
spolio, -are, -avi, -atus: rob
superus, -a, -um: above; previous
tempus, temporis *n.*: time; opportunity
tutus, -a, -um: safe
venenum, -i *n.*: poison
voco, -are, -avi, -atus: call; summon

Rex: King Ferdinand I of Naples (1423-1494)
Deiphoebi: Deifobo, son of Count Everso
quippe qui: "since he"
ab eo: referring to Deifobo
superiore bello: abl. of time within which, "during the previous war"
petitus fuerat: pluperf. pass. (CL *petitus erat*, see Introduction 7.D)
ut ... proficiscantur: ind. command
primo quoque tempore: abl. of time when, "at each (of their) first opportunity"
Deiphoebum et Franciscum: sons of Count Everso
vocatos: agreeing with *Deiphoebum et Franciscum*
ut ... servarent: ind. command
latronibus: abl. of separation
ne ... spoliarentur: neg. purpose clause
Romam: acc. of place to which
utque ... redderent: ind. command, dependent on *monuerat; ut + que* coordinates with the *et* above

43

Vici quondam filio Caprarolam, quod oppidum est, redderent, cum omnia fere ipsius praefecti bona possiderent. Utrunque vero non modo facere recusarunt, verum etiam minas addidere, iactantes saepius se comitis Aversae filios esse, nec lacessentibus parcituros.

The sons of Count Everso are defeated; one escapes but the other is captured

28 Tum vero Paulus clanculum paratis rebus omnibus ad bellum necessariis, supervenientibus etiam regiis copiis, quintodecimo die

---

addo, -ere, addidi, additus: add

bona, -orum *n.*: goods, possessions; wealth (*pl.*)

Caprarola, -ae *f.*: Caprarola, a town in Lazio, north of Rome

clanculum: (*adv.*) secretly

comes, comitis *m.*: companion; Count

copia, -ae *f.*: abundance; troops (*pl.*)

dies, diei *m./f.*: day

fere (*adv.*): nearly

iacto, -are, -avi, -atus: boast

lacesso, -ere, -ivi, -itus: provoke

minae, -arum *f.*: threats

modo (*adv.*): only

necessarius, -a, -um: necessary

oppidum, -i *n.*: town

parco, -ere, peperci, parcitus (CL *parsum*): spare, forgive (+ *dat.*)

paro, -are, -avi, -atus: prepare

possideo, -sidere, -sedi, -sessus: possess, occupy

praefectus, -i *m.*: commander; prefect

quintodecimus, -a, -um: fifteenth

quondam (*adv.*): formerly, one time

recuso, -are, -avi, -atus: refuse

reddo, -ere, reddidi, redditus: return; restore

regius, -a, -um: royal

supervenio, -venire, -veni, -ventus: come upon, arrive

uterque, utraque, utrunque (CL *utrumque*): each of two, both

vero: but, however

verum: but

Vicus, -i *m.*: Vico Equense, a town just south of Naples

Securanciae praefecti Vici … filio: "Securanza the son of the former (*quondam*) prefect of Vico Equense"

quod: Caprarola is antecedent, *quod* is neuter "which (thing)"

cum … possiderent: causal *cum* clause; the fiefs at Caprarola, a site north of Rome, belonged to the Prefect of Vico's fiefdom and had been taken by Deifobo and Francesco

Utrunque: "either thing"; namely, keeping the road safe and returning Caprarola

recusarunt: syncopated from *recusa(ve)runt*

addidere: alt. form of *addiderunt*

saepius: compar. of *saepe*

se … esse … parcituros: ind. statement introduced by *iactantes*

paratis rebus omnibus … necessariis: abl. abs.

ad bellum: "for war," in CL dat. *bello* (see Introduction 7.B)

supervenientibus … regiis copiis: abl. abs.; *regiis* here, "belonging to the Kingdom of Naples"

quintodecimo die: abl. of time when

posteaquam incohatum est, bello eos incautos et nil tale opinantes oppressit, redactis in potestatem Ecclesiae novem castellis: quorum de numero aliqua ita munita natura et arte erant, ut vix opera hominum expugnari posse crederentur. Deiphoebus autem veritus ne captus ad regem mitteretur, salutem sibi fuga quaesivit. Capitur autem Franciscus frater cum filio, et quinquennio in arce Hadriani retentus, demum creato Sixto liberatur.

---

aliquis, -qua, -quod: some
ars, artis *f.*: skill, craft
arx, arcis *f.*: citadel
capio, -ere, cepi, captus: seize; capture
castellum, -i *n.*: castle
creo, -are, -avi, -atus: create; elect
demum (*adv.*): finally
Ecclesia, -ae *f.*: the Church
expugno, -are, -avi, -atus: assault; conquer
fuga, -ae *f.*: flight, escape
incautus, -a, -um: incautious (+ *dat.*)
incoho, -are, -avi, -atus: begin
libero, -are, -avi, -atus: free; release
munio, -ire, -ivi, -itus: fortify
novem (*indecl.*): nine
numerus, -i *m.*: number

opera, -ae *f.*: work
opinor, -ari, -atus sum: imagine, expect
opprimo, -ere, oppressi, oppressus: crush, overwhelm; take by surprise
posteaquam (*conj.*): after
potestas, -tatis *f.*: power, rule
quaero, -ere, quaesivi, quaesitus: seek
quinquennium, -i *n.*: period of five years
redigo, -ere, redegi, redactus: drive back; reduce
retineo, -ere, retinui, retentus: keep; detain
salus, -utis *f.*: health; safety
talis, -e: such; of that sort
vereor, -eri, -itus sum: respect; fear
vix (*adv.*): hardly

---

incohatum est: *bellum* is implied subject
bello: dat. with *incautos*; or perhaps abl. of means
eos: Count Everso's sons, Deifobo and Francesco
redactis ... castellis: abl. abs.; antecedent to *quorum*
natura et arte: abl. of means
ut ... crederentur: result clause
opera: abl. of means
hominum: subjective gen.
ne ... mitteretur: fear clause, "that having been captured, he *would* be sent"
fuga: abl. of means
quinquennio: abl. of extent of time (post-Classical, see Introduction 7.A)
arce Hadriani: the mausoleum of Emperor Hadrian (r. 117-138 AD), converted to a papal citadel and now called Castel Sant'Angelo, see fig. 4 (p. 83)
creato Sixto: abl. abs., "when Sixtus was elected." Pope Sixtus IV (1414-1484) succeeded Paul in 1471. He created the Vatican Library, made Platina the director, and was the dedicatee of Platina's *Lives of the Popes*

A dispute over tribute arises between Paul and King Ferdinand of Naples

29 Hinc postea inter Paulum et regem [375] ipsum ortae graves inimicitiae sunt, cum Ferdinandus hoc tanto merito peteret superiorum annorum tributum, quod Ecclesiae pendebat, sibi relaxari et, quod deinceps soluturus esset, diminui, cum regnum Siciliae patruus suus possideret, cuius ipse una cum regno Neapolitano vectigal penderet. Inspicienda dicens et sua merita et considerandum quid

---

annus, -i *m.*: year
considero, -are, -avi, -atus: consider
deinceps (*adv.*): thereafter
diminuo, -ere, -ui, -utus: diminish
Ecclesia, -ae *f.*: the Church
gravis, -e: heavy; serious
hinc (*adv.*): from here
inimicitia, -ae *f.*: enmity, hostility
inspicio, -ere, inspexi, inspectus: examine, consider
meritum, -i *n.*: merit, service
Neapolitanus, -a, -um: Neapolitan; of Naples
orior, -iri, ortus sum: arise
patruus, -i *m.*: (paternal) uncle

pendo, -ere, pependi, pensus: weigh out; pay
peto, -ere, -ivi, -itus: ask (for)
possideo, -sidere, -sedi, -sessus: seize; possess
postea (*adv.*): afterwards
regnum, -i *n.*: kingdom
relaxo, -are, -avi, -atus: lighten, alleviate
Sicilia, -ae *f.*: Sicily
solvo, -ere, solvi, solutus: loosen; pay off
superior, -is: previous
tributum, -i *n.*: tax, tribute
una (*adv.*): together
vectigal, -alis *n.*: tax, tribute

---

cum ... peteret: causal *cum* clause

Ferdinandus: Ferdinand I of Naples (1423-1494)

hoc tanto merito: abl. of cause, the *merito* refers to his aid against the sons of Count Everso (ch. 26-28)

tributum ... relaxari et ... diminui: ind. statement introduced by *peteret*

quod ... pendebat: antecedent is *tributum*

quod ... soluturus esset: subjunctive because the rel. clause is within ind. statement

cum ... possideret: causal *cum* clause

cuius: antecedent is *regnum Siciliae*

Inspicienda (esse) ... sua merita: pass. periphrastic in ind. statement, "that his own services must be considered"

considerandum (esse): pass. periphrastic in ind. statement, "and that it must be considered"

quid posset ... accidere: ind. question, "what could happen on the contrary" with *considerandum*

posset in contrarium accidere, cum diceret se continuo acies quasdam in armis habere, non magis sua quam pontificis Romani gratia, ut in bello contra Aversanos paulo ante noverat. Commemorabat vicissim Paulus merita Ecclesiae erga Ferdinandum; atque hoc modo altercationibus in longum res ipsa semper protracta est, cum uterque repetendi ius suum tempus quaereret.

---

accido, -ere, accidi, - : happen, occur
acies, aciei *f.*: edge, battle line
altercatio, -onis *f.*: contention, debate
arma, -orum *n.*: arms
commemoro, -are, -avi, -atus: recall, relate
continuo (*adv.*): immediately, continuously
contra: against (+ *acc.*)
contrarium, -i *n.*: opposite
Ecclesia, -ae *f.*: the Church
erga: towards (+ *acc.*)
ius, iuris *n.*: right
longus, -a, -um: long
magis (*adv.*): to greater extent, more
meritum, -i *n.*: merit, service

modus, -i *m.*: manner, way
nosco, -ere, novi, notus: learn, find out
paulo (*adv.*): by a little
pontifex, -ficis *m.*: pontiff, pope
protraho, -trahere, -traxi, -tractus: drag forward, prolong
quaero, -ere, quaesivi, quaesitus: search for, seek
quidam, quaedam, quoddam: certain
repeto, -ere, -ivi, -itus: regain, get back
tempus, -oris *n.*: time; opportunity, chance
uterque, utraque, utrumque: each (of two)
vicissim (*adv.*): in turn

---

cum diceret: causal *cum* clause
se ... habere: ind. statement
non magis sua quam pontificis Romani gratia: *gratia* goes first with *sua*, then the gen., "not more for his own sake than that of the Roman pontiff"
ut ... noverat: "as he had found out"
Aversanos: referring to Deifobo and Francesco Everso, sons of Count Everso
hoc modo: abl. of manner, "in this way"
altercationibus: abl. of cause
in longum: substantive adj., "for a long time"
cum ... quaereret: causal *cum* clause
repetendi: gen. gerund; dependent on *tempus*, acc. obj. is *ius suum*, "the opportunity of regaining his own right"

King Ferdinand invites Jacopo Piccinino to Naples, where he is jailed and murdered

30 Moliri res novas rex interim cavebat Iacobi Picennini, qui Sulmonem in Marsis et alia opida tenebat, potentiam veritus; quem postea Franciscus Sfortia socer ad regem misit data fide se quotiens libuisset incolumem rediturum. Verum aliter Iacobo quam putarat accidit. Captus enim Neapoli a Ferdinando cum filio, et in carcerem coniectus, non ita multo post vita privatur, figmento adhibito quod

---

accido, -ere, accidi, - : happen, occur
adhibeo, -ere, -ui, -itus: use, employ
aliter (*adv.*): otherwise, differently
capio, -ere, cepi, captus: take hold, capture
carcer, -eris *m.*: prison
caveo, -ere, cavi, cautus: take care (against), avoid
conicio, -ere, conieci, coniectus (CL *coniectus*): throw
fides, fidei *f.*: faith; a pledge of protection
figmentum, -i *n.*: fiction
incolumis, -e: unharmed, safe
interim (*adv.*): meanwhile
libet, -ere, -uit, -itus est (*impers.*): it pleases
Marsus, -a, -um: related to the Marsi, an ancient people in central Italy; here with an assumed *finibus* ("territory")"

molior, -iri, -itus sum: undertake
multo (*adv.*): much, by much
Neapolis, -is *f.*: Naples
novus, -a, -um: new
opidum, -i (CL *oppidum*) *n.*: town
postea (*adv.*): afterwards
potentia, -ae *f.*: power
privo, -are, -avi, -atus: deprive, rob
quotiens (*adv.*): as often as
redeo, -ire, -ivi(ii), -itus: return
soceri, soceri *m.*: father-in-law
Sulmo, -onis *f.*: Sulmona, a town in Italy
teneo, -ere, tenui, tentus: hold, possess
vereor, -eri, -itus sum: fear, dread
verum (*adv.*): however

Moliri: obj. inf. of *cavebat*
res novas: idiom, "a new political situation," acc. obj. of *Moliri*
Iacobi Picennini: possessive gen. with *potentiam*. Jacopo Piccinino was an Italian noble and *condottiero*, son of Niccolò Piccinino. He supported the French John of Anjou in the wars for Naples from 1459-1464 from his territory in Abruzzo
qui ... tenebat: rel. clause, antecedent is *Iacobi Picennini*
veritus: agrees with *rex*
Franciscus Sfortia: Francesco Sforza, Duke of Milan. Francesco was the founder of the Sforza dynasty in Milan and its surrounding territories. After spending most of the 1440s and 1450s fighting Niccolò Piccinino and his son Jacopo, Sforza married his daughter Drusiana to Jacopo and made an alliance
se ... rediturum (esse): ind. statement introduced by *data fide*
aliter ... quam: "differently than"
putarat: syncopated from *puta(ve)rat*
Neapoli: locative
multo: abl. of degree of difference
vita: abl. of separation
figmento adhibito: abl. abs. with concessive sense
quod ... fregisset: clause of alleged reason

in carcere ipso decidens crus fregisset, dum redeuntes ab Ischia (quam Aenariam antiqui vocabant) triremes regis de Gallis victrices studiosius quam cautius per fenestram inspicit.

Some believed the pope privy to the murder, but the idea is rejected since the pope had much to gain from Piccinino

31 Sunt qui arbitrantur hominem adhuc vivere; quod ego nullo modo credo, cum nullus esset in Italia aptior, si auctoritatem hominis in militia respicis, ad evertendum Ferdinandi regis imperium.

---

adhuc (*adv.*): still
Aenaria, -ae *f.*: Aenaria, ancient name for Ischia
antiquus, -a, um: ancient; (*substantively in pl.*) the ancients
aptus, -a, -um: suitable, proper
arbitror, -ari, -atus sum: believe, think
auctoritas, -tatis *f.*: power; reputation
carcer, -eris *m.*: prison, jail
caute (*adv.*): cautiously
crus, cruris *n.*: leg
decido, -ere, decidi, - : fall
everto, -ere, everti, eversus: overturn, overthrow
fenestra, -ae *f.*: window
frango, -ere, fregi, fractus: break, shatter
Gallus, -a, -um: Gallic, French

imperium, -i *n.*: command, rule
inspicio, -ere, inspexi, inspectus: examine, look at
Ischia, -ae *f.*: an island in the gulf of Naples
Italia, -ae *f.*: Italy
militia, -ae *f.*: army
modus, -i *m.*: manner, way
nullus, -a, -um: not any, no one
per: through (+ *acc.*)
redeo, -ire, -ivi(ii), -itus: return, go back
respicio, -ere, respexi, respectus: consider
studiose (*adv.*): eagerly
triremis, -is *f.*: trireme, ship
victrix, victricis: victorious
vivo, -ere, vixi, victus: be alive, live
voco, -are, -avi, -atus: call

---

de Gallis: "victorious over the Gauls"

victrices: agrees with *triremes*; the Neapolitan navy was returning from an engagement off Ischia, where they destroyed the fleet of John of Anjou with the help of the Aragonese navy

studiosus ... cautius: compar. adverbs

quam: compar., "than"

hominem ... vivere: ind. statement; on the use of *homo* see Introduction 7.E

quod ... credo: antecedent is previous clause, "a thing which I ... "

nullo modo: abl. of manner, "in no way"

cum ... esset: causal *cum* clause

aptior: compar. of *aptus*; construe closely with *ad evertendum*

ad evertendum imperium: *ad* + acc. gerundive expressing purpose, "in order for the power to be overthrown (i.e. to overthrow the power)"

Ferdinandi: King Ferdinand I of Naples (1423-1494)

Substiterat in via hac re cognita, Senis nanque erat, ducis Mediolani filia {234v} Neapolim ad maritum itura, ut fidem faceret nulla patris sui [376] culpa Ferdinandum in Iacobi Picennini necem conspirasse. Quid autem ea de re suspicati sint homines, optime novimus. Fuere etiam qui dicerent id prius a Paulo pontifice scitum fore, cum illis

---

cognosco, -noscere, -novi, -nitus: know, learn
conspiro, -are, -avi, -atus: plot, conspire
culpa, -ae *f.*: fault
dux, ducis *m.*: leader, duke
fides, fidei *f.*: faith
maritus, -i *m.*: husband
Mediolanum, -i *n.*: Milan
nanque (CL *namque*): for in fact
Neapolis, -is *f.*: Naples
nex, necis *f.*: death; murder

nosco, -ere, novi, notus: learn
nullus, -a, -um: nobody, nothing
optime (*superl. adv.*): best, very well
pontifex, -ficis *m.*: pontiff, pope
prius (*adv.*): earlier
scio, -ire, -ivi, -itus: know
Senae, -arum *f.*: Siena, a town in Tuscany
subsisto, -ere, substiti, - : halt, stop
suspicor, -ari, -atus sum: suspect, suppose
via, -ae *f.*: road, journey

Substiterat: subject is *filia*

hac re cognita: abl. abs.

Senis: locative

ducis Mediolani filia: Drusiana, daughter of Francesco Sforza, Duke of Milan, and wife of Jacopo Piccinino

Neapolim: acc. of place to which

itura: fut. act. participle of *eo*, fem. sing.

ut fidem faceret: purpose clause; *fidem facere* is an idiom, "to assure"

nulla ... culpa: abl. of means

Ferdinandum ... conspirasse: ind. statement introduced by *faceret*

Iacobi Picennini: Jacopo Piccinino, mercenary and ruler of Abruzzo by the time of his murder

conspirasse: syncopated from *conspira(vi)sse*

Quid ... suspicati sint homines: ind. question, "what men suspected"

novimus: *nosco* in perf. is "learned," therefore "now know"

Fuere: alternative form of *fuerunt*

qui dicerent: rel. clause of characteristic

id ... scitum fore: ind. statement, "that it would have been known," in the manuscripts, Platina had originally written "that this too was accomplished through Pope Paul's crafts" (*id quoque Pauli Pontificis artibus factum esse*)

cum ... commeaverit: causal *cum* clause

illis diebus: abl. of time within which

diebus archiepiscopus Mediolanensis a pontifice ad regem et a rege ad pontificem frequenter commeaverit, cunque Paulus ipse dixerit, audita hominis captivitate, appellationum iudicem e medio sublatum esse. Sed verum est illud Virgilianum: "Nescia mens hominum fati sortisque futurae." Nullius enim magis quam Iacobi Picennini opera reprimere Ferdinandi contumaciam Paulus potuisset, si tum in vita

---

appellatio, -onis *f.*: appeal (to higher authority)

archiepiscopus, -i *m.*: archbishop

audio, -ire, -ivi, -itus: hear, listen

captivitas, -tatis *f.*: captivity

commeo, -are, -avi, -atus: go (to), travel,

contumacia, -ae *f.*: obstinacy

cunque (CL *cumque*) (*adv.*): and since (*cum + -que*)

dies, diei *m./f.*: day

fatum, -i *n.*: fate, destiny

frequenter (*adv.*): often, frequently

futurus, -a, -um: future

iudex, iudicis *m.*: judge

magis (*adv.*): more

Mediolanensis, -e: Milanese, of Milan

medius, -a, -um: middle, midst

mens, mentis *f.*: mind

nescius, -a, -um: unaware, ignorant

nullus, -a, -um: no one; none

opera, -ae *f.*: work, aid, service

reprimo, -ere, repressi, repressus: repress, check

sors, sortis *f.*: lot, fate

tollo, -ere, sustuli, sublatus: remove

verus, -a, -um: true

Virgilianus, -a, -um: Virgilian, of Virgil

---

archiepiscopus Mediolanensis: Stefano Nardini, Archbishop of Milan. Paul II had made Nardini Papal Nuncio to the Kingdom of Naples, and so some suspected him of informing the pope of the plot on Jacopo's life

cunque ... dixerit: causal *cum* clause

audita ... captivitate: abl. abs.

iudicem ... sublatum esse: ind. statement introduced by *dixerit*

e medio: idiom, "from their midst"

illud Virgilianum: "that (saying) of Virgil"

Nescia ... futurae: Virgil *Aeneid* 10.501; the poet laments the limited knowledge of men, as Turnus boasts over the body of Pallas

Nullius: gen. of *nullus*, parallel to *Iacobi Picennini*

magis quam: "more than"

opera: abl. of means

potuisset, si ... fuisset: past contrafactual cond., "he would have been able ... if he had been ... "

51

fuisset quando inter eos de solvendo tributo contentio est orta ac bellum prope certum.

Paul and Ferdinand settle their differences

32 Nam celebratis nurus ac filii nuptiis hac una re et Iacobi morte stabilito regno, Ferdinandus cum pontifice instat ut et tributum ei diminuatur et quaedam oppida, quae de regno possidebat Ecclesia, ei redderentur. Misit eo Paulus Bartholomeum Roverellam

---

celebro, -are, -avi, -atus: celebrate, proclaim
certus, -a, -um: certain, sure
contentio, -onis *f.*: tension, controversy
diminuo, -ere, -ui, -utus: lessen, diminish
Ecclesia, -ae *f.*: the Church
insto, -are, institi, - : threaten, press hard
mors, mortis *f.*: death
nuptiae, -arum *f.*: marriage
nurus, -us *f.*: daughter-in-law
oppidum, -i *n.*: town
orior, -iri, ortus sum: arise, emerge

pontifex, -ficis *m.*: pontiff, pope
possideo, -sidere, -sedi, -sessus: possess, take possession of
prope (*adv.*): nearly
quando (*adv.*): when
reddo, -ere, reddidi, redditus: return, restore
regnum, -i *n.*: royal power, kingdom
solvo, -ere, solvi, solutus: loosen, pay off
stabilio, -ire, -ivi, -itus: make firm, establish
tributum, -i *n.*: tax, tribute

---

de solvendo tributo: gerundive phrase, "about the tribute to be paid off (i.e. about paying off the tribute)"
contentio: nom., subject of *est orta*
bellum (erat) prope certum: verb elided
celebratis ... nuptiis: abl. abs.
nurus ... filii: *nurus* (gen. sing.) is Ippolita Maria Sforza, daughter of Francesco Sforza of Milan; *fili* is Alfonso II, son of Ferdinand of Naples. The marriage allied the two powers and secured the Kingdom of Naples' strength and safety
hac una re et ... morte: ablatives of means
Iacobi: Jacopo Piccinino, *condottiero*
stabilito regno: abl. abs.
Ferdinandus: King Ferdinand I of Naples (1423-1494)
cum ... instat: circumstantial *cum* clause
ut ... diminuatur ... redderentur: ind. command dependent on *instat*
ei (*twice*): dat. of reference referring to Ferdinand
eo: dat. of reference referring to Ferdinand
Bartholomeum Roverellam: Bartolomeo Roverella (1406-1476), papal legate to the Kingdom of Naples for Popes Pius II and Paul II

legatum, tituli Sancti Clementis presbyterum cardinalem, qui regis mentem aliqua ex parte lenivit.

Francesco Sforza dies; he was Duke of Milan, and had taken possession of Genoa

33 Verebatur tum, credo, uterque ne solis ac lunae ecthlipses, quae tunc fuere cum maxima hominum admiratione, regnorum mutationem portenderent. Moritur tamen (ne corpora caelestia frustra pati existimes) sequenti anno Franciscus Sfortia Insubriae et Lyguriae dux. Nam Genuae dominatum biennio ante adeptus

---

adipiscor, adipisci, adeptus sum: gain, overtake
admiratio, -onis *f.*: astonishment
aliqui, -qua, -quod: some
annus, -i *m.*: year
biennium, -i *n.*: two years
caelestis, -e: heavenly, celestial
cardinalis, -is *m.*: cardinal
corpus, -oris *n.*: body
dominatus, -us *m.*: rule
dux, ducis *m.*: leader, duke
ecthlipsis, -is (CL *eclipsis*) *f.*: eclipse
existimo, -are, -avi, -atus: think, suppose
frustra (*adv.*): in vain
Genua, -ae *f.*: Genoa
Insubria, -ae *f.*: Insubria, the region surrounding Milan
legatus, -i *m.*: envoy, ambassador

lenio, -ire, -ivi, -itus: calm, placate, appease
luna, -ae *f.*: moon
Lyguria, -ae *f.*: Liguria, the region surrounding Genoa
mens, mentis *f.*: mind
mutatio, -onis *f.*: change
pars, partis *f.*: part; portion
patior, pati, passus sum: suffer, submit
portendo, -tendere, -tendi, -tentus: predict, foretell
presbyter, -i *m.*: priest
regnum, -i *n.*: kingdom; royal power
sanctus, -i *m.*: saint
sequens, -entis: following, next
sol, solis *m.*: sun
titulus, -i *m.*: title; here "titular church"
uterque, utraque, utrumque: each (of two)
vereor, -eri, -itus sum: fear, dread

---

legatum: appositive, "as an envoy"
Sancti Clementis: San Clemente, a titular church
presbyterum cardinalem: a rank of cardinal
aliqua ex parte: idiom, "to some degree"
uterque: subject of *Verebatur*, refers to Paul and Ferdinand
ne ... portenderent: fear clause dependent on *Verebatur*
fuere: alt. form of *fuerunt*; here with sense of "existed" or "happened"
ne ... existimes: neg. purpose clause
sequenti anno: abl. of time when; 1466
Franciscus Sfortia: Francesco Sforza of Milan, powerful *condottiero*
Genuae ... fuerat: Genoa had been under the control of the Milanese Francesco Sforza since 1464, after he had aided the Genoese in their rebellion against the French and had installed a puppet ruler
biennio: abl. of degree of difference, take with *ante*

fuerat, dedentibus sese civibus, diutino bello, partim intestino et gravi partim externo, agitatis. Gallorum enim dominatum (quem sponte petierant) reiicientes, ad sex millia Gallici [377] nominis ante oculos Renati regis interfecere, qui cum triremibus aliquot bene armatis aderat recuperandae urbis causa, quae iam a Gallis defecerat.

---

adsum, -esse, -fui, -futurus: be present
agito, -are, -avi, -atus: stir up, impel
aliquot (*indecl.*): some
armatus, -a, -um: armed
bene (*adv.*): well
civis, -is *m./f.*: citizen
dedo, -ere, dedidi, deditus: give up, surrender
deficio, -ere, defeci, defectus: revolt, defect
diutinus, -a, -um: long, long lasting
dominatus, -us *m.*: rule
externus, -a, -um: external, foreign
Gallicus, -a, -um: Gallic, French
Galli, -orum *m.*: the Gauls; the French

gravis, -e: painful, serious
iam (*adv.*): now, already
interficio, -ficere, -feci, -fectus: kill, destroy
intestinus, -a, -um: internal, domestic
mille, millia (CL *mille, milia*): thousand
oculus, -i *m.*: eye
partim (*adv.*): partly
peto, -ere, -ivi(ii), -itus: desire, ask for
recupero, -are, -avi, -atus: regain
reiicio, -ere, reieci, reiectus: refuse, reject
sex: six
spons, spontis *f.*: free will
triremis, -is *f.*: trireme

---

dedentibus ... civibus: abl. abs.
sese: "themselves," acc. obj. of *dedentibus*
bello: abl. of means with *agitatis*
agitatis: agrees with *civibus*
Gallorum: subjective gen.; substantive adj., "of the Gauls"
dominatum: acc. obj. of *reiicientes*
sponte: abl. of manner, lacks *cum* in this expression; so "willingly," "of their own accord"
reiicientes: the Genoese; subject of *interfecere*
ad sex millia: *ad* + number, "around"; obj. of *interfecere*
Gallici nominis: "of the Gallic name (i.e. French)"
Renati: René of Anjou, who claimed the title King of Naples
interfecere: alt. form of *interfecerunt*
cum triremibus ... armatis: abl. of accompaniment
recuperandae ... causa: *causa* + gen. gerundive to express purpose, "for the sake of the city to be regained (i.e. to regain the city)"

Paul resolves to maintain order in Italy and moves to assure a smooth succession in Milan

34 Mortuo itaque Francisco Sfortia Mediolanensium Duce, cardinales statim Paulus ad se vocat, quid esset agendum consulit. Censuere omnes mittendas esse litteras et nuncios ad principes Italiae, ad populos, qui eos adhortarentur nil novi moliri sed pacem ante initam servare, maxime vero tam iniquo tempore, quo a Thurco

---

adhortor, -ari, -atus sum: encourage, rally
ago, -ere, egi, actus: act, do
ante (*adv.*): earlier
cardinalis, -is *m.*: cardinal
censeo, -ere, censui, census: decide, determine
consulo, -sulere, -sului, -sultus: consult, deliberate, consider
dux, ducis *m.*: leader; duke
ineo, -ire, -ivi(ii), -itus: enter, establish
iniquus, -a, -um: uneven, hostile
Italia, -ae *f.*: Italy
litterae, -arum *f.*: letter (epistle)
maxime (*adv.*): especially, most

Mediolanensis, -e: Milanese
molior, -iri, -itus sum: undertake, plan
novus, -a, -um: new
nuncius, -i (CL *nuntius*) *m.*: messenger
populus, -i *m.*: people, nation
princeps, -cipis *m.*: leader, prince
servo, -are, -avi, -atus: preserve
statim (*adv.*): at once, immediately
tam (*adv.*): so
tempus, -oris *n.*: time
Thurcus, -a, -um: Turkish
vero (*adv.*): truly
voco, -are, -avi, -atus: call

Mortuo … Francisco Sfortia … Duce: abl. abs.; Francesco Sforza (1401-1466)

Mediolanensium: substantive adj., "of the Milanese"

vocat … consulit: asyndeton

quid esset agendum: pass. periphrastic in ind. question dependent on *consulit*, "what ought to be done"

Censuere: alternate form of *censuerunt*

omnes: the cardinals; subject of *censuere*

mittendas esse: *mittendas* modifies both *litteras* and *nuncios*, but takes its gender from the closer word; phrase is pass. periphrastic in ind. statement "that letters … ought to be sent"

qui eos adhortarentur: rel. clause of purpose, "in order to urge them"

novi: partitive gen., nothing "(of) new"

moliri sed … servare: obj. infinitives of *adhortarentur*

iniquo tempore: abl. of time when, antecedent to *quo*, an abl. of time within which

a Thurco … hoste: the Ottomans conquered Constantinople in 1453. The sacking of a city many Christians thought unconquerable signaled the end of the Byzantine Empire and sent shockwaves through the Christian world. The Popes who reigned in the years following, including Paul II, would be preoccupied with planning to retake Constantinople from the Turks

communi Christianorum hoste vexaremur.   Praeterea vero episcopum Conchensem Mediolanum mittit oratum populum illum ut
nil antiquius fide putaret quam Galeatio Francisci filio praestiterat.

*Galeazzo Sforza, son of Francesco, returns from France and takes control of Milan
with his mother's help*

35 Aberat tum Galeatius iussu patris in Galliam cum exercitu
missus, dum rex Alovisius cum principibus regni dicto suo haud

---

absum, abesse, afui, afuturus: be away, be
   absent
antiquus, -a, -um: old, time-honored
Christianus, -a, -um: Christian
communis, -e: common
Conchensis, -e: of Cuenca, a town in Spain
dictum, -i *n.*: word; command
episcopus, -i *m.*: bishop
exercitus, -us *m.*: army
fides, fidei *f.*: loyalty; pledge of protection
Gallia, -ae *f.*: Gaul, France
haud (*adv.*): not at all
hostis, -is *m./f.*: enemy

iussus, -us *m.*: order
Mediolanum, -i *n.*: Milan
nil *n.* (*indecl.*): nothing
oro, -are, -avi, -atus: beg
populus, -i *m.*: people, populace
praesto, -are, -stiti, -stitus: supply; vouch
   for; maintain
praeterea (*adv.*): in addition
princeps, principis *m.*: leader; prince
regnum, -i *n.*: kingdom
vero (*adv.*): in fact
vexo, -are, -avi, -atus: harass

---

communi: agrees with *Thurco … hoste*
vexaremur: subjunctive in a rel. clause in ind. statement
episcopum Conchensem: Giacopo Antonio Venier, Bishop of Cuenca and Papal
   Nuncio to Francesco Sforza in Milan starting in 1460
Mediolanum: acc. of place to which
oratum: acc. supine expressing purpose
ut … putaret: purpose clause
antiquius: neut. acc. sing., compar. of *antiquus*
fide: abl. of comparison
quam: antecedent is *fide*
Galeatio Francisci filio: Galeazzo Sforza, son of Francesco Sforza; dat. of ind. obj.
Galeatius: Galeazzo Sforza was in France aiding King Louis XI against King Charles I
   of Burgundy
iussu: abl. of cause, "at the command"
Alovisius: Louis XI, King of France (r. 1461-1483)
cum principibus: abl. of accompaniment, here translated "against"
dicto suo: dat. with the compound verb *obtemperantibus*
haud quaquam: idiom, "not at all"

quaquam obtemperantibus bellum gerit. Ex foedere enim dum Genuam in pheudum accipit, praesidia regi Franciscus subministrabat. Requirebat et hoc affinitas inter eos contracta, cum Galeatius reginae ac ducis Sabaudiae sororem in uxorem {235R} accępisset. Qui cognita patris morte, relicto bello, quod regio nomine contra Burgundiae ducem incohaverat, Lugduno abiens, ac cum paucis

---

abeo, -ire, -ivi(ii), -itus: depart
accipio, -ere, accępi (CL *accepi*), **acceptus**: take, receive
affinitas, -tatis *f.*: relation by marriage
cognosco, -noscere, -novi, -nitus: learn
contra: against (+ *acc.*)
contraho, -trahere, -traxi, -tractus: contract
dux, ducis *m.*: leader; duke
foedus, foederis *n.*: treaty
Genua, -ae *f.*: Genoa
gero, -ere, gessi, gestus: bear, carry
incoho, -are, -avi, -atus: begin
Lugdunum, -i *n.*: Lyon, a town in France
mors, mortis *f.*: death
obtempero, -are, -avi, -atus: obey (+ *dat.*)

paucus, -a, -um: few
pheudum, -i (or *feudum*) *n.*: fiefdom; feudal allegiance
praesidium, -i *n.*: assistance; auxiliary forces (*pl.*)
regius, -a, -um: of a king, royal
relinquo, -ere, reliqui, relictum: leave behind, abandon
requiro, -ere, requisivi, requisitus: require
Sabaudia, -ae *f.*: Savoy, a territory in the Western Alps in today's Rhone-Alpes region
subministro, -are, -avi, -atus: supply
uxor, -oris *f.*: wife

---

obtemperantibus: agrees with *principibus*
bellum gerit: "wages war"
ex foedere: here, "by the treaty"
regi: dat. of advantage, "for the benefit of the king"
Franciscus: Francesco Sforza (1401-1466)
Requirebat: subject is *affinitas*
hoc: acc. obj. of *Requirebat*, referring to Galeazzo's intervention in France
cum … accępisset: causal *cum* clause
ducis Sabaudiae sororem: Bona of Savoy, member of the noble Italian House of Savoy and second wife to Galeazzo Sforza
in uxorem: "in wedlock"
cognita … morte: abl. abs.
relicto bello: abl. abs.
quod: acc. obj. of *incohaverat*; antecedent is *bello*
regio nomine: abl. of attendant circumstance, "under the king's name"
Burgundiae ducem: Philip III of Burgundy (r. 1419-1467), which was located in the Low Countries and Switzerland
Lugduno: abl. of place from which
cum paucis: substantive adj. "with a few people"

permutata veste in patriam rediens, ditione paterna auxilio matris, quae populos in fide continuerat, sine ulla contentione potitur.

Paul considers aiding the Knights of Rhodes

36 Paulus vero compositis hoc modo Italiae rebus, cum intellegeret militiam Rhodiorum Militum ob inopiam ad nihilum redigi, eorum magistrum ac primates religionis ad se vocat corrigendi erroris

---

auxilium, -i *n.*: help
compono, -ponere, -posui, -positus: arrange
contentio, -onis *f.*: contention
contineo, -tinere, -tinui, -tentus: maintain, preserve
corrigo, -rigere, -rexi, -rectum: amend, reform
ditio, -onis (CL *dicio*) *f.*: power
error, -oris *m.*: error
fides, fidei *f.*: faith, loyalty
inopia, -ae *f.*: need, poverty
intellego, -legere, -lexi, -lectus: realize
Italia, -ae *f.*: Italy
magister, -tri *m.*: master
miles, militis *m.*: soldier
militia, -ae *f.*: army
modus, -i *m.*: manner

nihilum, -i *n.*: nothing
paternus, -a, -um: ancestral
patria, -ae *f.*: native land
permuto, -are, -avi, -atus: swap, exchange
populus, -i *m.*: people
potior, -iri, -itus sum: obtain (+ *abl.*)
primas, primatis: leader, primate
redeo, -ire, -ivi(ii), -itus: go back, return
redigo, -ere, redegi, redactus: reduce
religio, -onis *f.*: religion
Rhodius, -a, -um: Rhodian, of Rhodes
sine: without (+ *abl.*)
ullus, -a, -um: any
vero: but, however
vestis, -is *f.*: clothes
voco, -are, -avi, -atus: call

---

permutata veste: abl. abs.

ditione paterna: abl. with *potitur*

auxilio: abl. of means

populos: CL would use sing.

compositis … rebus: abl. abs., "when the affairs of Italy had been settled," referring to Paul's actions in the papal states (ch. 26-28), his struggles with Naples (ch. 29-32), and the succession in Milan (ch. 33-35)

hoc modo: abl. of manner

cum intellegeret: circumstantial *cum* clause

militiam … redigi: ind. statement introduced by *intellegeret*

Rhodiorum Militum: the Knights of Rhodes, a group of Knights Hospitallers who lived on the island of Rhodes under the threat of an Ottoman invasion from Sultan Mehmet II

Militum: gen. pl. with *militiam*

corrigendi … causa: *causa* + gen. gerundive indicates purpose, "for the sake of their error to be corrected (i.e. to correct their error)"

causa, qui post frequentes conventus ad S. Petrum habitos tedio animi et senio confectus moritur, sepeliturque in basilica Sancti Petri non longe a sacello Sancti Andreae; in cuius locum Carolus Ursinus suffectus, Rhodum ad tuendam insulam propere mittitur.

Paul punishes several local heretics

37 Interim vero cum Paulo nunciatum [378] esset, in Poli, oppido in Equicolis posito, multos haereticos inesse, dominum loci

---

animus, -i *m.*: soul
basilica, -ae *f.*: basilica
conficio, -ficere, -feci, -fectus: consume
conventus, -us *m.*: meeting
dominus, -i *m.*: lord, master
Equicolus, -a, -um (CL *Aequiculus*): related to the Aequi, a people just east of Rome in ancient Italy; here with an assumed *finibus* ("territory")"
frequens, -entis: numerous
haereticus, -i *m.*: heretic
insula, -ae *f.*: island
insum, -esse, -fui, -futurus: be in
interim (*adv.*): meanwhile
locus, -i *m.*: place; position
longe (*adv.*): far (off)

nuncio, -are, -avi, -atus (CL *nuntio*): announce
oppidum, -i *n.*: town
Poli (*indecl.*): Poli, a town East of Rome
pono, -ere, -ui, -itus: place; locate
properus, -a, -um: quick, speedy
Rhodus, -i *f.*: Rhodes, island in the Aegean Sea
sacellum, -i *n.*: shrine
sanctus, -i *m.*: saint
senium, -i *n.*: condition of old age
sepelio, -ire, sepelivi, sepultus: bury
sufficio, -ficere, -feci, -fectus: appoint, replace
tedium, -i (CL *taedium*) *n.*: weariness
tueor, -eri, -itus sum: protect
vero (*adv.*): in fact, moreover

---

post frequentes conventus ... habitos: "after numerous meetings held"
ad: here, "near"
S(anctum) Petrum: the Basilica of St. Peter, in Rome
Sancti Andreae: St. Andrew, gen.
Carolus Ursinus: Carlo Orsini, a member of the Orsini family, which was powerful in Rome
Rhodum: acc. of place to which
ad tuendam: *ad* + acc. gerundive expressing purpose, "for the island to be protected (i.e. to protect the island)"
cum ... nunciatum esset: circumstantial *cum* clause
nunciatum esset: impers., "it was announced"
oppido: appositive to *Poli*
haereticos: Fraticelli, who believed that popes and prelates were illegitimate unless they followed the poverty of Jesus
inesse: ind. statement introduced by *nunciatum esset*

cum viris octo et foeminis sex comprehensos, et ad se perductos, cognito hominum errore, ignominia notavit, et quidem gravissima, eos potissimum qui pertinaciores fuere. Nam mitius cum his est actum qui errorem confessi veniam petiere. Erant enim eius sectae quam a perversa mentis opinione esse dicimus, quod dicerent nullum verum Christi vicarium esse eorum qui post Petrum fuere, nisi qui paupertatem Christi imitati sunt.

---

ago, -ere, egi, actum: do, handle
Christus, -i *m.*: Christ
cognosco, -noscere, -novi, -nitus: recognize, learn
comprehendo, -hendere, -hendi, -hensus: seize, arrest
confiteor, -fiteri, -fessus sum: confess, admit
error, -oris *m.*: wandering, error
foemina, -ae (CL *femina*) *f.*: woman
gravis, -e: heavy, painful, serious
ignominia, -ae *f.*: disgrace, dishonor
imitor, -ari, -atus sum: imitate, copy, follow
mens, mentis *f.*: mind
mite (*adv.*): mildly
noto, -are, -avi, -atus: brand

nullus, -a, -um: no, no one
octo (*indecl.*): eight
opinio, -onis *f.*: belief, opinion
paupertas, -tatis *f.*: poverty, need
perduco, -ere, -duxi, -ductus: lead
pertinax, -acis: tenacious, stubborn
perversus, -a, -um: askew, perverse
peto, -ere, -ivi(ii), -itus: seek, ask (for)
potissimum (*adv.*): chiefly, principally, especially
secta, -ae *f.*: party, sect
sex (*indecl.*): six
venia, -ae *f.*: favor, pardon
verus, -a, -um: true, real, genuine
vicarius, -i *m.*: vicar

---

comprehensos … perductos: these participles modify *dominum* and so technically should be sing., but the pl. is used because of the accompanying 8 men and 6 women
hominum: = *eorum* (see Introduction 7.E)
pertinaciores: compar. of *pertinax*
fuere: alt. form of *fuerunt*
mitius: compar. adv.
est actum: impers., "it was handled"
errorem confessi: *confiteor* (deponent) takes the acc., *confessi* is in apposition to *qui*
petiere: alt. form of *petierunt*
eius sectae: gen. of description
quam: antecedent is *sectae*
quod dicerent: causal *quod* clause of alleged reason, "on the grounds that they say"
nullum … esse: ind. statement
Christi vicarium: The Vicar of Christ, one of the titles of the pope
post Petrum: Peter the apostle, the first pope (according to Catholic tradition)
fuere: alt. form of *fuerunt*

Paul creates several new cardinals

38 Aucto deinde cardinalium numero, ad X enim eodem tempore creavit, quorum de numero ii fuere: Franciscus Savonensis ordinis Minorum generalis, M. Barbo praesul Vicentinus, cuius opera et consilio magnis in rebus semper est usus, Oliverius archiepiscopus Neapolitanus, A. episcopus Aquilanus, Theodorus Monferratus: reliqui partim Galli partim Ungari et Angli sunt habiti.

Angli, -orum *m.*: English
Aquilanus, -a, -um: of Aquila, in central Italy
archiepiscopus, -i *m.*: archbishop
augeo, -ere, auxi, auctus: increase
cardinalis, -is *m.*: cardinal
consilium, -i *n.*: consultation, advice, counsel
creo, -are, -avi, -atus: create; appoint
deinde (*adv.*): then, afterward
episcopus, -i *m.*: bishop
Galli, -orum *m.*: French
generalis, -is *m.*: general (here, meaning leader)
idem, eadem, idem: same
Monferratus, -a, -um: of Monferrato, in the Piedmont region of northern Italy

Neapolitanus, -a, -um: Neapolitan, of Naples
numerus, -i *m.*: number
opera, -ae *f.*: work, aid
ordo, ordinis *m.*: order (of monks)
partim (*adv.*): partly
praesul, praesulis *m./f.*: prelate
reliquus, -a, -um: rest of, remaining
Savonensis, -e: of Savona, a town near Genoa
tempus, -oris *n.*: time
Ungari, -orum *m.*: Hungarian
utor, uti, usus sum: use, enjoy; (+ *abl.*)
Vicentinus, -a -um: of Vicenza, a town in Northern Italy

Aucto ... numero: abl. abs.

ad X: *ad* + numeral expresses approximation, "around ten"; obj. of *creavit*

eodem tempore: abl. of time when; late 1467 and 1468

fuere: alt. form of *fuerunt*

Franciscus Savonensis: Francesco della Rovere, General of the Franciscan Order; he succeeded Paul II as Sixtus IV (r. 1471-1484); Platina dedicated his *Lives of the Popes* to him

ordinis Minorum: of the "order of the Lesser ones," i.e. the Franciscan Order, a group of monks known for living in poverty

M. Barbo: Marco Barbo (a relative of Paul II), a humanist famous for his sizable library

praesul Vicentinus ... est usus: in the manuscripts, Platina added this phrase in the margin

magnis: here, "important"

est usus: subject is Paul

Oliverius ... Neapolitanus: Oliviero Carafa, the Archbishop of Naples

A(micus) ... Aquilanus: Amico Agnifili, Bishop of Aquila, tutor of Pope Paul II

Theodorus Monferratus: Teodoro di Monferrato

reliqui: namely, Jean de la Balue, Bishop of Angers and close counselor of Louis XI of France; Stephan Varda, Archbishop of Kalocsa; Thomas Bourchier, Archbishop of Canterbury

The Battle of Molinella: Florentine exiles try to return with the help of Venice and Bartolomeo Colleoni; Florence fights back with the help of Naples and Galeazzo Sforza

39 Senatu itaque in hunc modum aucto ad componendam Italiae pacem totus convertitur. Nam [379] cum Florentini quidam, a factione Petri Medices civili discordia pulsi (ut Detesalvus Neronius, et Angelus Accioiolus, ac Nicolaus Sudorinus), Bartholemeum Bergomatem concitassent, qui magnam vim equitum ac peditum habebat, ut in Hętruriam cum exercitu movens se ac extorres omnes

---

augeo, -ere, auxi, auctus: increase, enlarge

civilis, -e: civil

compono, -ponere, -posui, -positus: put together, order; settle

concito, -are, -avi, -atus: stir up

converto, -vertere, -verti, -versus: turn, direct attention

discordia, -ae *f.*: disagreement, discord

eques, equitis *m.*: knight; calvalry (*pl.*)

exercitus, -us *m.*: army, force

extorris, -e: exiled

factio, -onis *f.*: party, faction

Florentinus, -a , -um: Florentine, of Florence

Hętruriae, -ae (CL *Etruria*) *f.*: Etruria (or Tuscany), a region in Italy

Italia, -ae *f.*: Italy

modus, -i *m.*: manner, measure

moveo, -ere, movi, motus: move

pedes, peditis *m.*: foot soldier; infantry (*pl.*)

pello, -ere, pepuli, pulsus: drive out, banish

senatus, -us *m.*: here, College of Cardinals

totus, -a, -um: whole, entire

vis, vis *f.*: strength; (+ *gen.*) abundance of

Senatu ... aucto: abl. abs.

in hunc modum: "to this measure"

ad componendam ... pacem: *ad* + acc. gerundive expressing purpose, "in order for the peace to be settled (i.e. to settle the peace)"

totus: modifying the understood subject, Paul; nom. adjectives can be translated adverbially, "entirely"

cum ... concitassent: circumstantial *cum* clause; *concita(vi)ssent* is the syncopated form

Petri Medices: gen. of Piero Medici (*Medices* is indeclinable), a member of the powerful *Medici* faction in Florentine politics, son of Cosimo de' Medici and father of Lorenzo the Magnificent

civili discordia: abl. of means

pulsi: antecedent is *Florentini*

ut: "as (for instance)" beginning the list of three exiled Florentines

Detesalvus Neronius, Angelus Accioiolus, Nicolaus Sudorinus: the *quidam Florentini* who were exiled by Piero Medici for attempting a coup in 1466

Bartholomeum Bergomatem: Bartolomeo Colleoni, an Italian *condottiero* who fought for both the Milanese Sforza and the Venetians

qui: antecedent is *Bartholomeum*

ut ... reduceret: ind. command dependent on *concitassent*

in patriam reduceret; adiuvantibus etiam Venetis, occulte tamen, primo quidem impetu posse et velle subvertere totam Italiam visus est. Verum cum in Flamminea Galeacium ducem Mediolanensem obvium habuisset cum regis ac Florentini populi copiis, habenas inhibuit, et cunctando potius quam pugnando vincere annixus est. Pugnatum est tamen semel, atque acriter comitis Urbinatis auspiciis

---

acriter (*adv.*): sharply; fiercely
adiuvo, -are, adiuvi, adiutus: help, aid
annitor, anniti, annixus sum: strive
auspicium, -i *n.*: auspices (*pl.*)
comes, comitis *m.*: companion; count
copia, -ae *f.*: abundance; troops (*pl.*)
cuncto, -are, -avi, -atus: delay
dux, ducis *m.*: leader; duke
Flamminea, -ae (CL *Flaminia*) *f.*: the region around the Via Flaminia, near Rimini in northern Italy
habena, -ae *f.*: reins (*pl.*)
impetus, -us *m.*: attack, assault
inhibeo, -ere, -ui, -itus: restrain, hold back
Italia, -ae *f.*: Italy
Mediolanensis, -e: Milanese, of Milan
obvius, -a, -um: in the way

occulte (*adv.*): secretly
patria, -ae *f.*: native land
populus, -i *m.*: people, state
potius (*adv.*): rather
primus, -a, -um: first
pugno, -are, -avi, -atus: fight
reduco, -ere, reduxi, reductus: lead back; restore
semel: at one time, once and for all
subverto, -vertere, -verti,-versus: overturn, overthrow
totus, -a, -um: whole, all
Urbinas, -atis: of Urbino
Venetus, -a, -um: Venetian
verum (*adv.*): but; however
vinco, -ere, vici, victus: conquer, win
volo, velle, volui, - : want; be willing

---

adiuvantibus … Venetis: abl. abs. with causal sense

posse et velle: complementary infinitives with *visus est*

subvertere: complementary inf. with *posse et velle*

visus est: subject is Bartolomeo Colleoni; *video* in passive is "he seemed"

cum … habuisset: causal *cum* clause, subject is Bartholomeo Colleoni

Galeacium: Galeazzo Sforza, Duke of Milan; on the spelling see Introduction 6.A

ducem: appositive to *Galeacium*

cum regis ac Florentini populi copiis: abl. of accompaniment, "with the troops of the King (of Naples) and of the Florentine people"

inhibuit: the main verb of the sentence; subject is Bartolomeo Colleoni

cunctando … pugnando: gerunds; ablatives of means, "by delaying … by fighting"

potius quam: "rather than"

Pugnatum est: impers., "it was fought" or "there was a fight"; refers to the Battle of Molinella

comitis Urbinatis: Federico da Montefeltro, Count of Urbino. He was a highly successful *condottiero* who oversaw the construction of a great library in Urbino

auspiciis: abl. of attendant circumstance, "under the auspices" (i.e. the count of Urbino was in charge)

in agro Bononiensi ad Ricardinam (id ei loco nomen est) dum castrametatur. Quo quidem tempore de Bergomate actum certe erat, si tum Galeacius affuisset, qui Florentiam compenendae rei bellicae causa profectus paulo ante fuerat. Ferunt, qui tanto proelio interfuere, nusquam aetate nostra maiore contentione {235v} certatum esse, nec prelium antea fuisse in quo plures desiderati fuerint.

---

aetas, -tatis *f.*: lifetime, age
ager, agri *m.*: field, country
ago, -ere, egi, actus: drive, urge, conduct, act
assum, adesse, affui, affuturus: be present, be in attendance
bellicus, -a, -um: of war, military
Bononienis, -e: Bolognese, of Bologna
castrametor, -ari, -atus sum: encamp
certe (*adv.*): surely, certainly, without doubt
certo, -are, -avi, -atus: fight
compendo, -pendere, -pensi, -pensus: weigh, settle
contentio, -onis *f.*: intensity

desidero, -are, -avi, -atus: desire; lose
fero, ferre, tuli, latus: bring; tell
Florentia, -ae *f.*: Florence
intersum, -esse, -fui, -futurus: be present, take part in
locus, -i *m.*: position; place
nusquam (*adv.*): nowhere, on no occasion
paulo (*adv.*): by a little, a little
proelium, -i *n.*: battle
proficiscor, -ficisci, -fectus sum: depart, set out
prelium, -i (CL *proelium*) *n.*: battle
tempus, -oris *n.*: time

agro Bononiensi: "the territory of Bologna"
ad Ricardinam: "near Riccardina," a village in Northern Italy
ei loco: dat. of the possessor
Quo ... tempore: abl. of time when with *quo* acting as a connective rel., "and at this time"
Bergomate: Bartolomeo Colleoni
actum ... erat: "it would have been done (i.e. he would have died)"; the apodosis of the past contrafactual cond. is indic. to vividly present a fact
Galeacius: Galeazzo Sforza, Duke of Milan
Florentiam: acc. of place to which
compenendae rei bellicae causa: *causa* + gen. gerundive expressing purpose, "for the sake of a military matter to be settled (i.e. to settle a military matter)"
profectus ... fuerat: pluperf. (CL *profectus erat*, see Introduction 7.D)
qui: antecedent is assumed *ii*, subject of *ferunt*
interfuere: alt. form of *interfuerunt*
nusquam ... certatum esse ... fuisse: ind. statement introduced by *ferunt*
aetate nostra: abl. of time within which
maiore contentione: abl. of manner
certatum esse: impers., "there was a fight"
quo ... desiderati fuerint: rel. clause in ind. statement
plures: compar. of *multus*, substantive

Amid complex military and political maneuvering, Paul brokers a peace

40 Tum autem Veneti sibi potius quam homini caventes, cohortibus aliquot et turmis ei in auxilium missis, pacem enixius quaerere, eius conficiendae arbitrium omne in pontificem deferentes. Qui rei suae quoque admodum timens si victoria ad regem et ducem recideret, ut pax [380] conficeretur instabat. Erat enim opinio quorundam

---

admodum (*adv.*): greatly
aliquot (*indecl.*): a few
arbitrium, -i *n.*: judgment, decision
auxilium, -i *n.*: help, assistance
caveo, -ere, cavi, cautus: beware, take precautions
cohors, -hortis *f.*: cohort, armed force
conficio, -ficere, -feci, -fectus: complete, accomplish
defero, -ferre, -tuli, -latus: defer
dux, ducis *m.*: leader; duke
enixe (*adv.*): earnestly, with strenuous efforts

insto, -are, institi, - : urge
opinio, -onis *f.*: belief, idea, opinion
pontifex, -ficis *m.*: pontiff, pope
potius (*adv.*): more
quaero, -ere, quaesivi, quaesitus: seek
quidam, quaedam, quoddam: a certain one
recido, -ere, recidi, recasus: fall back, go
timeo, -ere, -ui, - : fear, be afraid
turma, -ae *f.*: troop, squadron
Venetus, -a, -um: Venetian
victoria, -ae *f.*: victory

---

potius quam: "rather than"
homini: Bartolomeo Colleoni
cohortibus ... turmis ... missis: abl. abs. with concessive sense
in auxilium: acc. denoting purpose, "for help"
enixius: compar. adv.
quaerere: historical inf., "began to seek"
eius conficiendae: gen. gerundive phrase, "of this (peace) to be accomplished (i.e. of accomplishing this peace)"
in pontificem: *in* + acc., "to the pope"
Qui: connecting rel., "And he" (i.e. the pope)
rei suae: "his own situation," dat. of reference with *timens*
timens si ... recideret: imperf. subjunctive used for fut. more vivid conditionals in (implied) ind. statement in secondary sequence, "fearing (what would happen) if victory would go to ..."
regem et ducem: King Ferdinand of Naples and Duke Galeazzo Sforza of Milan
ut ... conficeretur: ind. command dependent on *instabat*

hominum non vulgarium, Bartholemeum connivente pontifice Padum traięcisse, quo mutato Florentinorum statu inferre bellum Ferdinando regi commodius posset, cui ita infensus erat, ut accire contra eum novos quoque in Italiam hostes cogitaverit. Vocatis itaque ad se omnium principum legatis, pacem his rationibus composuit: ut utraque pars quae bello cęperat redderet, utque Bartholemeus copias suas in Cisalpinam Galliam reduceret, servareturque pax

---

accio, -ire, -ivi, -itus: invite

capio, -ere, cępi (CL *cepi*), **captus**: seize, occupy

cogito, -are, -avi, -atus: consider; devise how, plot to

commode (*adv.*): conveniently

compono, -ponere, -posui, -positus: arrange

conniveo, -ere, -ivi, - : blink; turn a blind eye

contra: against (+ *acc.*)

copia, -ae *f.*: abundance; troops (pl.)

Florentinus, -a, -um: Florentine, of Florence

hostis, -is *m./f.*: enemy

infensus, -a, -um: hostile

infero, inferre, intuli, illatus: bring in; inflict

Italia, -ae *f.*: Italy

legatus, -i *m.*: envoy, ambassador

muto, -are, -avi, -atus: move, change, exchange

novus, -a, -um: new

Padus, -i *m.*: Po river

pars, partis *f.*: party

pontifex, -ficis *m.*: pontiff, pope

princeps, principis *m.*: leader; prince

ratio, -onis *f.*: reasoning, plan

reddo, -ere, reddidi, redditus: return

reduco, -ere, reduxi, reductus: lead back, bring back

servo, -are, -avi, -atus: protect, keep, preserve

status, -us *m.*: situation, condition

traicio, -ere, traięci (CL *traieci*), **traiectus**: transfer, cross

uterque, utraque, utrumque: each, either

voco, -are, -avi, -atus: to call

vulgaris, -e: common

Bartholemeum ... traięcisse: Bartolomeo Colleoni; ind. statement introduced by *opinio*

connivente pontifice: abl. abs. Platina originally wrote that Bartolomeo crossed the Po with Paul "egging him on" (*adhortante*), which he later softened to "turning a blind eye" (*connivente*)

quo ... posset: rel. clause of purpose, "in order that he be able ..."

mutato ... statu: abl. abs.

Ferdinando regi: dat. of ind. obj. with *inferre*; King Ferdinand I of Naples

commodius: compar. adv.

ut ... cogitaverit: result clause

Vocatis ... legatis: abl. abs.

his rationibus: abl. of description, "with these terms"; *his* looks forward to the subsequent *ut* clause

ut ... redderet, utque ... reduceret, (ut) servareturque ... : noun clause, "that ... would return, and that ... would bring back, and that ... would be kept"

Bartholemeus: Bartolomeo Colleoni

Cisalpinam Galliam: Cisalpine Gaul (Northern Italy above the Po river)

illa, quae antea inter Franciscum Sfortiam et Venetos apud Laudam
Pompeianam composita fuerat.

*Galeazzo Sforza does not want the Duke of Savoy to be included in the peace; the
King of France ultimately settles things*

41 In una re tantum addubitatum est, excludereturne a pace
Italiae Sabaudiae dux, vel Philippus frater, qui eo anno Venetorum
stipendiis militaverat, provinciam Galeacii bello vexerat. Petebant
Veneti ut inter foederatos is quoque censeretur. Negabat id fieri

---

addubito, -are, -avi, -atus: doubt, be
  uncertain
annus, -i *m.*: year
antea (*adv.*): before, in the past
censeo, -ere, censui, census: judge, count
compono, -ponere, -posui, -positus: place
  together, arrange
dux, ducis *m.*: leader; duke
excludo, -ere, exclusi, exclusus: shut out,
  exclude
fio, feri, factus sum: happen
foederatus, -a, -um: allied
Italia, -ae *f.*: Italy

milito, -are, -avi, -atus: serve as soldier
nego, -are, -avi, -atus: refuse, say ... not
peto, -ere, -ivi, -itus: fall upon; desire, ask
  (for)
provincia, -ae *f.*: province
Sabaudia, -ae *f.*: Savoy, region in northwest
  Italy
stipendium, -i *n.*: pay, (military) wages
tantum (*adv.*): only
unus, -a, -um: one
veho, -ere, vexi, vectus: bear, drag
Venetus, -a, -um: Venetian

---

pax illa: "that famous peace," the Peace of Lodi (1454), an agreement signed between
  Milan, Venice, and Florence that solidified the balance of power in Northern Italy
  and ushered in years of relative peace
Franciscum Sfortiam: Francesco Sforza, Duke of Milan
Laudam Pompeianam: Lodi, a town in Lombardy
composita fuerat: pluperf. (CL *composita erat*, see Introduction 7.D)
addubitatum est: impers., "it was doubted" or "there was doubt"
excludereturne: -*ne* introduces ind. question "whether he be excluded..."
Sabaudiae dux ... Philippus frater: Louis I, Duke of Savoy from 1440-1465, and
  his brother, Philip
eo anno: abl. of time within which
stipendiis: abl. of attendant circumstance, "under the wages"
Galeacii: Galeazzo Sforza, Duke of Milan
bello: abl. of means
ut ... censeretur: ind. command
is: the Duke of Savoy (and his brother, Philip)
id: that Savoy be included among those allied. Also subject acc. of *posse* in ind.
  statement

posse Galeacius, cum diceret eum se nunquam pro amico et socio habiturum, quem rex Franciae hostem haberet. Verum tantum valuit Paulus blanditiis et pollicitacionibus ut legatum Galeacii contra principis sui decretum in sententiam sui ipsius traxerit. Hanc ob rem iratus Galeacius et Laurentium Pisauriensem legatum suum exilio mulctavit et Sabaudienses ita bello vexavit, ut eos pacem exposcere coęgerit; quae quidem ex arbitrio regis Franciae postea composita

---

arbitrium, -i *n.*: arbitration, authority

blanditiae, -arum *f.*: flatteries, enticements

cogo, -ere, coęgi (CL *coegi*), **coactus**: force, compel

compono, -ponere, -posui, -positus: arrange, settle

contra: against, contrary to (+ *acc.*)

decretum, -i *n.*: decree

exilium, -i *n.*: exile

exposco, -ere, expoposci, - : request, ask for

Francia, -ae *f.*: France

hostis, -is *m./f.*: enemy

iratus, -a, -um: angry, enraged

legatus, -i *m.*: ambassador, legate

mulcto, -are, -avi, -atus: punish

nunquam (*adv.*): never

pollicitacio, -onis (CL *pollicitatio*) *f.*: promise

postea (*adv.*): afterwards

princeps, principis *m.*: leader; prince

pro: on behalf of, as (+ *abl.*)

Sabaudiensis, -e: Savoyard, of Savoy

sententia, -ae *f.*: opinion, purpose

tantum (*adv.*): so much

traho, -ere, traxi, tractus: draw, draw in

valeo, -ere, -ui, -itus: be influential, prevail

verum (*adv.*): however

vexo, -are, -avi, -atus: harass

---

cum diceret: causal *cum* clause

eum ... habiturum (esse): ind. statement introduced by *diceret*; a simpler order would be *se nunquam habiturum (esse) eum pro amico ... quem*; i.e., Galeazzo would not ally with Savoy because the King of France - Milan's ally - considered Savoy an enemy

quem ... haberet: rel. clause of characteristic

blanditiis et pollicitacionibus: ablatives of means

ut ... traxerit: result clause

principis sui: not technically reflexive because not referring to subject, but a sense of "his own prince (i.e. Galeazzo)"

sui ipsius: emphatic pronoun added to distinguish from the previous use of the reflexive, "of he himself (i.e. Paul)"

et ... et: "both ... and"

Laurentium Pisauriensem: Lorenzo of Pesaro, Galeazzo's legate

legatum: appositive to *Laurentium Pisauriensem*

exilio: abl. of means

Sabaudienses: substantive adj.

bello: abl. of means

ut ... coęgerit: result clause

exposcere: inf. object of *coęgerit*

est, intervenientibus et reginae et uxoris Galeacii precibus, quae
ducis Sabaudiae sorores sunt.

*Paul and his vice-chamberlain, Vianesio Albergati, put on a lavish Carnival cele-
bration in Rome*

42 Compositis autem hoc modo rebus, Paulus ad ocium conversus, populo Romano ad imitationem veterum, ludos quam magnificentissimos et epulum lautissimum instituit, procurante eam rem
Vianesio Bononiensi pontificis vicecamerario. Ludi autem erant

---

compono, -ponere, -posui, -positus:
  arrange, settle
convertor, -verti, -versus sum: turn
dux, ducis *m.*: leader; duke
epulum, -i *n.*: feast; public banquet
imitatio, -onis *f.*: imitation
instituo, -ere, -ui, -utus: set up
intervenio, -venire, -veni, -ventus: intervene
lautus, -a, -um: sumptuous, luxurious
ludus, -i *m.*: game
magnificus, -a, -um: splendid, magnificent

modus, -i *m.*: manner, way
ocium, -i (CL *otium*) *n.*: leisure, peace, rest
pontifex, -ficis *m.*: pontiff, pope
populus, -i *m.*: people
prex, precis *f.*: prayer, request
procuro, -are, -avi, -atus: manage; attend to
Sabaudia, -ae *f.*: Savoy, region in northwest
  Italy
uxor, -oris *f.*: wife
vetus, veteris: ancient
vicecamerarius, -i *m.*: vice-chamberlain

---

reginae: Charlotte of Savoy, wife of Louis XI of France, sister to Louis I, Duke of
  Savoy
uxoris Galaecii: Bona of Savoy, wife of Galeazzo Sforza, sister of Louis I, Duke of
  Savoy
intervenientibus … precibus: abl. abs. with causal sense, "because of the intervening
  prayers of the queen and of Galeazzo's wife"
Compositis … rebus: abl. abs.
hoc modo: abl. of manner
populo Romano: dat. of advantage
ad imitationem: *ad* + acc. often replaces the dat. of CL (see Introduction 7.B); here a
  dat. of purpose, "as an imitation"
veterum: substantive, "the ancients"
quam magnificentissimos et … lautissimum: "as magnificent and … sumptuous as
  possible"
procurante … Vianesio Bononiensi: abl. abs.
Vianesio Bononiensi: Vianesio Albergati of Bologna, Paul II's vice-chamberlain, a
  post which at that time included administration of the city of Rome

pallia octo, quae cursu certantibus in Carnisprivio proponebantur
singulis diebus. Currebant senes, adoloscentes, iuvenes, Iudei, ac
seorsum pastillis primo quidem pleni quo tardiores in cursu essent.
Currebant et equi, equae, asini, bubali tanta cum omnium voluptate, ut omnes prae risu pedibus stare vix possent. Cursus autem et

---

adoloscens, -entis (CL *adulescens*) *m./f.*:
  young adult
asinus, -i *m.*: ass, donkey
bubalus, -i *m.*: antelope, gazelle; wild ox
Carnisprivium, -i *n.*: Carnival
certor, -ari, -atus sum: compete
curro, -ere, cucurri, cursus: run
cursus, -us *m.*: running; race
dies, diei *m./f.*: day
equa, -ae *f.*: mare
equus, -i *m.*: horse
Iudeus, -i (CL *Iudaeus*) *m.*: Jew
iuvenis, -is *m./f.*: youth
octo (*indecl.*): eight
pallium, -i *n.*: coverlet; a race

pastillus, -i *m.*: pastry
pes, pedis *m.*: foot
plenus, -a, -um: full
prae: because of (+ *abl.*)
primo (*adv.*): at the beginning
propono, -ponere, -posui, -positus: propose;
  put or place forward
risus, -us *m.*: laughter
senex, senis *m.*: old man
seorsum (*adv.*): separately
singulus, -a, -um: individual, each
sto, -are, steti, status: stand
tardus, -a, -um: slow
vix (*adv.*): scarcely
voluptas, -tatis *f.*: pleasure, enjoyment

---

pallia: a coverlet given as a prize in races; used metonymically to refer to the race itself

cursu: abl. of means

certantibus: dat. of ind. obj. with *proponebantur*

Carnisprivio: festival of excess preceding Lent

singulis diebus: abl. of time when

Currebant … essent: Jews were treated very badly in Rome under the rule of Pope
  Paul II. During Carnival they were fed rich meals and forced to run through the
  streets for the entertainment of the Roman people and the pope

seorsum … essent: refers to *Iudei*, so that the Jews are the ones full with pastries

quo … essent: rel. clause of purpose, "in order that by means of this they might be
  slower"

tardiores: nom. pl. compar. of *tardus*

tanta cum omnium voluptate: "with such great pleasure (on the part) of all"

ut … possent: result clause

Cursus … et stadium erat: *erat* is singular due to the nearest noun, *stadium*, but
  is best translated in the plural "were" to include *cursus*. This route is the modern
  Corso, which takes its name from these races

stadium erat ab Arcu Domiciani usque ad aedes Sancti Marci, unde pontifex ipse solidam voluptatem percipiebat. Hac etiam in pueros coeno oblitos post cursum munificentia usus, ut singulis carlenum (nummi argentei id genus est) condonaret.

Paul is warned of a conspiracy between Callimachus (of the Roman Academy) and Luca Tozzoli (an exile in Naples); panic sets in

43 Sed ecce in tam publica omnium laeticia subitus terror Paulum occupat. Nunciatur ei quosdam adolescentes duce Calimacho

---

adolescens, -entis (CL *adulescens*)*m./f.*: young adult

aedes, aedis *f.*: temple; house (*pl.*)

arcus, -us *m.*: arch

argenteus, -a, -um: made of silver

carlenum, -i *n.*: a Carlino, a silver coin

coenum, -i (CL *caenum*) *n.*: mud

condono, -are, -avi, -atus: give (away); make a present of

cursus, -us *m.*: race

Domicianus, -i (CL *Domitianus*) *m.*: Domitian, Emperor 81-96 CE

dux, ducis *m.*: leader

ecce: look!

genus, generis *n.*: kind

hac (*adv.*): here

laeticia, -ae (CL *laetitia*) *f.*: joy, happiness

munificentia, -ae *f.*: bountifulness, munificence

nummus, -i *m.*: coin

nuncio, -are, -avi, -atus (CL *nuntio*): announce, report

oblino, -are, oblinavi, oblitus: smear over

occupo, -are, -avi, -atus: seize; overtake

percipio, -cipere, -cepi, -ceptus: perceive, observe; take

pontifex, -ficis *m.*: pontiff, pope

publicus, -a, -um: public

quidam, quaedam, quoddam: certain

sanctus, -i *m.*: saint

singulus, -a, -um: each one; individual

solidus, -a, -um: full; real

stadium, -i *n.*: stadium; race course

subitus, -a, -um: sudden

tam (*adv.*): so, so much

terror, -oris *m.*: terror, panic

unde (*adv.*): from where

usque (*adv.*): all the way

utor, uti, usus sum: use, make use of (+ *abl.*)

voluptas, -tatis *f.*: pleasure, enjoyment

Arcu Domiciani: the Arch of Domitian; Platina is probably referring to the Arco di Portogallo on the Corso, destroyed in the 17th century

aedes Sancti Marci: Palazzo San Marco (now called Palazzo Venezia), the palace Paul built for himself, see fig. 3 (p. 72)

in: here, "towards"

coeno: abl. of means

ut ... condonaret: result clause

singulis: dat. of ind. obj. with *condonaret*

nummi argentei: partitive gen. dependent on *genus*

Nunciatur: impers.

duce Calimacho: abl. abs.

Calimacho: Filippo Buonaccorsi, also known as Callimachus (1437-1496), a humanist and member of the Roman Academy

FIGURE 3:   Palazzo San Marco, also called Palazzo Venezia (photo by authors)

In 1455 Pietro Barbo built the *aedes Sancti Marci* to adjoin the church of San Marco, where he was cardinal priest (see ch. 1). The façade of church is made up of the double rows of three arches at left. While cardinal, Barbo made further improvements, creating the imposing structure whose tower and battlements dominate the square below. In 1564, Pope Pius IV gave the Palazzo San Marco to the Republic of Venice for use as its embassy, after which it became known as the Palazzo "of" Venezia. From 1929 until 1943, the building served as the headquarters for the Fascist Party, and some of Mussolini's most famous speeches were delivered from a balcony on the second floor (center right).

in eum conspirasse, cui prae timore vix [381] {236ʀ} respiranti nescioquo fato novus etiam terror additur. Advolat enim quidam cognomento Philosophus, homo facinorosus et exul, qui vitam primo et reditum in patriam deprecatus, nunciat, ac falso quidem, Lucam Totium, Romanum civem Neapoli exulantem, cum multis exulibus in nemoribus Veliternis, a se visum ac paulo post affuturum.

---

addo, -ere, addidi, additus: add
adsum, adesse, affui, affuturus: be present
advolo, -are, -avi, -atus: rush forth
civis, -is *m./f.*: citizen
cognomentum, -i *n.*: surname
conspiro, -are, -avi, -atus: plot
deprecor, -ari, -atus sum: pray, beg (for)
exul, -ulis *m./f.*: exile
exulo, -are, -avi, -atus: live in exile
facinorosus, -a, -um: wicked, criminal
falso (*adv.*): falsely
fatum, -i *n.*: fate
Neapolis, -is *f.*: Naples
nemus, nemoris *n.*: wood
nescioquis, nescioquid: some

novus, -a, -um: new
nuncio, -are, -avi, -atus (CL *nuntio*): announce; report
patria, -ae *f.*: homeland
paulo (*adv.*): by a little
prae: because of (+ *abl.*)
primo (*adv.*): at first
quidam, quaedam, quoddam: a certain
reditus, -us *m.*: return
respiro, -are, -avi, -atus: breathe
terror, -oris *m.*: terror, panic
timor, -oris *m.*: fear; dread
Veliternus, -a, -um: of Velletri (a suburb of Rome)
vix (*adv.*): scarcely

---

in eum: here, "against him"
conspirasse: syncopated from *conspera(vi)sse*, inf. in ind. statement introduced by *nunciatur*
cui: dat. of ind. obj. with *additur*
respiranti: agrees with *cui*
cognomento: abl. of respect
Philosophus: a Roman named Andreas but known as "Philosophus"
homo ... exul: appositives with *Philosophus*
Lucam Totium: Luca Tozzoli, an exile in league with the Orsini, a powerful Roman family opposed to Paul
Neapoli: locative
visum (esse): perf. pass. inf. of *video* in ind. statement introduced by *nunciat*; acc. subject is *Lucam Totium*
affuturum (esse): fut. inf. in ind. statement introduced by *nunciat*

Timere Paulus ac magis trepidare tum coepit, veritus ne domi et foris opprimeretur.

In the ensuing panic, many are arrested and jailed; some individuals opportunistically take advantage of the situation

44 Capiuntur permulti in urbe, tum ex aulicis, tum ex Romanis. Augebat hominis timorem Vianesius. Augebant [382] et alii eius familiares, qui ex tanta perturbatione aditum ad maiorem dignitatem et uberiorem fortunam sibi quaerebant. Irrumpebant cuiusvis

---

aditus, -us *m.*: access; opportunity
augeo, -ere, auxi, auctus: increase
aulicus, -i *m.*: courtier
capio, -ere, cepi, captus: seize; arrest
coepio, -ere, coepi, coeptus: begin
dignitas, -tatis *f.*: honor; rank
domus, -i *f.*: home, household
familiaris, -is *m./f.*: member of household
foris (*adv.*): out of doors
fortuna, -ae *f.*: fortune; circumstances
irrumpo, -ere, irrupi, irruptus: invade; break in
magis (*adv.*): more
opprimo, -primere, -pressi, -pressus: overwhelm; seize; catch by surprise

permultus, -a, -um: very much; very many (*pl.*)
perturbatio, -onis *f.*: disturbance; commotion
quaero, -ere, quaesivi, quaesitus: seek, strive for
quivis, quaevis, quodvis: whoever, whatever; anyone
timeo, -ere, -ui, - : fear; be afraid
timor, -oris *m.*: fear; dread
trepido, -are, -avi, -atus: tremble
uber, uberis: rich, abundant
urbs, urbis *f.*: city
vereor, -eri, -itus sum: fear; dread

---

ne ... opprimeretur: fear clause
domi: locative; *domi et foris* is "both at home and abroad"; that is, by Callimachus and the young men in Rome, and by Luca Tozzoli with foreign backers
tum ... tum: "both ... and"
Romanis: i.e. the non-curial citizens of Rome
Augebat hominis timorem Vianesius: in the manuscripts, Platina had removed this sentence, but then he added it back in before printing
Vianesius: Vianesio Albergati of Bologna, vice-chamberlain to Paul II
maiorem: compar. of *magnus*
uberiorem: compar. of *uber*
sibi: reflexive, dat. of advantage
cuiusvis: gen. sing., "of anyone at all"

domum sine discrimine. Trahebant in carcerem* quos suspectos coniurationis habuissent*.

Platina is arrested and brought before Paul

45 Et ne ego tantae calamitatis expers essem, domum ubi habitabam, multis satellitibus noctu circundant, fractis foribus ac fenestris, vi irrumpunt, Demetrium Lucensem familiarem meum comprehendunt; a quo ubi scivere me apud cardinalem Mantuanum

---

calamitas, -tatis *f.*: misfortune, disaster

carcer, -is *m.*: prison, jail

cardinalis, -is *m.*: cardinal

circundo, -dare, -dedi, -datus (CL *circumdo*): surround

comprehendo, -hendere, -hendi, -hensus: seize; arrest

coniuratio, -onis *f.*: conspiracy, plot

discrimen, -minis *n.*: distinction, discrimination

domus, -i *f.*: home, household

expers, expertis: free from (+ *gen.*)

familiaris, -is *m./f.*: household servant

fenestra, -ae *f.*: window

foris, -is *f.*: door, gate

frango, -ere, fregi, fractus: break, shatter

habito, -are, -avi, -atus: inhabit; live

irrumpo, -ere, irrupi, irruptus: invade, break in

Mantuanus, -a, -um: of Mantua

noctu (*adv.*): at night

satelles, -itis *m./f.*: attendant

scisco, -ere, scivi, scitus: come to know, learn

sine: without (+ *abl.*)

suspectus, -a, -um: suspected (+ *gen.*)

traho, -ere, traxi, tractus: draw, drag

ubi (*adv.*): where; when

vis, vis *f.*: violence, force

---

carcerem* … habuissent*: Platina originally wrote and then later crossed out before printing: *carcerem non quos … habuissent, sed quos aut ipsi oderant ob aliquam simultatem, aut divellere a complexu coniugum explendae libidinis suae causa cupiebant* ("they dragged into jail not those suspected of conspiracy, but those whom they themselves either hated because of some rivalry, or desired to tear away from the embrace of their spouses for the sake of satisfying their own pleasure.")

ne … essem: neg. purpose clause

domum: acc. obj. of *cirdundant*

noctu: abl. of time when, adverbial

Demetrium Lucensem: Demetrius Guazzelli of Lucca, a household member and student of Platina

scivere: alt. form of *sciverunt*

cardinalem Mantuanum: Francesco Gonzaga (1444-1483), Cardinal of Mantua (1461-1483), had helped secure Platina's release from prison after Platina was accused of treason the first time; see Introduction 2 and ch. 18

cęnare, statim accurunt, et me, in cubiculo hominis captum, ad Paulum confestim trahunt.

Platina denies that Callimachus was contriving a conspiracy

46 Qui ubi me vidit: "Ita," inquit, "duce Calimacho in nos coniurabas?" Tum ego frętus innocentia mea, ita constanti animo respondi ut nullum conscientie signum in me deprehendi posset. Instabat ille discinctus et pallidus, et nisi verum faterer, nunc tormenta mihi, nunc mortem proponebat. Tum ego cum viderem

---

accurro, -ere, accucurri, accursus: charge
animus, -i *m.*: mind; soul
capio, -ere, cepi, captus: seize; arrest
confestim (*adv.*): immediately
coniuro, -are, -avi, -atus: conspire, plot
conscientia, -ae *f.*: knowledge; (guilty) conscience
constans, constantis: steadfast, resolute
cubiculum, -i *n.*: chamber; apartment
cęno, -are, -avi, -atus (CL *ceno*): dine
deprehendo, -hendere, -hendi, -hensus: discover; reveal
discinctus, -a, -um: ungirt; half dressed
dux, ducis *m.*: leader
fateor, -eri, fassus sum: admit, confess (+ *acc.*)
frętus, -a, -um (CL *fretus*): relying on, supported by (+*abl.*)

innocentia, -ae *f.*: innocence
inquam, -, -, -: say
insto, -are, institi, - : pursue, threaten
mors, mortis *f.*: death
nullus, -a, -um: no; none
nunc (*adv.*): now
pallidus, -a, -um: pale, yellow-green
propono, -ponere, -posui, -positus: propose
respondeo, -ere, respondi, responsus: respond
signum, -i *n.*: sign
statim (*adv.*): immediately
tormentum, -i *n.*: torture
traho, -ere, traxi, tractus: drag
ubi (*adv.*): where; when
verum, -i *n.*: truth

---

me ... cęnare: ind. statement introduced by *scivere*
hominis: = *eius* (see Introduction 7.E), referring to *cardinalem Mantuanum*
duce Calimacho: abl. abs.; Callimachus, a member of the Roman Academy accused of leading the conspiracy (ch. 43)
constanti animo: abl. of manner
ut ... posset: result clause
conscientie: gen. sing. (CL *conscientiae*, see Introduction 6.B)
deprehendi: pass. inf., complementary with *posset*
nisi ... faterer: fut. more vivid cond., expressed in imperf. subj. in virtual ind. statement in secondary sequence, "unless I would confess"
cum viderem: circumstantial *cum* clause

omnia armis et tumultu circunsonare, veritus ne quid gravius ob formidinem et iram in nos consuleretur, rationes attuli quam ob rem crederem Calimachum nil aliquid tale unquam moliturum, nedum meditatum fuisse, quod consilio, lingua, manu, solicitudine, opibus, copiis, clientelis, armis, pecuniis, oculis postremo careret. Caeculus enim erat, et P. Lentulo somniculosior, ac L. Crasso ob

---

affero, afferre, attuli, allatus: convey, offer

aliquis, aliquid: someone, something; anything

arma, -orum *n.*: weapons

caeculus, -a, -um: near blind

careo, -ere, -ui, -itus: be without, lack (+ *abl.*)

circunsono, -are, -avi, -atus (CL *circumsono*): resound on every side

clientela, -ae *f.*: group of clients

consilium, -i *n.*: plan; intelligence

consulo, -sulere, -sului, -sultus: deliberate; adopt

copia, -ae *f.*: abundance; troops (*pl.*)

formido, -dinis *f.*: fear, terror

gravis, -e: heavy; serious

ira, -ae *f.*: anger

lingua, -ae *f.*: tongue; speech

manus, -us *f.*: hand; literary skill

meditor, -ari, -atus sum: contemplate, think

molior, -iri, -itus sum: plan, contrive

nedum (*adv.*): still less

nil *n.* (*indecl.*): nothing

oculus, -i *m.*: eye

ops, opis *f.*: power; resources (*pl.*)

postremo (*adv.*): finally

ratio, -onis *f.*: reasoning

solicitudo, -dinis (CL *sollicitudo*) *f.*: concern; responsibility

somniculosus, -a, -um: sleepy, drowsy

talis, -e: so great

tumultus, -us *m.*: commotion, uproar

unquam (*adv.*): ever

vereor, -eri, -itus sum: fear, dread

---

omnia ... circunsonare: ind. statement introduced by *viderem*

ne ... consuleretur: fear clause

quid: *aliquid*, "something" (after *si*, *nisi*, *num* and *ne*, "*ali*" takes a holiday)

gravius: neut. compar., agrees with *quid*

quam ob rem crederem: ind. question

nil: here adverbial, "in no way"

aliquid tale: "any such thing"

moliturum (esse): ind. statement introduced by *crederem*, "that he would contrive"

meditatum fuisse: ind. statement coordinated with *moliturum*, acc. obj. of both is *aliquid*; "that he (actually) had planned"

quod ... careret: "because ..."; *careret* is subjunctive in a subordinate clause in ind. statement

Caeculus: diminutive of *caecus*; Callimachus was often described by Platina as almost blind

P. Lentulo ... L. Crasso: abl. of comparison with *somniculsior* and *tardior*; P. Cornelius Lentulus Sura and M. Licinius Crassus, two men involved in the Catilinarian Conspiracy (Sallust *Cat.* 17), a plot by the senator Catiline to overthrow the republic, put down by Cicero in 63 BCE; *lentulus* means slow and *crassus* means large; Platina is making a pun on their names

adipem tardior. Omitto quod nec civis quidem Romanus erat qui patriam liberaret, nec praesul qui pontificatum sibi Paulo interempto desumeret. Quid poterat Calimachus? Quid auderet? Eratne lingua et manu promptus? Habebatne ad tantam rem conficiendam certos homines delectos et descriptos, quorum opera uteretur? Nisi forte vellent Glaucum et Petreium, fugae suae comites, alteros Gabinios ac Statilios esse.

---

adeps, adipis *m./f.*: fatness; corpulence
audeo, -ere, ausus sum: dare
certus, -a, -um: trusty
civis, -is *m./f.*: citizen
comes, comitis *m./f.*: comrade, companion
conficio, -ficere, -feci, -fectus: accomplish
delectus, -a, -um: chosen
descriptus, -a, -um: organized, arranged
desumo, -ere, desumpsi, desumptus: take
forte (*adv.*): by chance
fuga, -ae *f.*: escape; exile
interemo, -emere, -emi, -emptus: kill

libero, -are, -avi, -atus: liberate
lingua, -ae *f.*: tongue; speech
manus, -us *f.*: hand
omitto, -ere, omisi, omissus: omit; disregard
opera, -ae *f.*: work, service
patria, -ae *f.*: homeland
pontificatus, -us *m.*: pontificate
praesul, -is *m./f.*: prelate
promptus, -a, -um: ready, quick
tardus, -a, -um: slow
utor, uti, usus sum: use, enjoy (+ *abl.*)
volo, velle, volui, - : wish, want

---

quod: introducing a substantive clause, "the fact that"
nec ... nec: neither ... nor
qui ... liberaret, qui ... desumeret: rel. clauses of characteristic
poterat: "capable of"
Quid auderet: deliberative, "what would he have dared?"
Eratne ... Habebatne: *-ne* attached to first word of a sentence to indicate a question
lingua et manu: abls. of respect; referring to speech and action
ad tantam rem conficiendam: *ad* + acc. gerundive expressing purpose, "in order for such a thing to be accomplished (i.e. to accomplish such a thing)"
quorum ... uteretur: rel. clause of characteristic
vellent ... esse: potential subjunctive followed by ind. statement, "they would wish that Glaucus and Petreius be another set of Gabinii and Statilii"
Glaucum: Lucio Condulmaro, member of the Roman Academy and friend of Callimachus; he took the ancient name "Glaucus"
Petreium: Pietro Marso, member of the Roman Academy
comites: appositive with *Glaucum et Petreium*
Gabinios ac Statilios: P. Gabinius Capito and Statilius, two of the Catilinarian conspirators (Sall. *Cat.* 17)

Paul calls for Platina to be tortured and imprisons him in Castel Sant'Angelo

47 Tum Paulus ad Vianesium conversus: "Hic," inquit (me torvis oculis aspiciens), "tormento cogendus est verum fateri; nam coniurandi artem optime novit." *Utinam consideratius mecum egisset Paulus*; non enim me statim tormento subięcisset. Nam cum verum conięctura quaeritur nec de facto constat, in coniuratione potissimum, et quae ante suscęptum negocium et post sint gesta,

---

ago, -ere, egi, actus: act
ars, artis *f.*: skill, art
aspicio, -ere, aspexi, aspectus: look
bene (*adv.*): well
cogo, -ere, coegi, coactus: force, compel
coniuratio, -onis *f.*: conspiracy, plot
coniuro, -are, -avi, -atus: conspire, plot
conięctura, -ae (CL *coniectura*) *f.*: conjecture
considerate (*adv.*): thoughtfully, maturely
consto, -stare, -stiti, -status: to stand; be established
convertor, -verti, -versus sum: turn
factum, -i *n.*: fact
fateor, -eri, fassus sum: admit, confess
gero, -ere, gessi, gestus: carry; accomplish
inquam, - , - , - : say

negocium, -i (CL *negotium*) *n.*: trouble; business
nosco, -ere, novi, notus: learn
oculus, -i *m.*: eye
potissimum (*adv.*): chiefly, especially
quaero, -ere, quaesivi, quaesitus: seek; ask
statim (*adv.*): immediately
subicio, -icere, -ięci (CL *subieci*), -iectus: subject
suscipio, -cipere, -cepi, -cęptus (CL *susceptus*): undertake; take up
tormentum, -i *n.*: torture
torvus, -a, -um: pitiless; wild; piercing
utinam: if only, would that
verum, -i *n.*: truth

Vianesium: Vianesio Albergati of Bologna, vice-chamberlain to Paul II
Hic ... cogendus est: pass. periphrastic, "He must be forced"
tormento: dat. of agent with pass. periphrastic
coniurandi: gen. gerund, "of conspiring"
optime: superl. of *bene*
novit: "has learned," therefore, "knows"
Utinam ... egisset Paulus: optative subjunctive, "If only ... Paul had acted"; Platina originally wrote a different phrase, which he crossed out before printing: *Utinam Paulus aliquando rhetoricam didicisset* ("If only Paul had at some point learned rhetoric"); the implication is that Paul did not understand Platina's references to the Catilinarian conspiracy and his puns highlighting Callimachus's harmlessness
consideratius: compar. of *considerate*
subięcisset: potential subjunctive
cum ... quaeritur ... constat: temporal *cum* clause
conięctura: abl. of origin, "from conjecture"
constat: impers.
quae ... sint gesta: ind. question "what things were done before the business was taken up, and after"

quaeritur. Consideratur vita coniurantis; considerantur mores, ambitio, cupiditas tum facultatum tum honorum, et si quid antea dictum, scriptum, aut factum sit, quod eo tendat. Horum {236v} nihil consideravit Paulus; in carcerem nos coniicit.

Paul learns that Luca Tozzoli never left Naples

[383] **48** Verum cum admoneretur ab his qui bene sentiebant, quibusque exploratum erat, Lucam Totium nusquam pedem Neapoli

---

admoneo, -ere, -ui, -itus: advise
ambitio, -onis *f.*: ambition
bene (*adv.*): well
carcer, -eris *m.*: prison, jail
coniicio, -iicere, -ieci, -iectus: throw
coniuro, -are, -avi, -atus: conspire, plot
considero, -are, -avi, -atus: examine; investigate
cupiditas, -tatis *f.*: passion, ambition
eo (*adv.*): there, in that direction
exploro, -are, -avi, -atus: investigate, confirm

facultas, -tatis *f.*: capability; resources (*pl.*)
honor, -oris *m.*: honor; office
mos, moris *m.*: habit; (*pl.*) morals, character
nusquam (*adv.*): nowhere; on no occasion
pes, pedis *m.*: foot
quaero, -ere, quaesivi, quaesitus: seek, ask
scribo, -ere, scripsi, scriptus: write
sentio, -ire, sensi, sensus: understand
tendo, -ere, tetendi, tensus: extend, tend
verum (*adv.*): but; however

---

quaeritur: impers.
mores, ambitio, cupiditas: subjects of *considerantur*
tum ... tum: "both ... and"
facultatum ... honorum: obj. genitives
si ... dictum (sit), scriptum (sit), aut factum sit: ind. quest., "if anything before has been said, written, or done"
si quid: "if anything" (after *si, nisi, num* and *ne*, "*ali*" takes a holiday)
quod eo tendat: rel. clause of characteristic, "which might extend to that (i.e. that looks that way)"
Horum: partitive gen.
cum admoneretur: circumstantial *cum* clause
quibusque: abl. of agent, the *-que* coordinates with *ab his*
exploratum erat: impers.
Lucam Totium ... movisse: ind. statement introduced by *admoneretur*; acc. obj. is *pedem*; Luca Tozzoli was rumored to be waiting outside Rome with troops to overthrow the pope
Neapoli: abl. of place from which

movisse, ne tantum tumultum cum suo discrimine concitaret, revocat edictum tertio die quo proemia illis proponebat, qui Lucam reum maiestatis, vel vivum vel mortuum, in potestatem suam redęgissent; non tamen Quadratios fratres, quos ob eam suspicionem cęperat et torserat, dimisit. Subesse aliquam latentem causam videri volebat, ne levitatis argueretur.

---

aliqui, -qua, -quod: some
arguo, -ere, -ui, -utus: prove, accuse (+ *gen.*)
capio, -ere, cępi (CL *cepi*), **captus**: seize; arrest
concito, -are, -avi, -atus: stir up; cause
dies, diei *m./f.*: day
dimitto, -ere, dimisi, dimissus: send away, release
discrimen, -minis *n.*: crisis, danger
edictum, -i *n.*: proclamation; edict
latens, latentis: hidden; secret
levitas, -tatis *f.*: levity; fickleness
maiestas, -tatis *f.*: greatness; high treason
mortuus, -a, -um: dead
moveo, -ere, movi, motus: move

potestas, -tatis *f.*: power
proemium , -i (CL *praemium*) *n.*: prize; reward
propono, -ponere, -posui, -positus: propose
redigo, -ere, redęgi (CL *redegi*), **redactus**: drive back; render
reus, -a, -um *m.*: guilty, accused
revoco, -are, -avi, -atus: call back
subsum, -esse, -fui, - : be underneath
suspicio, -onis *f.*: suspicion
tertius -a -um: third
torqueo, -ere, torsi, tortus: torture
tumultus, -us *m.*: commotion; disturbance
vivus, -a, -um: alive
volo, velle, volui, - : wish, want

---

ne ... concitaret: neg. purpose clause
cum suo discrimine: "with his own danger (i.e. with danger to himself)"
revocat: subject is *Paulus* from the previous sentence
tertio die: abl. of time when
quo: "from (that day) on which"
illis: dat. of ind. obj. with *proponebat*
qui ... redęgissent: rel. clause of characteristic, "who would have rendered"; antecedent is *illis*
Quadratios fratres: other members of the Roman Academy
videri: pass. inf. in ind. statement, "seem"
ne ... argueretur: neg. purpose clause

Vianesio tortures many humanists

49 Liberatus hoc metu Paulus ad nos statim animum adiicit. Mittit in arcem Hadriani Vianesium cum Iohanne Francisco, Clugiensi Sanga, et satellite, qui nos quovis genere tormentorum adigat ea etiam fateri quae nusquam sciebamus. Torquentur prima et sequenti die multi, quorum pars magna prae dolore in ipsis cruciatibus concidit. Bovem Phalaridis sepulchrum Hadriani tum

---

adigo, -ere, adegi, adactus: force
adiicio, -ere, adieci, adiectus: add; apply
animus, -i *m.*: mind
arx, arcis *f.*: citadel; stronghold
bos, bovis *m./f.*: bull
Clugiensis, -e: of Chiozza
concido, -cidere, -cidi, - : fall down, collapse; faint
cruciatus, -us *m.*: torture device
dies, diei *m./f.*: day
dolor, -oris *m.*: pain, suffering
fateor, -eri, fassus sum: admit, confess (+ *acc.*)
genus, -eris *n.*: kind, sort
libero, -are, -avi, -atus: free; liberate
metus, -us *m.*: fear, anxiety
nusquam (*adv.*): on no occasion
pars, partis *f.*: part
prae: because of (+ *abl.*)
primus, -a, -um: first
quivis, quaevis, quodvis: any, whatever
satelles, -itis *m./f.*: attendant
scio, -ire, -ivi, -itus: know
sepulchrum, -i *n.*: grave, tomb
sequens, sequentis: following; next
statim (*adv.*): immediately
tormentum, -i *n.*: torture
torqueo, -ere, torsi, tortus: torture

---

hoc metu: abl. of separation
arcem Hadriani: the Mausoleum of Hadrian, now called the Castel Sant'Angelo, see fig. 4 (p. 83)
Hadriani: Hadrian, Roman Emperor (r. 117-138 CE)
Vianesium: Vianesio Albergati of Bologna, vice-chamberlain to Pope Paul II
Iohanne Francisco, Clugiensi Sanga: Giovanni Francesco and Sanga of Chiozzo, Vianesio's assistants
qui ... adigat: rel. clause of purpose dependent on *mittit*
fateri: inf. obj. of *adigat*; acc. subj. is *nos* and acc. obj. is *ea*
prima et sequenti die: abl. of time when
multi: subject of *torquentur*, substantive
quorum: partitive gen.
Bovem Phalaridis: a bronze bull in which the tyrant Phalaris roasted people alive
(esse) sepulchrum Hadriani: Castel Sant'Angelo, the fortress built onto Hadrian's Mausoleum

FIGURE 4:   Castel Sant'Angelo (photo by authors)

The structure that Platina calls the *arx Hadriani* (ch. 28 and 49), the *sepul-chrum Hadriani* (ch. 49), and the *moles Hadriani* (ch. 59) was originally built as a mausoleum for the emperor Hadrian (r. 117-138) and his descendants. Only the lower portion of the drum-shaped structure dates back to this early time. The mausoleum was subsequently built into a fortress for the popes, who used it both for defense and for incarceration. (Before Paul II imprisoned the humanists there, he also used it to jail Francesco, son of Count Everso (ch. 28).) The name Castel Sant'Angelo goes back to a tradition about the Archangel Michael appearing above the structure and sheathing his sword at the end of a plague. This photo is taken from the bridge on which Platina observed Paul II standing with the Holy Roman Emperor in ch. 59.

putasses, adeo resonabat fornix ille concavus vocibus miserorum adolescentum. Torquebatur Lucidus homo omnium innocentissimus. Torquebatur Marsus, Demetrius, Augustinus, Campanus optimus adolescens et unicum saeculi nostri decus, si ingenium et litteraturam inspicis; quibus cruciatibus et dolore animi mortuum postea crediderim.

---

adeo (*adv.*): to such an extent

adolescens, -entis (CL *adulescens*) *m./f.*: young adult

animus, -i *m.*: mind; soul

concavus, -a, -um: hollow

cruciatus, -us *m.*: cruelty; torture

decus, decoris *n.*: glory

dolor, -oris *m.*: pain, suffering

fornix, -icis *m.*: arch, vault, cellar

ingenium, -i *n.*: nature; talent

innocens, innocentis: harmless, innocent

inspicio, -ere, inspexi, inspectus: consider, inspect

litteratura, -ae *f.*: writing; scholarship

miser, -a, -um: miserable, wretched

postea (*adv.*): afterwards

resono, -are, -avi, -atus: resound

saeculum, -i *n.*: age; generation

torqueo, -ere, torsi, tortus: torture

unicus, -a, -um: only, sole, unique

vox, vocis *f.*: voice

---

putasses: syncopated from *puta(vi)sses*, potential subjunctive, "you would have thought"

Lucidus: Marco Lucido Fazini

homo: functioning as a rel. pronoun

omnium: partitive gen.

Marsus, Demetrius, Augustinus, Campanus: Pietro Marso, Demetrio Guazzelli, Agostino Maffei, Antonio Settimuleio Campano; friends of Platina

optimus: superl. of *bonus*

unicum ... decus: appositive to *Campanus*, as is *optimus adolescens*

si ... inspicis: protasis in a simple cond. with the apodosis elided

quibus cruciatibus et dolore: abl. of means

mortuum (esse): ind. statement introduced by *crediderim*; subject is an assumed *eum* (Campano)

crediderim: potential subjunctive, sense of "I believe (if I'm not mistaken)"

Vianesio tortures Platina

50 Fessi tortores non tamen satiati. Nam ad viginti fere eo biduo questioni subięcerant; me quoque ad poenam vocant. Accingunt se operi carnifices; parantur tormenta; spolior, laceror, trudor tanquam crassator et latro. Sedet Vianesius tanquam alter Minos stratis tapetibus, ac si in nuptiis esset, vel potius in coena Atrei et Tantali.

---

accingo, -ingere, -inxi, -inctus: equip (oneself)
biduum, -i *n.*: two days
carnifex, -ficis *m.*: butcher, torturer
coena, -ae (CL *cena*) *f.*: dinner; meal
crassator, -oris (CL *grassator*) *m.*: rioter; robber
fere (*adv.*): almost, nearly
fessus, -a, -um: tired
lacero, -are, -avi, -atus: whip
latro, -onis *m.*: bandit
nuptia, -ae *f.*: wedding (*pl.*)
opus, operis *n.*: work
paro, -are, -avi, -atus: prepare
poena, -ae *f.*: punishment
potius (*adv.*): rather
questio, -onis (CL *quaestio*) *f.*: questioning
satio, -are, -avi, -atus: satisfy, satiate
sedeo, -ere, sedi, sessus: sit
spolio, -are, -avi, -atus: strip
sterno, -ere, stravi, stratus: spread, strew
subicio, -icere, -ięci (CL *subieci*), **-iectus**: throw under; subject
tanquam (CL *tamquam*): just as
tapes, -etis *m.*: coverlet
tormentum, -i *n.*: torture device
tortor, -oris *m.*: torturer
trudo, -ere, trusi, trusus: push, shove, beat
viginti (*indecl.*): twenty
voco, -are, -avi, -atus: call

---

satiati (sunt): perf. pass.
ad viginti: *ad* + a number expresses approximation, "about twenty (humanists)"; direct obj. of *subięcerant*
eo biduo: abl. of time within which
subięcerant: to subject something (direct obj. here *ad viginti* rather than an acc.) to something (here dat. *questioni*)
ad poenam: *ad* + acc. expressing purpose, "for punishment"
carnifices: subject of *Accingunt*
Vianesius: Vianesio Albergati of Bologna, vice-chamberlain to Pope Paul II
Minos: mythical king of Crete, judge of the dead in the underworld
ac si ... esset: *ac si* "as if"; pres. contrafactual cond. clause of comparison
Atrei: Atreus, mythical ruler of Mycenae, grandson of Tantalus, murdered his nephews and fed them to their father
Tantali: Tantalus, mythical ruler of Mycenae who tried to feed his son Pelops to the gods

Homo, inquam, sacris initiatus, et quem sacri canones vetant de laicis questionem habere: ne si mors subsequatur, quod in tormentis interdum accidere solet, irregularis (ut eorum verbo utar) et impius habeatur.

Vianesio questions Platina about Callimachus's alleged conspiracy, about why Pomponio Leto called him 'Holiest Father,' and about whether he had written to any princes to call a council

51 Neque hoc quidem contentus, dum penderem miser in ipsis cruciatibus, [384] monilia Sangae Clugiensis attrectans, hominem rogabat a qua puella donum amoris habuisset. De amoribus locutus,

---

accidit, -ere, accidit, accisus est (*impers.*): happens

amor, -oris *m.*: love; love affairs (*pl.*)

attrecto, -are, -avi, -atus: handle

canon, -onis *m.*: canon, law

Clugiensis, -e: of Chiozza

contentus, -a, -um: content, satisfied (+ *abl.*)

cruciatus, -us *m.*: torture device

donum, -i *n.*: gift; offering

impius, -a, -um: wicked, impious

initio, -are, -avi, -atus: initiate

inquam, -, -, -: say

interdum (*adv.*): sometimes

irregularis, -e: irregular; contrary to Church rule

laicus, -i *m.*: layman, one not belonging to the priesthood

loquor, loqui, locutus sum: speak

miser, misera, miserum: miserable, wretched

monile, -lis *n.*: necklace

mors, mortis *f.*: death

pendeo, -ere, pependi, -: hang

questio, -onis (CL *quaestio*) *f.*: questioning

sacer, sacra, sacrum: sacred, holy

sacrum, -i *n.*: sacrifice; religious rites (*pl.*)

soleo, -ere, -ui, -itus: to be accustomed

subsequor, -sequi, -secutus sum: follow

tormentum, -i *n.*: torture

utor, uti, usus sum: use (+ *abl.*)

verbum, -i *n.*: word

veto, -are, -avi, -atus: forbid, prohibit

---

vetant ... habere: *veto* takes an obj. inf., "forbid him to hold an investigation of laymen"

de laicis: "concerning (i.e. over) laymen"

ne ... habeatur: neg. purpose clause, "lest he be considered"

accidere solet: *solet* + inf., "is accustomed to happen"

ut ... utar: purpose clause

contentus ... rogabat: subject is Vianesio

dum penderem: *dum* + imperf. subjunctive as "while" (see Introduction 7.C)

miser: adjectives in nom. often best translated adverbially, "miserably"

Sangae Clugiensis: Sanga of Chiozza, assistant of Vianesio

a qua ... habuisset: ind. question

ad me conversus instabat ut seriem coniurationis, vel fabulae potius a Calimacho confictae explicarem, diceremque quid causae esset, cur Pomponius, qui tum Venetiis erat, ad me scribens, patrem sanctissimum in suis litteris appellaret: "Te," inquit, "pontificem creaverant coniurati omnes?" Flagitat item, dederimne litteras Pomponio ad imperatorem, aut ad aliquem Christianum principem suscitandi scismatis aut concilii causa?

---

aliqui, -qua, -quod: some
appello, -are, -avi, -atus: call
Christianus, -a, -um: Christian
concilium, -i *n*.: council
confingo, -fingere, -finxi, -fictus: fabricate; invent
coniuratio, -onis *f*.: conspiracy
coniuratus, -i *m*.: conspirator
convertor, -verti, -versus sum: turn
creo, -are, -avi, -atus: create; elect
cur (*adv*.): why
explico, -are, -avi, -atus: explain
fabula, -ae *f*.: story, fable
flagito, -are, -avi, -atus: demand urgently

imperator, -oris *m*.: emperor; Holy Roman Emperor
inquam, - , - : say
insto, -are, institi, - : insist
item (*adv*.): likewise
litterae, -arum *f*.: a letter (epistle)
pontifex, -ficis *m*.: pontiff, pope
potius (*adv*.): rather
princeps, -cipis *m*.: leader, prince
sanctus, -a, -um: sacred, holy
scisma, -atis *n*.: schism
scribo, -ere, scripsi, scriptus: write
series, seriei *f*.: series, order of events
suscito, -are, -avi, -atus: stir up; kindle
Venetiae, -arum *f*.: Venice

Calimacho: Callimachus, a member of the Roman Academy who was accused of leading the conspiracy
ut ... explicarem, diceremque: ind. command
quid ... esset: ind. question
causae: partitive gen., "what of a reason (i.e. what reason)"
cur ... appellaret: ind. question
Pomponius: Pomponio Leto, humanist and founder of the Roman Academy
Venetiis: locative
patrem sanctissimum: a term reserved for the pope
dederimne: subjunctive in ind. question, *-ne* (enclitic) attached to first word of a sentence to indicate a question, "whether I gave"
suscitandi scismatis ... causa: *causa* + gen. gerundive expressing purpose, "for the sake of a schism to be stirred up (i.e. to stir up a schism)"

Platina denies all charges: he did not even like Callimachus, he cannot speak for Pomponio Leto, and he sent no letters

52 Respondeo me nunquam consiliorum Calimachi participem fuisse, quippe cum inter nos simultas esset haud parva. Nescire item cur Pomponius me patrem sanctissimum appellaret, sciturum ab eo; nam paulo post vinctum {237R} affuturum dicebat. De pontificatu vero non esse cur soliciti essent, quod vita privata semper contentus

---

adsum, adesse, affui, affuturus: be present; arrive
appello, -are, -avi, -atus: call
consilium, -i *n.*: plan
contentus, -a, -um: content, satisfied (+ *abl.*)
cur (*adv.*): why
haud (*adv.*): not at all, no
item (*adv.*): likewise
nescio, -ire, -ivi, -itus: to not know
nunquam (*adv.*): never
particeps, -cipis *m./f.*: sharer, partaker
paulo (*adv.*): a little

pontificatus, -us *m.*: pontificate, the office of pontifex
privatus, -a, -um: private; not in public office
quippe (*adv.*): indeed, as you see
respondeo, -ere, respondi, responsus: respond
sanctus, -a, -um: sacred, holy
scio, -ire, -ivi, -itus: know
simultas, -tatis *f.*: enmity; hatred
solicitus, -a, -um (CL *sollicitus*): concerned, anxious
vero (*adv.*): in fact, truly
vincio, -ire, vinxi, vinctus: bind

---

me ... fuisse: ind. statement
Calimachi: Callimachus, a member of the Roman Academy accused of leading the conspiracy
cum ... esset: causal *cum* clause
Nescire: ind. statement introduced by *respondeo*
cur ... appellaret: ind. question
Pomponius: Pomponio Leto, founder of the Roman Academy
sciturum (esse) ab eo: "he (Vianesio) would know this from him (Pomponius)"
affuturum (esse) dicebat: "he (Vianesio) was saying that he (Pomponius) would be present"
De pontificatu ... esse: ind. statement introduced by *respondeo*, "That truly concerning the pontificate there was no (reason) why"
cur ... essent: ind. question "why they should be concerned (with me)"
quod ... fuissem: subordinate clause within ind. statement, "because I had always been"

fuissem.   Ad imperatorem vero me nunquam litteras misisse, nec Pomponii opera ea in re usum esse, id etiam ab eo sciturum.

Platina is asked about his dealings with Sigismondo Malatesta; the questioning ends, but more torment is promised

53 Tandem vero delinitus aliquantulum tot meis cruciatibus, non tamen satiatus, deponi me iubet, vesperi maiores subiturum. Deferor in cubiculum semimortuus; nec ita multo post revocor a questoribus bene potis et pransis, aderat et Laurentius archiepiscopus

---

adsum, -esse, -fui, -futurus: be present
aliquantulum (*adv.*): some little bit
archiepiscopus, -i *m.*: archbishop
bene (*adv.*): well
cruciatus, -us *m.*: torture
cubiculum, -i *n.*: chamber
defero, -ferre, -tuli, -latus: carry down
delinio, -ire, -ivi, -itus: soothe
depono, -ere, deposui, depositus: let down
imperator, -oris *m.*: general; Holy Roman Emperor
iubeo, -ere, iussi, iussus: order
litterae, -arum *f.*: a letter (epistle)
multo (*adv.*): much
nunquam (CL *numquam*) (*adv.*): never
opera, -ae *f.*: work, service

poto, -are, potavi, potus: drink; (*pass.*) be filled with drink
prandeo, -ere, prandi, pransus: eat; (*pass.*) be filled with food
questor, -oris (CL *quaestor*) *m.*: questioner
revoco, -are, -avi, -atus: recall
satio, -are, -avi, -atus: satisfy, sate
scio, -ire, -ivi, -itus: know
semimortuus, -a, -um: half-dead
subeo, -ire, -ivi(ii), -itus: endure
tandem (*adv.*): finally
tot (*indecl.*): so many
utor, uti, usus sum: use, enjoy (+ *abl.*)
vero: but, however
vesperi (*adv*): in the evening

---

me ... misisse ... usum esse ... sciturum (esse): ind. statement introduced by *respondeo*
id: refers to the previous clause
deponi: obj. inf. (pres. pass.) with *iubet*, "that I be let down"; the torture was the strappado: hanging from one's hands, tied behind the back
maiores: acc. pl. compar. of *magnus*, substantive "greater (tortures)"
subiturum (esse): obj. inf. (fut. act.) with *iubet*, "that I undergo"
questoribus: in classical times, the *quaestor* was a public official in charge of financial affairs, in this context, it is an interrogator
potis et pransis: agreeing with *questoribus*
Laurentius archiepiscopus Spalatrensis: Lorenzo Zanni, Archbishop of Split (1452-1473)

Spalatrensis. Petunt quid mihi colloquii fuerit cum Sigismundo Malatesta, qui tum in urbe erat. "De litteris," inquam, "de armis, de praestantibus ingeniis tum veterum tum nostrorum hominum loquebamur, deque his rebus, quae in hominum colloquia cadere possunt." Minari tum Vianesius ac maiores cruciatus proponere, nisi verum faterer. Rediturum se die sequenti; meditarer interim ubi essem et quibuscum mihi esset agendum.

---

ago, -ere, egi, actus: do, act; deal
arma, -orum *n.*: arms
cado, -ere, cecidi, casus: fall; occur
colloquium, -i *n.*: conversation
cruciatus, -us *m.*: torture
dies, diei *m./f.*: day
fateor, -eri, fassus sum: admit, confess
ingenium, -i *n.*: nature; talent
inquam, -, -, -: say
interim (*adv.*): in the meantime
litterae, -arum *f.*: literature
loquor, loqui, locutus sum: speak

meditor, -ari, -atus sum: consider, think
minor, -ari, -atus sum: threaten
peto, -ere, -ivi, -itus: seek
praestans, praestantis: excellent
propono, -ponere, -posui, -positus: propose
redeo, -ire, -ivi(ii), -itus: return
sequens, sequentis: next
Spalat(r)ensis, -e: of Split, in modern Croatia
ubi (*adv.*): where; when
verum, -i *n.*: truth
vetus, veteris: ancient; the ancients (*pl.*)

---

quid ... fuerit: ind. question
quid ... coloquii: partitive gen., "what (of) conversation"
mihi: dat. of the possessor, "I had"
Sigismundo Malatesta: Sigismondo Pandolfo Malatesta (1417-1468), Prince of Rimini, powerful *condottiero*, patron of the arts, and sometimes enemy of Paul II. Vianesio suspected Malatesta's involvement in the alleged conspiracy
tum ... tum ...: "both ... and"
deque: *de* with the enclitic *-que*
in ... colloquia cadere: "fall into people's conversations (i.e. happen in people's conversations)"
Minari ... proponere: historic inf., "began to threaten and to propose"
maiores: compar. of *magnus*, agrees with *cruciatus*
nisi ... faterer: fut. more vivid cond., expressed in imperf. subjunctive in virtual ind. statement in secondary sequence, "unless I would confess"
Rediturum (esse): inf. in implicit ind. statement (Vianesio still speaking)
die sequenti: abl. of time when
meditarer: potential subj. with implied command, "I might consider"
ubi essem: ind. question
quibuscum ... agendum: subjunctive pass. periphrastic in ind. question "with whom it had to be dealt by me (i.e. with whom I had to deal)"
mihi: dat. of agent with pass. periphrastic

Back in his cell, Platina is cared for by Angelo and Marcello del Bufalo, who had been jailed for a murder relating to a feud

54 Reducor iterum ad cubile ubi tantus me repente dolor invasit, ut vitam cum morte cuperem commutare; recrudescentibus doloribus ob refrigerata membra, quassa vehementer ac laesa. Recreabat me tamen [385] non parum Angeli Bufali Romani equitis humanitas, quem anno ante Paulus in carcerem conięcerat, ob interfectum a Marcello filio Franciscum Cappocium. Id enim factum Angeli suasu

---

annus, -i *m.*: year
carcer, -eris *m.*: prison
commuto, -are, -avi, -atus: exchange
conicio, -icere, -ięci (CL *conieci*), **-iectus**: throw
cubile, -lis *n.*: bed
cupio, -ere, -ivi, -itus: desire
dolor, -oris *m.*: pain; grief
eques, equitis *m.*: knight
fio, feri, factus sum: happen, come about
humanitas, -tatis *f.*: kindness
interficio, -ficere, -feci, -fectus: kill
invado, -ere, invasi, invasus: enter
iterum (*adv.*): again

laedo, -ere, laesi, laesus: wound
membrum, -i *n.*: limb
mors, mortis *f.*: death
parum (*adv.*): very little
quatio, -ere, - , quassus: shake
recreo, -are, -avi, -atus: restore; revive
**recrudesco, -ere, recrudui, - **: break out again
reduco, -ere, reduxi, reductus: lead back
refrigero, -are, -avi, -atus: cool, become cold
repente (*adv.*): suddenly, unexpectedly
suasus, -us *m.*: advice
ubi (*adv.*): where; when
vehementer (*adv.*): vehemently

---

ut ... cuperem: result clause

recrudescentibus doloribus: abl. abs.

quassa ... laesa: both participles agree with *membra*

Angeli Bufali: possessive gen.; Angelo del Bufalo, knighted by Paul II in 1464, accused of being an accomplice of his son Marcello in the murder of Francesco Cappocio

Romani equitis: appositive to *Angeli ... Bufali*

anno: abl. of degree of difference

ob interfectum ... Franciscum Cappocium: "because of Francesco having been killed by ... " Platina had originally written a relative clause adding that Francesco "had committed adultery with his (Marcellus's) wife" (*qui eius uxori stuprum intulerat*); the phrase can still be read in A, but Platina later crossed it out very heavily in V and F

Marcello filio: Marcello del Bufalo, son of Angelo, was accused of murdering Francesco Cappocio because Francesco had slept with Marcello's wife and then mocked him with gestures *variis atque diversis* (according to Gaspar of Verona *De Gestis Pauli II* p. 45 Zippel)

Franciscum Cappocium: Francesco Cappocio, a noble Roman murdered by Marcello del Bufalo

factum (esse): perf. pass. inf. in ind. statement introduced by *dicebat*

Paulus dicebat. Angelus itaque ac Franciscus nepos, quibuscum in eodem cubiculo divertebam, quominus doloribus et inedia morerer, suis manibus et medelas et cibum mihi afferebant.

Paul's doctor tells Platina that he will be freed soon; instead, Paul charges him with heresy

55 Post biduum vero Christophorus Veronensis Pauli medicus ad me veniens, "Bono," inquit, "animo te esse iubet Paulus ac de se bene sperare, brevique liberum futurum." Sciscitor quando id fore speraret. Respondet homo liber audientibus omnibus qui tum aderant, non

---

adsum, -esse, -fui, -futurus: be present
affero, afferre, attuli, allatus: bring to, offer
animus, -i *m.*: mind; heart
audio, -ire, -ivi, -itus: hear, listen
bene (*adv.*): well
biduum, -i *n.*: two days
brevi (*adv.*): in a short time
cibus, -i *m.*: food
cubiculum, -i *n.*: chamber
diverto, -ere, diverti, diversus: lodge
dolor, -oris *m.*: pain, anguish
inedia, -ae *f.*: fasting, starvation
inquam, -, -, -, -: say
iubeo, -ere, iussi, iussus: order, bid

liber, libera, liberum: free
manus, -us *f.*: hand
medela, -ae *f.*: medical healing
medicus, -i *m.*: doctor, physician
nepos, -otis *m./f.*: nephew
quando (*adv.*): when
quominus: that not
respondeo, -ere, respondi, responsus: answer
sciscitor, -ari, -atus sum: ask
spero, -are, -avi, -atus: hope
vero (*adv.*): truly, in fact
Veronensis, -e: of Verona

Franciscus: Francesco, nephew of Angelo del Bufalo (different from Francesco Cappocio)
quibuscum ... divertebam: "with whom I was lodging in the same chamber"
quominus ... morerer: 1st sing. imperf. subjunctive in prevention clause dependent on *afferebant*
Christophorus Veronensis: Christopher of Verona, Paul II's personal doctor
Bono ... animo: abl. of description, "(be) of good heart"
esse ... sperare: *iubet* takes inf.
(te) liberum futurum (esse): ind. statement with implied *dicit Paulus* following *brevique*
quando ... speraret: ind. question
fore: alt. form of *futurum esse*, fut. inf. in ind. statement introduced by *speraret*
liber: adjectives in nom. often best translated adverbially, "freely"
audientibus omnibus: abl. abs.
non ... posse: ind. statement introduced by *Respondet*

ita cito fieri posse, ne levitatis et scaevitiae argueretur pontifex, quod illos, quos tanto tumultu concitato cępisset ac torsisset, statim veluti innoxios dimitteret. Neque hoc quidem contentus Paulus, quos paulo ante coniurationis et maiestatis accersierat, eosdem mutata sententia ob divulgatam fabulam haereseos accusat.

Pomponio Leto is extradited from Venice and faces questions about his use of ancient (pre-Christian) names

56 Trahitur ad urbem Pomponius [386] Venetiis captus; per totam Italiam, tanquam alter Iugurtha, ducitur in iudicium

---

accerso, -ere, -ivi(ii), -itus: summon; accuse

accuso, -are, -avi, -atus: accuse, charge (+ *gen.*)

arguo, -ere, -ui, -utus: accuse (+ *gen.*)

capio, -ere, cępi (CL *cepi*), **captus:** arrest, capture

cito (*adv.*): quickly

concito, -are, -avi, -atus: stir up, rouse

coniuratio, -onis *f.*: conspiracy, plot

contentus, -a, -um: content, satisfied (+ *abl.*)

dimitto, -ere, dimisi, dimissus: discharge; release

divulgo, -are, -avi, -atus: disseminate; gossip

fabula, -ae *f.*: story

fio, fieri, factus sum: happen

haeresis, haereseos *f.*: heresy

innoxius, -a, -um: harmless

Italia, -ae *f.*: Italy

iudicium, -i *n.*: trial

levitas, -tatis *f.*: levity; fickleness

maiestas, -tatis *f.*: treason

muto, -are, -avi, -atus: change

paulo (*adv.*): a little

per: through (+ *acc.*)

pontifex, -ficis *m.*: pontiff, pope

scaevitia, -ae (CL *saevitia*) *f.*: violence; cruelty

sententia, -ae *f.*: opinion

statim (*adv.*): immediately

tanquam (CL *tamquam*): just as if

torqueo, -ere, torsi, tortus: torture

totus, -a, -um: whole, all

traho, -ere, traxi, tractus: drag

tumultus, -us *m.*: commotion, uproar

veluti (*adv.*): just as, as if

Venetiae, -arum *f.*: Venice

---

ne ... argueretur: neg. purpose clause

quod ... dimitteret: clause of reported reason, "on the grounds that he immediately released"

quos ... cępisset ... torsisset: subjunctive by attraction in subordinate clause

coniurationis et maiestas: gen. of the charge, "(on a charge) of conspiracy and treason"

haereseos: alt. form of gen.

Pomponius: Pomponio Leto (1428-1498), founder of the Roman Academy

Venetiis: locative, construe closely with *captus*

captus: Leto had already been arrested on charges of sodomy

Iugurtha: King of Numidia, who fought a war with Rome and was captured and executed, as recounted by Sallust; as above (ch. 46), the Sallustian reference suggests an incongruity in members of the Academy being treated like Rome's greatest enemies

ducitur: asyndeton with *Trahitur*

Pomponius, vir simplicis ingenii, neque coniurationis neque alicu-
ius sceleris conscius. Rogatus cur nomina adoloscentibus immutaret, ut homo liber erat, "Quid ad vos," inquit, "et Paulum si mihi
Foeniculi nomen indo, modo id sine dolo et fraude fiat?" Amore
nanque vetustatis antiquorum {237v} praeclara nomina repetebat,
quasi quaedam calcharia, quae nostram iuventutem aemulatione ad
virtutem incitarent.

---

adoloscens, -entis (CL *adulescens*) *m./f.* :
 young adult
aemulatio, -onis *f.*: ambition; emulation
aliqui, -qua, -quod: any
amor, -oris *m.*: love
antiquus, -a, -um: old, ancient
calchar, -aris (CL *calcar*) *n.*: spur (for horse)
coniuratio, -onis *f.*: conspiracy
conscius, -a, -um: aware of; sharing (secret)
 knowledge
cur (*adv.*): why
dolus, -i *m.*: trick
fio, feri, factus sum: happen
foeniculum, -i *n.* (CL *feniculum*): fennel
fraus, fraudis *f.*: fraud
immuto, -are, -avi, -atus: change
incito, -are, -avi, -atus: inspire

indo, -ere, indidi, inditus: put on; give to
ingenium, -i *n.*: nature; character
inquam, -, - , - : say
iuventus, -tutis *f.*: youth
liber, libera, liberum: free; frank
modo (*adv.*): provided that (+ *subjunctive*)
nanque (CL *namque*): for in fact
praeclarus, -a, -um: very clear; famous
quasi (*adv.*): just as if
quidam, quaedam, quoddam: certain; a
 kind of
repeto, -ere, -ivi, -itus: return to; recall
scelus, sceleris *n.*: crime
simplex, -plicis: simple
sine: without (+ *abl.*)
vetustas, -tatis *f.*: antiquity
virtus, -tutis *f.*: strength; virtue

---

simplicis ingenii: gen. of description with *vir*
conscius: appositive to *Pomponius* and *vir*, modified by *coniurationis* and *sceleris*
cur … immutaret: ind. question
ut … erat: *ut* as causal conjunction, "since he was …"
Quid ad vos (est): "what is it to you?" (CL *quid vobis est*), see Introduction 7.B
modo … fiat: proviso clause, "as long as it … happens"
Amore: abl. of cause
antiquorum: substantive, "the ancients," take with *praeclara nomina*
quaedam calcharia: *quaedam (essent) calcharia*, pres. contrafactual, "as if they were a
 kind of spur"
quae … incitarent: subjunctive in a rel. clause of purpose, "in order that they might
 inspire"

Lucillus is also charged, based on his authorship of a letter with homoerotic content

57 Trahitur et Lucillus ad urbem tanquam reus maiestatis, qui in Sabinis tetricam illam vitam ducebat, quod ad Campanum scribens, quae litterae postea deprehensae sunt, Heliogabali cuiusdam amores reprehendebat, ita occulte tamen ut nisi a conscio dignosci res ipsa non posset.

amor, -oris *m.*: love; (*pl.*) love affairs	**quidam, quaedam, quoddam**: a certain
conscius, -i *m/f.*: accomplice, confidant	**reprehendo, -hendere, -hensi, -hensus**:
deprehendo, -hendere, -hensi, -hensus:	blame, criticize
seize, catch	**reus, -a, -um**: accused; guilty
dignosco, -noscere, -novi, -notus: discern,	**Sabinus, -a, -um**: Sabine, a people in central
recognize	Italy
litterae, -arum *f.*: a letter (epistle)	**scribo, -ere, scripsi, scriptus**: write
maiestas, -tatis *f.*: treason	**tanquam** (CL *tamquam*): as, just as, just as if
occultus, -a, -um: hidden, secret	**tetricus, -a, -um**: gloomy, reserved
postea (*adv.*): afterwards	**traho, -ere, traxi, tractus**: draw, drag, haul

Lucillus: a fellow humanist, who was arrested because of a letter he wrote that was intercepted

reus maiestatis: defendant on a charge of treason

Sabinis: substantive, assumes *finibus* ("territory"); refers to the geographic location previously occupied by the Sabines in the Apennines

vitam: Platina originally added, then crossed out, *caste ac sancte* ("chastely and in holiness")

quod ... reprehendebat: "because he was criticizing ... " explaining why Lucillus was jailed

Campanum: Settimuleio Campano, a student of Pomponio Leto, imprisoned with other humanists in Castel Sant'Angelo at age nineteen, see ch. 49

quae litterae: "a letter which," the antecedent has been attracted into the rel. clause

Heliogabali: Elagabalus, Roman emperor (r. 218-222 CE), known for (among other things) his gender non-conformity

ut ... posset: result clause

dignosci: pass. inf., complementary with *posset*

Vianesio again tortures the humanists

58 Vianesius autem diligens pastor ad nos cum tormentis [387] saepius rediens, torto etiam Petreio, Calimachi comite, in fuga comprẹhenso ac nihil confesso, quod diceret ebriosam illam Calimachi collocutionem nullius momenti existimandam fuisse, omnia oculis collustrans, ne refractis parietibus tanquam Daedali ex alta arce volaremus, carcerem subterraneum meditatur, ac fabris statim locat;

---

altus, -a, -um: high, lofty
arx, arcis *f.*: citadel, stronghold
carcer, -eris *m.*: prison
collocutio, -onis *f.*: conversation
collustro, -are, -avi, -atus: look over, survey
comes, comitis *m./f.*: companion
comprehendo, -prehendere, -prehendi,
  -prẹhensus (CL *comprehensus*): catch; arrest
confiteor, -fiteri, -fessus sum: confess, admit
diligens, diligentis: diligent
ebriosus, -a, -um: drunken
existimo, -are, -avi, -atus: value, judge
faber, fabri *m.*: craftsman
fuga, -ae *f.*: flight, escape
loco, -are, -avi, -atus: arrange, contract (for)

meditor, -ari, -atus sum: devise, plan
momentum, -i *n.*: importance
nullus, -a, -um: no, none
oculus, -i *m.*: eye
paries, -etis *m.*: wall
pastor, -oris *m.*: shepherd, pastor
redeo, -ire, -ivi(ii), -itus: return, go back
refringo, -ere, refregi, refractus: break open
saepius (*compar. adv.*): quite often
statim (*adv.*): at once, immediately
subterraneus, -a, -um: subterranean
tanquam (CL *tamquam*): as, just as, just as if
tormentum, -i *n.*: torture device, torment
torqueo, -ere, torsi, tortus: twist, torture
volo, -are, -avi, -atus: fly

Vianesius: Vianesio Albergati of Bologna, Paul II's vice-chamberlain
diligens pastor: in the manuscripts, this sarcastic comment was taken out, then restored
torto … Petreio: abl. abs.; Pietro Marso, member of the Roman Academy
Calimachi: Callimachus (1437-1496), member of the Roman Academy, was accused of leading the alleged conspiracy
comprẹhenso ac … confesso: circumstantial abl. abs. with *Petreio*, "after being caught in flight and having confessed nothing"
quod diceret: clause of alleged reason
nullius momenti: gen. of indefinite value
existimandam: pass. periphrastic, "must be valued"
collustrans: agrees with *Vianesius*; in asyndeton with *rediens*
ne … volaremus: neg. purpose clause dependent on *meditatur*
Daedali: Daedalus, the mythical figure who escapes from prison on Crete with his son Icarus by flying with wings that he built

eoque coniicit Franciscum Anguillaram, Gattalusium, Franciscum Alvianum, Iacobum Ptolemaeum quadriennio ante molestia carceris maceratos. De libertate nostra interim nullum verbum fiebat.

Paul lavishly hosts the Holy Roman Emperor; Platina watches from his cell

59 Erat tum imperator in urbe; voti enim gratia venerat cum magno comitatu, quem Paulus magna cum impensa honorificentissime suscępit, expensis decem et octo millibus nummum aureorum. Ambos ex mole Hadriani sub eodem pallio a Laterano redeuntes,

---

ambi, -ae, -a: both
aureus, -a, -um: golden
comitatus, -us *m.*: company, retinue
coniicio, -iicere, -ieci, -iectus: throw (together)
eo (*adv.*): there
expendo, -ere, expendi, expensus: pay, pay out
fio, fieri, factus sum: happen, occur
honorificus, -a, -um: honorable
idem, eadem, idem: the same
impensa, -ae *f.*: expense, cost
imperator, -oris *m.*: general; emperor
interim (*adv.*): meanwhile
libertas, -tatis *f.*: freedom, liberty

macero, -are, -avi, -atus: make soft, wear down
mille, millia: thousand (CL abl. *milibus*)
moles, molis *f.*: mass, large structure
molestia, -ae *f.*: trouble
nullus, -a, -um: no, not any
nummus, -i *m.*: coin
pallium, -i *n.*: coverlet, canopy
quadriennium, -i *n.*: period of four years
redeo, -ire, -ivi(ii), -itus: return, go back
suscipio, -cipere, -cępi (CL *suscepi*), **-ceptus**: undertake, receive
verbum, -i *n.*: word
votum, -i *n.*: vow, pledge

---

eoque: *eo* ("there") + *-que* ("and")
quadriennio: abl. of degree of difference; take with *ante*
maceratos: agrees with *Franciscum* and the others listed
imperator: Frederick III, Holy Roman Emperor (r. 1452-1493)
voti ... gratia: "for the sake of a vow"
magna ... impensa: abl. of manner
honorificentissime: superlative adv.
expensis ... millibus: abl. abs.
decem et octo millibus: 18,000
nummum aureorum: *nummum* syncopated from *numm(or)um*, appositional gen., "18,000 (of) gold coins"
mole Hadriani: Castel Sant'Angelo, the fortress built onto the ruins of the mausoleum of Hadrian, see fig. 4 (p. 83)
Hadriani: Hadrian, Roman Emperor (r. 117-138 CE)
Laterano: St. John Lateran Basilica in Rome

comitante honorato quoque, inspexi. Substitit Paulus in ponte, donec imperator equites aliquot crearet.

After the Emperor departs, Paul accuses Platina and the humanists of debating the immortality of the soul and of being Platonists

60 Abeunte deinde [388] imperatore, cum iam metu omni liberatus esset (nam et equitum et peditum suorum magnam partem in urbem vocaverat, veritus ne quid tumultus a populo Romano excitaretur, presente imperatore) decimo mense post captivitatem nostram in arcem veniens, ne tantum tumultus frustra concitasse

---

abeo, -ire, -ivi(ii), -itus: depart, go away
aliquot (*indecl.*): some
arx, arcis *f.*: citadel, stronghold
captivitas, -tatis *f.*: captivity
comito, -are, -avi, -atus: accompany
concito, -are, -avi, -atus: stir up, disturb, rush
creo, -are, -avi, -atus: create, appoint
decimus, -a, -um: tenth
deinde (*adv.*): then
donec: while
eques, equitis *m.*: horseman, knight
excito, -are, -avi, -atus: stir up
frustra (*adv.*): in vain
honoratus, -a, -um: honored; (substantively) the nobility

iam (*adv.*): now
imperator, -oris *m.*: general; emperor
inspicio, -ere, inspexi, inspectus: observe
libero, -are, -avi, -atus: free, liberate
mensis, -is *m.*: month
metus, -us *m.*: fear
pars, partis *f.*: part; party
pedes, peditis *m.*: foot soldier
pons, pontis *m.*: bridge
populus, -i *m.*: people
presens, -sentis (CL *praesens*): present, at hand
subsisto, -sistere, -stiti, - : halt, stand
tumultus, -us *m.*: commotion, disturbance
vereor, -eri, -itus sum: fear
voco, -are, -avi, -atus: to call, summon

---

comitante honorato: abl. abs
aliquot: take with *equites*
crearet: subjunctive of circumstance introduced by *donec*
cum ... liberatus esset: circumstantial *cum* clause
metu omni: abl. of separation
ne quid tumultus ... excitaretur: fear clause; *quid* is *aliquid* (after *si, nisi, num* and *ne*, "*ali*" takes a holiday); *tumultus* is partitive gen., "that any(thing of) tumult ... be stirred up"
decimo mense: abl. of time when
ne ... videretur: neg. purpose clause, "lest he seem"
tumultus: partitive gen. with *tantum* "so much of a tumult"; *tantum* is acc. obj. of *concitasse*
concitasse: syncopated from *concita(vi)sse*

videretur, multa nobis obiicit, sed illud potissimum, quod de immor-
talitate animorum disputaremus, teneremusque opinionem Platonis,
quam divus Augustinus Christianae religioni simillimam esse censet.
"Merito," inquit Aurelius, "Cicero deum inter philosophos Platonem
vocat, qui certe cunctos ingenio et sapientia superavit"; hunc mihi
delegi, quocum disputarem, qui et de ultimo hominis fine et de

---

animus, -i *m.*: soul
Augustinus, -i *m.*: Augustine
Aurelius, -i *m.*: Augustine (Aurelius
  Augustinus)
censeo, -ere, censui, census: think, judge
certe (*adv.*): surely, certainly
Christianus, -a, -um: Christian
Cicero, -onis *m.*: Cicero
cunctus, -a, -um: all
deligo, -ere, delegi, delectus: choose
deus, -i *m.*: god
disputo, -are, -avi, -atus: debate, argue
divus, -a, -um: divine, blessed, saint
finis, -is *m.*: end, goal
immortalitas, -tatis *f.*: immortality

ingenium, -i *n.*: nature, talent
inquam, -, -, -: say
merito (*adv.*): deservedly, rightly
obiicio, -ere, obieci, obiectus: throw before
opinio, -onis *f.*: belief, idea, opinion
philosophus, -i *m.*: philosopher
Plato, -onis *m.*: Plato
potissimum (*adv.*): especially
religio, -onis *f.*: religion
sapientia, -ae *f.*: wisdom
similis, -e: similar
supero, -are, -avi, -atus: overcome, surpass
teneo, -ere, tenui, tentus: hold, support
ultimus -a -um: ultimate
voco, -are, -avi, -atus: call

---

quod ... disputaremus, teneremusque: *quod* noun clause, "the fact that (so he
  says)..."; clause of alleged reason
Platonis: Plato, the Greek philosopher (c. 429-347 BCE); Augustine was a
  Neoplatonist
Augustinus: *Aurelius Augustinus*, Augustine (354-430 CE), Bishop of Hippo and
  Christian philosopher, wrote the *Confessions* and *City of God*
Christianae religioni: dat. with *simillimam*
simillimam: acc. sing. superlative of *similis*; predicate of *quam*, "which ... (he) judges
  to be most similar"
censet: note switch to indic.
Cicero: Marcus Tullius Cicero, 106-43 BCE, Roman orator and statesman
quocum disputarem: rel. clause of purpose, "in order to debate with him"
qui: subj. of *philosophatur*; antecedent is Plato

divina natura melius quam cęteri philosophatur. "In dubium," inquit Paulus, "disputando Deum vocabatis."

Platina defends himself on various grounds

61 Quod quidem omnibus philosophis et theologis nostrorum temporum obiici potest, qui et animos et Deum et omnes intelligentias separatas, disputandi ac veri inveniendi causa, in dubium plerunque vocant. Praeterea vero haeretici sunt, ut ait Augustinus, qui quod prave sapiunt pertinaciter defendunt. "Sanam disciplinam

---

aio, -, -, - : say, assert

animus, -i *m.*: mind, soul

cęterus, -a, -um (CL *ceterus*): the other

defendo, -ere, defendi, defensus: defend

Deus, -i *m.*: God

disciplina, -ae *f.*: teaching, instruction, education

disputo, -are, -avi, -atus: discuss, debate

divinus, -a, -um: divine

dubium, -i *n.*: doubt, question

haereticus, -i *m.*: heretic, teacher of false doctrine

inquam, -, -, - : say

intelligentia, -ae *f.*: intelligence

invenio, -ire, inveni, inventus: discover

obiicio, -ere, obieci, obiectus: throw before, oppose

pertinaciter (*adv.*): tenaciously

philosophor, -ari, -atus sum: philosophize

philosophus, -i *m.*: philosopher

plerunque (CL *plerumque*) (*adv.*): generally, commonly

praeterea (*adv.*): besides

prave (*adv.*): wrongly, perversely

sanus, -a, -um: sound, healthy, sensible

sapio, -ere, -ivi, - : taste of, understand; believe

separo, -are, -avi, -atus: separate

tempus, temporis *n.*: time

theologus, -i *m.*: theologian

vero (*adv.*): truly, in fact

verum, -i: truth

voco, -are, -avi, -atus: call

---

melius quam: compar. adv. + *quam*, "better than"

cęteri: substantive, "the others"

In dubium … vocabatis: "you were calling into doubt"

disputando: gerund, abl. of means

Quod: "which thing" (referring to Paul's statement), subj. of *potest*. It is not entirely clear whether this and the rest of ch. 61 are Platina the author's remarks to the reader, or Platina the character's remarks to Paul; we have added quotation marks to signal our best guesses

omnibus … theologis: dat. with compound verb *obiici*

obiici: pass. inf.

disputandi: gerund, "of disputing"

veri inveniendi: gerundive phrase, "of the truth to be discovered (i.e. of discovering the truth)"

ut … Augustinus: *ut* + indicative, "as"

Augustinus: Augustine (354–430 CE), the famous early Christian author

qui: subj. of both *sapiunt* and *defendunt*

nunquam aspernati sumus, quod facere consueverunt (ut ait Leo)
{238ʀ} erroris magistri, qui seorsum ab Ecclesia sentientes, haeretici merito (Hieronymo teste) sunt appellati. Rationem vitae meae,
posteaquam sapere per etatem coepi usque ad hec tempora, reddere
vobis possum. Nullum mihi facinus impingi potest, non furtum, non
latrocinium, non sacrilegium, non depeculatus, non parricidium,
non rapina, non simonia. Vixi ut Christianum decebat, confessionem

---

aio, -, -, - : say
appello, -are, -avi, -atus: call
aspernor, -ari, -atus sum: despise, scorn
Christianus, -i *m.*: Christian
coepio, -ere, coepi, coeptus: begin
confessio, -onis *f.*: confession
consuesco, -suescere, -suevi, -suetus:
   accustom oneself
deceo, -ere, -uit, - (*impers.*): befit (+ *acc.*)
depeculatus, -us *m.*: fraud
Ecclesia, -ae *f.*: the Church
error, -oris *m.*: error
etas, -tatis (CL *aetas*) *f.*: age; period of life
facinus, -noris *n.*: crime, outrage
furtum, -i *n.*: theft
haereticus, -i *m.*: heretic
Hieronymus, -i *m.*: Jerome
impingo, -ere, impegi, impactus: thrust
   upon; tied to
latrocinium, -i *n.*: robbery

magister, magistri *m.*: teacher
merito (*adv.*): deservedly, rightly
nullus, -a, -um: no, not any
nunquam (*adv.*): at no time, never
parricidium, -i *n.*: parricide
per: through (+ *acc.*)
posteaquam (*adv.*): after
rapina, -ae *f.*: plunder
ratio, -onis *f.*: account
reddo, -ere, reddidi, redditus: return, render
sacrilegium,-i *n.*: sacrilege
sapio, -ere, -ivi, - : taste of, understand, have
   sense
sentio, -ire, sensi, sensus: perceive, think
seorsum (*adv.*): separately
simonia, -ae *f.*: simony
tempus, temporis *n.*: time
testis, -is *m./f.*: witness
usque (*adv.*): up to
vivo, -ere, vixi, victus: be alive, live

---

quod ... consueverunt: antecedent is previous clause
ut ... Leo: *ut* + indicative "as"; Leo the Great, pope from 440-461 CE
erroris: obj. gen., teachers "of error"
sentientes: modifies *qui*
Hieronymo teste: abl. abs.; Jerome (340-420), early Christian scholar and author,
   who produced the Vulgate Bible
Rationem: acc. obj. of *reddere*
sapere: complementary inf. with *coepi*
hec: neut. pl. acc. (CL *haec*, see Introduction 6.B)
reddere vobis: "relate to you"
mihi: dat. of disadvantage
impingi: pres. pass. inf.
non furtum ... simonia: nom. sings. governed by *potest impingi*
simonia: simony, the buying or selling of ecclesiastic privileges
ut ... decebat: *ut* + indicative, "as"

et communionem, in anno semel praesertim, intermisi nunquam. Nil ex ore meo excidit, quod contra symbolum esset, aut haeresim saperet. Non sum imitatus Simoniacos, Carpocratianos, Ophitas, Severianos, Alogios, Paulinos, Manicheos, Macedonianos aliamve haereticorum sectam."

---

annus, -i *m.*: year
communio, -onis *f.*: communion
contra: against (+ *acc.*)
excido, -ere, excidi, - : fall out
haeresis, -is *f.*: heresy
haereticus, -i *m.*: heretic
imitor, -ari, -atus sum: imitate; follow
intermitto, -mittere, -misi, -missus: interrupt; omit

nil *n.* (*indecl.*): nothing
nunquam (CL *numquam*) (*adv.*): never
os, oris *n.*: mouth
praesertim (*adv.*): especially, particularly
sapio, -ere, -ivi, - : taste of, resemble, suggest
secta, -ae *f.*: sect, faction
semel (*adv.*): once
symbolum, -i *n.*: orthodox doctrine
-ve: or (*enclitic*)

---

communionem: Eucharist taken during Mass

in anno semel praesertim: "at least once a year"

quod ... esset ... saperet: rel. clause of characteristic

quod: antecedent is *nil*

Simoniacos ... Macedonianos: acc. objects of *sum imitatus*, a chronological and somewhat recherché list of heresies from the early Church (none later than the fourth century)

Simoniacos: followers of Simon Magus, who were associated with a number of unorthodox beliefs, most famously selling spiritual gifts, whence the term 'simony' for selling Church offices

Carpocratianos: Carpocratian, an early form of Gnostic Christianity accused of avowing a kind of sexually transgressive sacrality

Ophitas: Ophyte, an early Christian sect that venerated the serpent from the Garden of Eden

Severianos: Severian, an early form of ascetic Gnostic Christianity

Alogios: Alogian, member of an early Christian sect which denied the legitimacy of the Gospel of John

Paulinos: Paulians, an early group who believed that God existed in one person (monarchianism) rather than three

Manicheos: Manichaean, follower of the religion founded by the Persian prophet Mani (216-276 CE)

Macedonianos: an early sect of Christianity with unorthodox beliefs about the Holy Spirit

Paul accuses Platina of an excessive love of pagan Antiquity, which Platina says is hypocritical, since Paul loved ancient artworks

62 Praeterea vero Paulus crimini nobis dabat, quod nimium gentilitatis amatores essemus, cum nemo eo huius rei studiosior esset, quippe qui et statuas veterum, undique ex tota urbe conquisitas, in suas illas aedes, quas sub Capitolio extruebat, congereret, avecto etiam ex sancta Agnete beatae Constantiae sepulchro, frustra

---

aedes, aedis *f.*: temple; (*pl.*) house
amator, -oris *m.*: lover, admirer
aveho, -ere, avexi, avectus: carry away
beatus, -a, -um: blessed
Capitolium, -i *n.*: Capitol, Capitoline Hill in Rome
congero, -gerere, -gessi, -gestus: collect, amass
conquiro, -quirere, -quisivi, -quisitus: seek out, collect
crimen, -minis *n.*: accusation; crime
extruo, -ere, extruxi, extructus: pile up, build up
frustra (*adv.*): in vain
gentilitas, -tatis *f.*: abstract noun relating to the "gentiles" (non-Christians), i.e. paganism

nemo, neminis *m./f.*: no one, nobody
nimium (*adv.*): too, too much
praeterea (*adv.*): besides, thereafter, in addition
quippe (*adv.*): of course, as you see
sanctus, -a, -um: sacred, holy
sepulchrum, -i *n.*: grave, tomb
statua, -ae *f.*: statue
studiosus, -a, -um: eager
totus, -a, -um: whole
undique (*adv.*): from every place
vero: but, however
vetus, veteris *n.*: old, ancient

---

crimini nobis: double dat. with *dabat* (reference and purpose), ascribed it "to us as a crime"
quod ... essemus: noun clause with subjunctive of alleged reason, "the fact that (according to him) ..."
cum ... esset: concessive *cum* clause
eo: abl. of comparison referring to himself (Paul)
huius rei: obj. gen. with *studiosior*
studiosior: nom. sing. m., compar. of *studiosus*
quippe qui: "since he," verb is *congereret*
veterum: gen. pl. form of *vetus*; substantive, "of the ancients"
in suas illas aedes: "into that famous house of his," the Palazzo San Marco (now called Palazzo Venezia), see fig. 3 (p. 72)
congereret: Platina originally wrote, then crossed out, *ne sanctis etiam parceret* ("lest he even spare the saints")
avecto ... sepulchro: abl. abs.
sancta Agnete: the Church of Saint Agnes Outside the Walls, built by Pope Honorius I in the 7th century
beatae Constantiae: Saint Constance, eldest daughter of Roman emperor Constantine

reclamantibus monachis loci, qui postea mortuo Paulo sepulchrum illud porphyreticum a Sixto Pontifice repetiere. Praeterea vero numismata prope infinita ex auro, argento, aereve, sua imagine signata, sine ullo senatusconsulto in fundamentis aedificiorum suorum more veterum collocabat, veteres* potius hac in re quam Petrum, Anacletum, et Linum imitatus*.

---

aedificium, -i *n.*: building
aes, aeris *n.*: bronze
argentum, -i *n.*: silver
aurum, -i *n.*: gold
colloco, -are, -avi, -atus: place; establish
fundamentum, -i *n.*: foundation
imago, -ginis *f.*: likeness, image
imito, -are, -avi, -atus: imitate
infinitus, -a, -um: endless, infinite
locus, -i *m.*: place, location
monachus, -i *m.*: monk
mos, moris *m.*: custom
numisma, -atis *n.*: coin
pontifex, -ficis *m.*: pontiff, pope
porphyreticus, -a, -um: made of porphyry (scarlet stone)

postea (*adv.*): afterwards
potius (*adv.*): more so (than)
praeterea (*adv.*): moreover, besides
prope (*adv.*): near, nearly, almost
reclamo, -are, -avi, -atus: cry out in protest
repeto, -ere, -ivi, -itus: get back; ask for something back
senatusconsultum, -i *n.*: decree of the Senate
sepulchrum, -i *n.*: grave, tomb
signo, -are, -avi, -atus: mark, stamp
sine: without (+ *abl.*)
ullus, -a, -um: any
vero (*adv.*): truly, in fact
vetus, veteris *m.*: old; (substantively) the ancients

---

qui postea: antecedent is *monachis*
Sixto Pontifice: Pope Sixtus IV (r. 1471-1484), Francesco della Rovere, who succeeded Paul II and to whom Platina dedicated the *Lives of the Popes*
repetiere: alt. form of *repetierunt*
signata: neut. pl. acc. agreeing with *numismata*
more: abl. of respect, "in accordance with the custom"
veteres* ... imitatus*: Platina originally wrote, but then crossed out before printing, *collocabat, Tiberium potius hac in re quam Petrum et Claudium quam Anacletum et Neronem quam Linum imitatus* ("in this matter imitating Tiberius rather than Peter, Claudius rather than Anacletus, and Nero rather than Linus")
potius ... quam: "more than"
Petrum, Anacletum, et Linum: Peter, Anacletus, and Linus were the first three popes. Platina criticizes Paul for imitating the early emperors of Rome rather than the early popes

Two bishops and two monks come to try Platina; Leonardo of Perugia speaks against him and Francesco of Assisi for him

63 Cum vero nostra de re inter Palatinos episcopos et duos fratres esset aliquando disceptatum, quorum alter erat ordinis Francisci, alter Dominici, venerunt fere omnes in hanc sententiam, nihil esse in nobis, quod haeresim saperet*. [389]

Paul then excludes Francesco in an attempt to influence the proceedings

64 Verum cum Paulus in arcem venisset, excludereturque de industria Franciscus patronus noster veritatis assertor, quo liberius

---

aliquando (*adv.*): finally
arx, arcis *f.*: citadel, fortress
assertor, -oris *m.*: defender, advocate
discepto, -are, -avi, -atus: dispute, debate
duo, -ae, -o: two
episcopus, -i *m.*: bishop
excludo, -ere, exclusi, exclusus: shut out, exclude
fere (*adv.*): nearly
haeresis, -is *f.*: heresy, heretical doctrine

industria, -ae *f.*: diligence
liber, -a, -um: free, unrestrained
ordo, ordinis *m.*: order (of monks)
Palatinus, -a, -um: Palatine, of the palace
patronus, -i *m.*: advocate
sapio, -ere, -ivi, - : taste of
sententia, -ae *f.*: opinion, feeling
veritas, -tatis *f.*: truth
vero: but, however
verum (*adv.*): but yet, however

Cum … esset … disceptatum: circumstantial *cum* clause
Palatinos episcopos: a kind of bishop with special rights and privileges
alter … alter: "one … the other"
ordinis Francisci: gen. of description, "of the order of Francis" (i.e. Franciscan)
Dominici (ordinis): gen. of description, "of the order of Dominic," (i.e. Dominican)
nihil esse: ind. statement introduced by *venerunt in sententiam*, "that there was nothing in us which …"
quod … saperet*: rel. clause of characteristic. Platina originally wrote, then crossed out the sentence *Solus Leonardus Perusinus ordinis Praedicatorum Paulo rem gratam facturus, quod ab eo episcopatum vel locum generalis ordinis sui expetebat, impugnare nos ausus est: cuius argumenta omnia Franciscus Assisius ordinis Minorum confutavit et infregit* ("Only Leonardo of Perugia of the Dominican order, trying to please Paul, because he was seeking from him a bishopric or the position of General of his Order, dared to impugn us: all of whose arguments Francesco from Assisi of the Order of Friars Minor refuted and shattered")
cum … venisset, excludereturque: circumstantial *cum* clause
de industria: idiom, "on purpose"
Franciscus: subj. of *excluderetur*
quo … liceret: rel. clause of purpose, "in order that by this it might be granted to Leonardo to speak more freely"
liberius: compar. adv. of *liber*

Leonardo loqui liceret*, eadem dicit quae pridie. Rogati sententiam, qui tum aderant et si ad nutum pontificis aliqua ex parte loquebantur, nostram tamen causam leviorem faciebant, ac pontificem mitiorem reddere conabantur. Solus autem inter omnes Laelius Valle, Romanus civis et advocatus concistorialis, nostram causam libere tutatus est. Confutat omnia quae a Leonardo dicta erant, queque partim affirmaverat alter advocatus, Andreas Sanctae Crucis*.

---

adsum, -esse, -fui, -futurus: be present

advocatus, -i *m.*: counselor, advocate

affirmo, -are, -avi, -atus: assert

aliqui, -qua, -quod: some, any

civis, -is *m./f.*: citizen

concistorialis, -e (or *consistorialis*): of the consistory (the assembly of cardinals)

confuto, -are, -avi, -atus: refute

conor, -ari, -atus sum: attempt

crux, crucis *f.*: cross

idem, eadem, idem: the same

levis, -e: light

libere (*adv.*): freely; generously

licet, -ere, -uit, -itus est (*impers.*): it is permitted

loquor, loqui, locutus sum: speak

mitis, -e: mild

nutus, -us *m.*: nod; will

pars, partis *f.*: part

partim (*adv.*): partly

pontifex, -ficis *m.*: pope, pontiff

pridie (*adv.*): day before

reddo, -ere, reddidi, redditus: render

sanctus, -a, -um: sacred, holy

sententia, -ae *f.*: opinion

solus, -a, -um: alone

tutor, -ari, -atus sum: defend

Leonardo: dat. of reference with *liceret*

loqui: subject inf. with *liceret*

liceret*: Platina originally wrote, then crossed out, *pretium iusti sanguinis ob eam rem accepturo* ("who would receive a reward for just blood because of this affair")

dicit: main verb, subj. is *Leonardus*

quae pridie: *quae* (*dixerat*) *pridie*

qui: antecedent is *Rogati*

si ... loquebantur: coordinated with *qui*, "those who were present and who spoke ..."

ad nutum: figuratively, "in line with the will"

aliqua ex parte: idiom, "to some degree"

leviorem ... mitiorem: note the parallelism between these two compar. adjs., each a predicate, and their respective phrases

Laelius Valle: Lelio della Valle (d. 1476)

a Leonardo: abl. of agent, the accuser of Platina and the other humanists

queque ... affirmaverat: *queque* is neut. pl. *quae* + *-que* (on the diphthong see Introduction 6.B); coordinated with *quae ... dicta erant*; antecedent of both is *omnia*

Andreas Sanctae Crucis*: nom. sing. m.; Andrea di Iacopo di Santa Croce, a clergyman and advocate of the *Camera Apostolica*. Platina had originally written the appositive *homo surdaster et loquax* ("a man unlistening and always speaking")

The Roman Academy is mentioned and receives criticism

65 Fit autem inter dicendum de Academia mentio. Inclamat tum M. Barbus, Sancti Marci cardinalis, nos non academicos esse sed foedatores Academiae. Quid turpitudinis autem a nobis in Academiam prodierit, certe non video, cum nec fures, nec latrones, nec incendiarii, nec decoctores essemus. Veteres academicos sequebamur, novos contemnentes, {238v} qui in rebus ipsis nil certi ponebant. Paulus tamen* haereticos eos pronunciavit qui nomen

---

Academia, -ae *f.*: the Academy, Plato's school	**inclamo, -are, -avi, -atus**: cry out
academicus, -a, -um: academic, a follower of Platonic philosophy	**inter**: among, amidst (+ *acc.*)
cardinalis, -is *m.*: cardinal	**latro, -onis** *m.*: bandit
certe (*adv.*): certainly	**mentio, -onis** *f.*: mention
certus, -a, -um: certain	**nil** (*indecl.*): nothing
contemno, -temnere, -tempsi, -temptus: disdain	**novus, -a, -um**: new
decoctor, -oris *m.*: defaulting debtor	**pono, -ere, posui, positus**: propose, posit
fio, feri, factus sum: happen, come about	**prodeo, -ire, -ivi(ii), -itus**: go out
foedator, -is *m.*: befouler, defiler	**pronuncio, -are, -avi, -atus** (CL *pronuntio*): declare
fur, furis *m./f.*: thief	**sequor, sequi, secutus sum**: follow
haereticus, -i *m.*: heretic	**turpitudo, -dinis** *f.*: ugliness, shame
incendiarius, -i *m.*: arsonist	**vetus, veteris**: old

---

inter dicendum: gerund, "amidst the speaking"

M. Barbus ... cardinalis: Marco Barbo, Paul II's relative, cardinal priest of St. Mark's Basilica in Rome, a patron of humanists and owner of a large library

sed (nos esse) foedatores Academiae: *Academiae* is obj. gen.

Quid turpitudinis: partitive gen., "What (of) shame"

Quid ... prodierit: ind. question dependent on *video*

cum ... essemus: causal *cum* clause

Veteres academicos: the "Old Academy," Plato and his fourth-century BCE successors

novos contemnentes: the "New Academy" embraced skepticism, which could be criticized from a Christian perspective as a lack of faith

qui ... ponebant: causal rel. clause

nil certi: partitive gen. with implied *esse*, "that there was nothing (of) certain"

tamen*: Platina originally wrote, but then crossed out before printing, a sarcastic comment: *tamen tantae doctrinae erat* (Paul "was nevertheless of such great learning")

haereticos: predicate, "declares those men to be heretics"

qui ... commemorarent: rel. clause of characteristic; antecedent of *qui* is *eos*

Academiae vel serio vel ioco deinceps commemorarent. Inusta est haec ignominia Platoni; ipse se tueatur.

Paul attempts to mock Pomponio Leto about his name; Pomponio responds with a joke that Paul fails to get

66 Volebat Paulus rebus in omnibus videri acutus et doctus*; volebat item videri facetus; deridebat fere omnes contemnebatque. Interrogat tum Pomponium, hominem irridens: quod ei a teneris annis nomen imposuerant parentes? Respondet Pomponius se

---

Academia, -ae *f.*: the Academy
acutus, -a, -um: sharp, wise
annus, -i *m.*: year; age
commemoro, -are, -avi, -atus: mention
contemno, -temnere, -tempsi, -temptus: disdain
derideo, -ere, derisi, derisus: mock, deride
deinceps (*adv.*): in order, thereafter
doctus, -a, -um: learned
facetus, -a, -um: witty
fere (*adv.*): almost
ignominia, -ae *f.*: disgrace; punishment
impono, -ere, imposui, impositus: impose, assign
interrogo, -are, -avi, -atus: ask

inuro, -ere, inussi, inustus: burn onto, brand
iocus, -i *m.*: joke
irrideo, -ere, irrisi, irrisus: ridicule
item (*adv.*): likewise
parens, -entis *m./f.*: parent
Plato, -onis *m.*: Plato
respondeo, -ere, respondi, responsus: answer
serius, -a, -um: serious
tener, tenera, tenerum: tender, young
tueor, -eri, tutus sum: look after, examine, defend
volo, velle, volui, - : wish, want

---

vel ... vel: either ... or
vel serio, vel ioco: abls. of manner; *serio* is used substantively, "in a serious comment"
tueatur: jussive subj.; more sarcasm
videri: compl. inf. with *volebat*, "to seem"
doctus*: Platina originally wrote but then crossed out *doctus, cum re vera natura et arte parum profecisset* ("although in actual fact by nature and skill he had little success")
contemnebatque: Platina originally wrote *contemnebat ac si ipse nil in se haberet quod reprehendi posset* ("as if he had nothing in himself which could be criticized")
Pomponium: Pomponio Leto, founder of the Roman Academy
hominem: acc. obj. of *irridens*, appositive of *Pomponium*
irridens: describes Paul, the implied subj. of *interrogat*
quod ... imposuerant parentes: ind. question that retains the indicative to emphasize its non-hypothetical character, "he asked ... what name his parents had (actually) given to him ..."
a teneris annis: abl. place from which with sense of time, "from his tender years"

Binomyum fuisse. Confusus novitate rei Paulus* substitit amplius de nomine quaerere.

Paul accuses Platina of many things, including ingratitude, which Platina reflects on sarcastically

67 Ad me autem conversus, [390] in omnem contumeliam prorupit; omitto quod mihi coniurationem, haeresim, maiestatis crimen obiiceret, quae omnia iam purgata erant; obiiciebat etiam ingratitudinem, quod in me licet ingratum officiossus fuisset. Si spoliare homines emptione sua incognita causa, si carcere, si tormentis,

---

amplius (*adv.*): further
binomyus, -a, -um (or *binomius*): two-named
carcer, -eris *m.*: prison
confusus, -a, -um: confused, perplexed
coniuratio, -onis *f.*: conspiracy
contumelia, -ae *f.*: abuse, insult
converto, -vertere, -verti, -versus: turn toward
crimen, criminis *n.*: charge; crime
emptio, -onis *f.*: purchase, property
haeresis, -is *f.*: heresy
iam (*adv.*): now; already
incognitus, -a, -um: unknown
ingratitudo, -dinis *f.*: ingratitude
ingratus, -a, -um: ungrateful

licet: although
maiestas, -tatis *f.*: treason
novitas, -tatis *f.*: newness, strangeness
obiicio, -ere, obieci, obiectus: throw before; charge to X (*dat.*) the fault Y (*acc.*)
officiossus, -a, -um (CL *officiosus*): dutiful
omitto, -ere, omisi, omissus: leave out, pass over
prorumpo, -rumpere, -rupi, -ruptus: break out
purgo, -are, -avi, -atus: clear
quaero, -ere, quaesivi, quaesitus: ask
spolio, -are, -avi, -atus: rob
subsisto, -sistere, -stiti, - : stop
tormentum, -i *n.*: torture

---

se ... fuisse: ind. statement introduced by *respondet*
Binomyum: that is, he has two names, his birth name (Giulio Sanseverino) and his chosen classicized name (Iulius Pomponius Laetus)
Confusus: Paul does not understand the word-play, as above in ch. 46
novitate: abl. of means
Paulus*: Instead of *Paulus* Platina originally wrote a sarcastic *homo doctus*, but changed it to the name before printing
quaerere: complementary inf. with *substitit*
quae omnia: "all (of) which," antecedents are the listed crimes of the previous clause
quod ... fuisset: clause of alleged reason, "because (so he said) he had been dutiful to me although (I was) ungrateful"
spoliare ... afficere: subject infs. of *est beneficium*
emptione sua: abl. of separation
incognita causa: abl. abs. with concessive sense

si ignominia, si calumnia afficere beneficium est, certe erga me
beneficus et liberalis dici potest Paulus, et ego ingratus, qui tanto-
rum maleficiorum immemor ab urbe non discesserim suis mandatis
obtemperans, suis pollicitationibus totiens frustratus.

*After a year of imprisonment, Platina is granted freedom of movement in Paul's
house, then the grounds of the Vatican, then all of Rome*

68 Abiit inde minabundus, et ob iram, quam tum concęperat,
nos usque ad integrum annum retinuit. Ita eum credo iurasse,
quando nos cępit et in carcerem conięcit; noluit periurus videri.

---

abeo, -ire, -ivi(ii), -itus: depart
afficio, -ere, affeci, affectus: afflict
annus, -i *m.*: year
beneficium, -i *n.*: kindness, benefit
beneficus, -a, -um: beneficent
calumnia, -ae *f.*: false accusation
capio, -ere, cępi (CL *cepi*), **captus**: take hold,
  capture
carcer, -eris *m.*: prison
certe (*adv.*): surely
concipio, -cipere, -cępi (CL *concepi*),
  -ceptus: conceive
coniicio, -iicere, -ięci (CL *conieci*),
  coniectus: put
discedo, -ere, discessi, discessus: depart
erga: towards (+ *acc.*)
frustro, -are, -avi, -atus: disappoint, deceive
ignominia, -ae *f.*: disgrace

immemor, -oris (*gen.*): forgetful
inde (*adv.*): thence
ingratus, -a, -um: ungrateful
integer, integra, integrum: whole
ira, -ae *f.*: anger
iuro, -are, -avi, -atus: swear
liberalis, -e: honorable, generous
maleficium, -i *n.*: evil deed
mandatum, -i *n.*: order
minabundus, -a, -um: threatening
nolo, nolle, nolui, - : wish not to
obtempero, -are, -avi, -atus: obey (+ *dat.*)
periurus, -i *m.*: a liar
pollicitatio, -onis *f.*: promise
quando (*adv.*): when
retineo, -ere, retinui, retentus: hold, restrain
totiens (adv.): so often
usque (*adv.*): all the way up to

certe ... Paulus: Platina's sarcasm is becoming more pronounced
dici: pres. pass. inf.
qui ... discesserim: causal rel. clause
suis mandatis ... suis pollicitationibus: referring to Paul
Abiit ... concęperat ... retinuit: Paul is the subj.
Ita: "thus"; i.e. that he would keep them jailed for a year
eum ... iurasse: ind. statement introduced by *credo*; *iurasse* syncopated from *iura(vi)sse*
videri: complementary pass. inf., "to seem"

Dimissos tandem in aedibus suis viginti diebus ita nos retinet, ut efferre pedem domo non liceret. Vagari deinde per Vaticanum sinit. Fatigatus postremo cardinalium precibus, liberos tandem nos facit.

Paul eventually allows Platina to leave Rome and go to the Baths to heal his arm, wounded from the torture; Platina returns afterwards, regaining Paul's trust

69 Vocor non ita multo post litteris a Lodovico Gonzaga principe Mantuano ad balnea Petriolana valitudinis causa, quam in

---

aedis, -is *f.*: temple; (*pl.*) home
balneum, -i *n.*: bath
cardinalis, -is *m.*: cardinal
deinde (*adv.*): then
dies, diei *m./f.*: day
dimitto, -ere, dimisi, dimissus: send away
domus, -i *f.*: house
effero, efferre, extuli, elatus: carry out
fatigo, -are, -avi, -atus: wear out
liber, libera, liberum: free
licet, -ere, -uit, -itus est (*impers.*): it is permitted
litterae, -arum *f.*: a letter (epistle)

multo (*adv.*): by much
per: through (+ *acc.*)
pes, pedis *m.*: foot
postremo (*adv.*): at last
prex, precis *f.*: prayer, request
princeps, -cipis *m.*: leader; prince
retineo, -ere, retinui, retentus: restrain
sino, -ere, sivi, situs: allow
tandem (*adv.*): finally
vagor, -ari, -atus sum: wander
valitudo, -dinis *f.* (CL *valetudo*): good health
Vaticanum, -i *n*: the Vatican
viginti (*indecl.*): twenty

Dimissos: agrees with *nos*
nos: acc. obj. of *retinet*, "he held us, dismissed, in this way …"
viginti diebus: abl. of extent of time (post-Classical, see Introduction 7.A)
ut … liceret: result clause
domo: abl. place from which, does not take a preposition with *domo*
sinit: (*nos*) *sinit*
liberos: predicate adj., "(makes us) free"
litteris: abl. of means
Lodovico Gonzaga: Ludovico III, Marquis of Mantua (r. 1444-1478), father of Platina's patron Francesco Gonzaga
balnea Petriolana: the baths of Petriolo, a province within Macerata in northeastern Italy
valitudinis: take with *causa*
quam: antecedent is *valitudinis*

carcere dextro humero debilitatus contraxeram. Eo ut proficiscerer, primo vetuit Paulus, quod diceret se brevi rei meae bene consulturum. Eo tamen ac redeo, spondente reditum meum Bessarione cardinali Niceno, viro praestantis ingenii et singularis litteraturae. Fidem meam commendat Paulus, ac crebro iactat optimam eius erga me voluntatem. Post discessum Borsii Estensis, quem ad urbem [391] cum magno equitatu venientem magnificentissime et laute

---

bene (*adv.*): well
brevi (*adv.*): in a short time
carcer, -eris *m.*: prison
cardinalis, -is *m.*: cardinal
commendo, -are, -avi, -atus: commend
consulo, -sulere, -sului, -sultus: make plans in the interest of (+ *dat.*)
contraho, -trahere, -traxi, -tractus: contract; diminish
crebro (*adv.*): often
debilitatus, -a, -um: maimed
dexter, -tra, -trum: right
discessus, -us *m*: departure
eo (*adv.*): there, to that place
equitatus, -us *m.*: cavalry
erga: towards, for (+ *acc.*)
fides, fidei *f.*: faith, loyalty

humerus, -i *m.*: upper arm
iacto, -are, -avi, -atus: boast (of)
ingenium, -i *n.*: talent
laute (*adv.*): elegantly
litteratura, -ae *f.*: erudition
magnifice (*adv.*): splendidly
Nicenus, -a, -um: Nicene, of Nicaea
praestans, praestantis: outstanding
primo (*adv.*): at first
proficiscor, -ficisci, -fectus sum: depart
redeo, -ire, -ivi(ii), -itus: return
reditus, -us *m.*: return
singularis, -e: singular
spondeo, -ere, spopondi, sponsus: promise
veto, -are, -ui, -itus: forbid
voluntas, -tatis *f.*: goodwill

---

dextro humero: abl. of respect; the wounded arm would have been the result of the *strappado* method of tortune: being hung by the arms after they have been tied behind the back, and then being dropped

debilitatus: agrees with 1st person subject

ut proficiscerer: ind. command

quod diceret: clause of alleged reason

se … consulturum (esse): ind. statement introduced by *diceret*, "that he would make plans shortly for my benefit"

spondente … Bessarione: abl. abs.

Bessarione cardinali Niceno: Basilios Bessarion (1403-1472), Cardinal of Nicaea, a longtime friend and supporter of Platina and the humanists

viro … litteraturae: *viro* in apposition to *Bessarione*; *praestantis ingenii* and *singularis litteraturae* gen. of description

iactat … voluntatem: *iactat* conveys disdain of Paul's actions, as Paul has clearly not demonstrated "his best kindness"

Borsii Estensis: Borso D'Este (1413-1471), made Duke of Ferrara in 1471 by Paul II

susceperat, ducemque Ferrariae creaverat, me brevi visurum quo in me animo esset. Idque etiam oratoribus tum Venetorum, tum ducis Mediolanensis, qui me ei commendaverant, saepe pollicitus fuerat.

Two years later, Paul dies

70 Biennio hac spe ductus vel frustratus potius, ire Bononiam institueram cum Cardinali Mantuano eiusdem civitatis legato. Quominus id facerem vetat Paulus; dicitque (ita erat urbanus et facetus) me satis sapere, et facultatibus potius quam {239R} litteratura

---

animus, -i *m.*: mind
biennium, -i *n.*: two years
Bononia, -ae *f.*: Bologna
brevi (*adv.*): in a short time
cardinalis, -is *m.*: cardinal
civitas, -tatis *f.*: city
commendo, -are, -avi, -atus: entrust, commend
creo, -are, -avi, -atus: create; invest
dux, ducis *m.*: leader; duke
facetus, -a, -um: clever
facultas, -tatis *f.*: means, wealth
Ferraria, -ae *f.*: Ferrara, a town in northern Italy
frustro, -are, -avi, -atus: disappoint, deceive

idem, eadem, idem: the same
instituo, -ere, -ui, -utus: set up, decide
legatus, -i *m.*: legate
litteratura, -ae *f.*: erudition
Mediolanensis, -e *m.*: Milanese, of Milan
orator, -oris *m.*: orator, ambassador
polliceor, -eri, -itus sum: promise
sapio, -ere, -ivi, - : have sense; know
satis (*adv.*): enough
spes, spei *f.*: hope
suscipio, -cipere, -cepi (CL *suscepi*), **-ceptus**: receive
urbanus, -a, -um: witty
Veneti, -orum *m.*: the Venetians
veto, -are, -ui, -itus: forbid

---

me ... visurum (esse): implied ind. statement, "that I would soon see"
quo ... esset: rel. clause of characteristic
in me: "toward me"
Idque: *id* + *-que*; acc. obj. of *pollicitus fuerat*
pollicitus fuerat: CL *pollicitus erat* (see Introduction 7.D)
Biennio: abl. of extent of time (post-Classical, see Introduction 7.A)
hac spe: abl. of means
Bononiam: acc. of place to which
Cardinali Mantuano: Platina's patron Francesco Gonzaga
eiusdem civitatis: obj. gen., referring back to Bologna; he was the pope's legate "for that same city"
legato: appositive to *Cardinali*
Quominus ... facerem: prevention clause, "forbid me from doing it"
me ... sapere: ind. statement introduced by *dicitque*
potius quam: "rather than"

indigere. Sed ecce, dum expecto ut mei tandem tot calamitatibus tot malis circumventi misereatur, pontifex ipse apoplexia moritur secunda hora noctis, solus in cubiculo nemine vidente, cum eo die laetus etiam concistorium habuisset, pontificatus sui anno sexto, mense decimo, quinto Calendas Augusti, MCCCCLXXI.

---

annus, -i *m.*: year
apoplexia, -ae *f.*: apoplexy
Augustus, -i *m.*: August
calamitas, -tatis *f.*: calamity
Calendae, -arum *f.*: Kalends, 1st of month
circumvenio, -venire, -veni, -ventus: surround; assail
concistorium, -i (CL *consistorium*) *n.*: consistory
cubiculum, -i *n.*: chamber
decimus, -a, -um: tenth
dies, diei *m./f.*: day
ecce: behold
expecto, -are, -avi, -atus: expect, wait
hora, -ae *f.*: hour
indigeo, -ere, -ui, - : lack (+ *abl.*)

laetus, -a, -um: happy, healthy
malum, -i *n.*: evil; misfortune
mensis, -is *m.*: month
misereor, -eri, -itus sum: have pity on (+ *gen.*)
nemo, neminis *m./f.*: no one
nox, noctis *f.*: night
pontifex, -ficis *m.*: pontiff, pope
pontificatus, -us *m.*: pontificate, time as pope
quintus, -a, -um: fifth
secundus, -a, -um: second
sextus, -a, -um: sixth
solus, -a, -um: alone
tandem (*adv.*): finally
tot (*indecl.*): so many

---

dum: temporal indicating simultaneous action, "while"
ut ... misereatur: noun clause, obj. of *expecto*, "await that he have pity on me ..."
tot calamitatibus tot malis: abls. of means
circumventi: agrees with *mei*
secunda hora: abl. of time when
nemine vidente: abl. abs. temporal
cum ... habuisset: concessive *cum* clause
concistorium: consistory, the assembly of the cardinals
pontificatus: gen. sing. masc.
anno sexto, mense decimo, quinto: abl. of time when
quinto (die ante) Calendas Augusti: *die ante* (as usual) is left out of this common formula; CL would use adj. *Augustas* (acc.) rather than noun *Augusti* (gen.); date is July 28, 1471

114

Paul was a large man, and took special care of his appearance

71 Fuit autem in homine, quantum ad corpus pertinet, maiestas pontifice digna. Erat enim magni ac vasti corporis, adeo ut dum ad rem divinam proficisceretur, solus emineret. Circa [392] cultum corporis, etsi morosus non erat, nequaquam tamen negligens habebatur. Fuere etiam qui dicerent eum, dum in publicum prodiret, faciem sibi fucis concinare.

---

adeo (*adv.*): to such a degree
circa: concerning (+ *acc.*)
concino, -are, -avi, -atus (CL *concinno*): put in order; prepare
corpus, -oris *n.*: body
cultus, -us *m.*: care
dignus, -a, -um: worthy of (+ *abl.*)
divinus, -a, -um: divine
emineo, -ere, -ui, - : stand out
etsi: although
facies, faciei *f.*: face
fucus, -i *m.*: dye; (as cosmetic) rouge
maiestas, -tatis *f.*: majesty; greatness
morosus, -a, -um: fastidious

negligo, -ligere, -lixi, -lictus (CL *neglego*): to disregard; to be negligent
nequaquam (*adv.*): by no means
pertineo, -tinere, -tinui, -tentus: relate to; pertain to
pontifex, -ficis *m.*: pontiff, pope
prodeo, -ire, -ivi(ii), -itus: to go out
proficiscor, -ficisci, -fectus sum: proceed; commence
publicus, -a, -um: public
quantum (*adv.*): so much as; as
solus, -a, -um: only; alone
vastus, -a, -um: vast, huge

---

maiestas pontifice digna: nom. *maiestas* agrees with *digna*, which determines abl. *pontifice*

magni ac vasti corporis: gen. of description; Platina originally characterized Paul's body as *obesi* ("obese")

ut ... emineret: result clause; he stands out because of his excessive size

dum ... proficisceretur: *dum* + imperf. subj., "while/when" (see Introduction 7.C)

ad rem divinam: CL uses this phrase for making a sacrifice to the gods; here rather to perform Christian liturgical functions

corporis: obj. gen. with *cultum*

nequaquam ... habebatur: "was by no means considered (to be)"; litotes implying he was quite concerned with his appearance

Fuere: alt. form of *fuerunt*

qui dicerent: rel. clause of characteristic

dum ... prodiret: *dum* + imperf. subj., "while/when" (see Introduction 7.C)

in publicum: substantive, "(to go out) in public"

sibi: dat. of advantage, "made his face up for himself with rouge"

Paul favored extravagant dress and liked to be seen

72 De apparatu pontificio non est cur ambigas maiores ab hoc uno superatos, regno praesertim, sive mitram velis appellare, in quam multas opes contulit, coemptis undique ac magnis preciis adamantibus, saphyris, smaragdis, chrysolitis, hyaspidibus, unionibus, et quicquid gemmarum in precio est, quibus ornatus tanquam alter Aron, in publicum forma humana augustiore prodibat. Inspici tum ab omnibus volebat et admirari. Hanc ob rem nonnunquam

---

adamas, -mantis *m.*: diamond
admiror, -ari, -atus sum: admire
ambigo, -ere, -, - : be in doubt
apparatus, -us *m.*: accoutrements
appello, -are, -avi, -atus: call; name
augustus, -a, -um: majestic
chrysolit(h)us, -i *m.*: topaz
coemo, -ere, coemi, coemptus: buy up
confero, -ferre, -tuli, -latus: bring together; devote
cur (*adv.*): why
forma, -ae *f.*: form, appearance
gemma, -ae *f.*: gem
humanus, -a, -um: human
hyaspis, hyaspidis (CL *iaspis*) *m.*: jasper
inspicio, -ere, inspexi, inspectus: look at, observe
maiores, -orum *m.*: ancestors
mitra, -ae *f.*: mitre, headdress for a Church official

nonnunquam (*adv.*): sometimes
ops, opis *f.*: power; wealth (*pl.*)
ornatus, -a, -um: adorned
pontificius, -a, -um: pontifical
praesertim (*adv.*): especially
precium, -i (CL *pretium*) *n.*: price; worth
prodeo, -ire, -ivi(ii), -itus: to go out
publicus, -a, -um: public
quisquis, quicquid: whoever, whatever
regnum, -i *n.*: kingdom; papal tiara
saphyrus, -i *m.*: sapphire
sive: or if
smaragdus, -i *m.*: emerald
supero, -are, -avi, -atus: overcome; surpass
tanquam (CL *tamquam*): just as if
undique (*adv.*): from everywhere
unio, -onis *m.*: pearl
volo, velle, volui, - : want, wish

---

non est cur: "there is no (reason) why"
ambigas: pres. subjunctive in ind. question
maiores … superatos (esse): ind. statement introduced by *ambigas*
regno: abl. of respect
quicquid gemmarum: partitive gen., "whatever (of) gems"
in precio: "in value," so highly regarded
alter Aron: Aaron, brother of Moses, was the first high priest. Josephus described him as having an elaborate headdress (*Ant.* III.vii.6).
in publicum: substantive, go out "in public"
forma … augustiore: abl. of description; *augustiore* is compar. adj.
humana: abl. of comparison "with an appearance more venerable than human"
Inspici: pres. pass. inf.
admirari: a deponent verb, but here with a true pass. sense

peregrinos in urbe retinuit, intermissa ostendendi sudarii consuetudine, quo a pluribus eodem tempore cerneretur.

*Paul also favored extravagant dress for the cardinals; some believed this splendor did
not serve Christianity*

73 Praeterea vero ne solus differre a cęteris videretur, publico
decreto mandavit proposita poena ne quispiam bireta coccinea (ita
appellant capitis tegmen) praeter cardinales ferret; quibus etiam

---

appello, -are, -avi, -atus: call; name
bi(r)retum, -i *n.*: biretta; a small, square
  Catholic clergy hat
caput, capitis *n.*: head
cardinalis, -is *m.*: cardinal
cerno, -ere, crevi, cretus: discern; see
coccineus, -a, -um: scarlet
consuetudo, -dinis *f.*: custom
cęterus, -a, -um (CL *ceterus*): the other; the
  rest
decretum, -i *n.*: decree
differo, differre, distuli, -dilatus: differ
fero, ferre, tuli, latus: bring; wear
idem, eadem, idem: the same
intermitto, -mittere, -misi, -missus:
  interrupt
mando, -are, -avi, -atus: order

ostendeo, -ere, ostendi, - : show; display
peregrinus, -i *m.*: pilgrim
poena, -ae *f.*: penalty
praeter: except (+ *acc.*)
praeterea (*adv.*): besides; in addition
propono, -ponere, -posui, -positus: propose
publicus, -a, -um: public
quispiam, quaepiam, quodpiam: anybody,
  anything
retineo, -ere, retinui, retentus: hold back;
  delay
solus, -a, -um: alone
sudarium, -i *n.*: handkerchief; here Veronica's
  Veil
tegmen, -minis *n.*: covering
tempus, temporis *n.*: time
vero (*adv.*): truly; in fact

---

intermissa ... consuetudine: abl. abs.
ostendendi sudarii: gerundive, "of the cloth to be displayed (i.e. of displaying the
  cloth)," Veronica's Veil was displayed once each year; Paul delayed the display to
  gather a crowd
quo ... cerneretur: rel. clause of purpose, "in order that (by this) he might be seen"
pluribus: compar. adj. of *multus*; here substantive, "more (people)"
eodem tempore: abl. of time when
ne ... videretur: neg. purpose clause, "so that he alone not seem"
proposita poena: abl. abs.
ne ... ferret: ind. command dependent on *mandavit*
quibus: connecting rel. referring to the cardinals, "and to them"

primo pontificatus sui anno pannum eiusdem coloris dono dedit, quo equos vel mulas sternerent dum equitant. Voluit praeterea in decretum referre, ut galeri cardinalium ex serico coccineo fierent; sed id quominus decerneretur vetuere illi, qui bene sentientes, diminuendam esse Ecclesiae pompam non augendam cum detrimento Christianae religionis praedicabant.

---

annus, -i *m.*: year
augeo, -ere, auxi, auctus: increase
bene (*adv.*): well
cardinalis, -is *m.*: cardinal
Christianus, -a, -um: Christian
coccineus, -a, -um: scarlet
color, -oris *m.*: color
decerno, -ere, decrevi, decretus: decide; determine; vote
decretum, -i *n.*: decree; vote
detrimentum, -i *n.*: damage
diminuo, -ere, -ui, -utus: diminish
donum, -i *n.*: gift
Ecclesia, -ae *f.*: Church
equito, -are, -avi, -atus: ride (horseback)
equus, -i *m.*: horse
fio, fieri, factus sum: be made
galerus, -i *m.*: ceremonial wide-brimmed hat, symbol of the rank of cardinal

idem, eadem, idem: the same
mula, -ae *f.*: mule
pannus, -i *m.*: cloth, garment
pompa, -ae *f.*: procession; pomp
pontificatus, -us *m.*: pontificate
praedico, -are, -avi, -atus: declare
praeterea (*adv.*): besides; in addition
primus, -a, -um: first
quominus: that not, from
refero, referre, rettuli, relatus: bring back; refer
religio, -onis *f.*: religion
sentio, -ire, sensi, sensus: perceive; think
sericum, -i *n.*: silk
sterno, -ere, stravi, stratus: lay out; saddle
veto, -are, -ui, -itus: forbid
volo, velle, volui, - : want, wish

---

primo ... anno: abl. of time when
pontificatus: gen. sing. masc.
dono dedit: dat. of purpose, "gave as a gift"
quo ... sternerent: rel. clause of purpose, "in order that (with it) they might saddle"
in decretum referre: that is, to refer the matter to a vote of the cardinals
ut ... fierent: ind. command
id: subj. of *decerneretur*, referring to the decree about the cardinals' hats
quominus decerneretur: prevention clause, introduced by *vetuere*
vetuere: alt. form of *vetuerunt*
illi: subj. of *vetuere*, antecedent of *qui*
diminuendam ... non augendam: pass. periphrastic, "(pomp) ought to be diminished, not increased"
cum detrimento: abl. of accompaniment, "with attendant damage to the Christian religion"
Christianae religionis: obj. gen. with *detrimento*

Paul had even promised summer palaces for all the cardinals, although he did not actually provide them

74 Ante pontificatum vero praedicare solebat, si sors unquam ei contigisset, singulis cardinalibus singula castella se donaturum, quo vitandi aestus urbani causa secedere percommode possent. Sed pontificatum adeptus, nil minus cogitavit.*

---

adipiscor, adipisci, adeptus sum: gain, obtain
aestus, -us *m.*: heat
cardinalis, -is *m.*: cardinal
castellum, -i *n.*: castle
cogito, -are, -avi, -atus: think
contingo, -tingere, -tigi, -tactus: happen; be granted to
dono, -are, -avi, -atus: give (gifts)
minus (*adv.*): less
nil *n.* (*indecl.*): nothing
percommodus, -a, -um: very convenient, very comfortable

pontificatus, -us *m.*: pontificate
praedico, -are, -avi, -atus: declare
secedo, -ere, secessi, secessus: withdraw
singulus, -a, -um: individual; one-a-piece
soleo, -ere, -itus sum: be accustomed to
sors, sortis *f.*: fate, fortune
unquam (CL *umquam*) (*adv.*): at any time, ever; at some time
urbanus, -a, -um: of the city; urban
vero (*adv.*): truly, in fact
vito, -are, -avi, -atus: avoid

---

si ... contigisset: protasis of a fut. more vivid cond. in ind. statement; after a main verb in secondary sequence, the fut. perf. indic. protasis becomes a pluperf. subjunctive.

sors: "the fate (of becoming pope)"

se donaturum (esse): apodosis of a cond. in ind. statement; the fut. inf. replaces what would be a fut. indic.

quo ... possent: rel. clause of purpose, "in order that they might withdraw there"

vitandi aestus urbani causa: gerundive phrase, "for the sake of the urban heat to be avoided (i.e. for avoiding the urban heat)"

pontificatum adeptus: Platina implicitly suggests both that Paul bribed the cardinals to get elected, and that he did not even hold up his part of the bargain

cogitavit*: Platina originally wrote, but then crossed out before printing: *Utinam non eos interdum sprevisset quos blanditiis in sententiam sui pellexerat* ("If only he had not sometimes scorned those whom he should have coaxed to his side with enticements")

Paul attempted to increase papal glory through influence and arms. The first example of the former is his mediation of a dispute between the Duke of Burgundy and the people of Liège

75 Pontificatus tamen maiestatem tum auctoritate tum armis augere conatus est. Nam Tricaricensem episcopum in Gallias misit, qui, cognita Leodiensium et ducis Burgundiae contentione, eos ad concordiam revocaret, sublato interdicto, quo Leodienses notati erant,

---

arma, -orum *n.*: arms
auctoritas, -tatis *f.*: authority
augeo, -ere, auxi, auctus: increase
Burgundia, -ae *f.*: Burgundy
cognosco, -noscere, -novi, -nitus: know; recognize
concordia, -ae *f.*: peace
conor, -ari, -atus sum: attempt
contentio, -onis *f.*: struggle
dux, ducis *m.*: leader; duke
episcopus, -i *m.*: bishop

Gallia, -ae *f.*: Gaul
interdictum, -i *n.*: prohibition
Leodiensis, -e: from Liège, in modern Belgium
maiestas, -tatis *f.*: greatness
noto, -are, -avi, -atus: mark; brand
pontificatus, -us *m.*: pontificate
revoco, -are, -avi, -atus: call back, recall
tollo, -ere, sustuli, sublatus: lift; remove
Tricaricensis, -e: of Tricaro, a town in southern Italy

Pontificatus: gen. sing. masc.

tum ... tum: "not only ... but also"

Tricaricensem episcopum: Onofrio de Santa Croce (d. 1471), whom Paul sent to make peace between Charles I and Burgundy and the people of Liège. Onofrio failed, but commissioned humanist Angelo Sabino to write the epic *De excidio civitatis Leodiensis*

Gallias: pl. because several Gallic territories were each called *Gallia*

qui ... revocaret: rel. clause of purpose, "sent (him) who would recall (i.e. in order that he might recall)"

cognita ... contentione: abl. abs.

Leodiensium: gen. pl., a substantive for the people of Liège

ducis Burgundiae: Charles I (the Bold), r. 1467-1477

sublato interdicto: abl. abs.; an *interdictum* is a penalty forbidding the administration of certain sacraments

ob pulsum iniuria episcopum suum. Verum, dum Tricaricensis haec quam accurate agit, ut id ad solum pontificem pertinere ostenderet, a Leodiensibus cum eorum episcopo capitur. Hanc ob rem dux [393] Burgundiae inita pace cum Lodovico, Franciae rege (tum enim bellum inter se gerebant), adiuvante ipso rege, Leodienses gravissimis caedibus persecutus, eorum urbem tandem evertit et captos episcopos liberavit.

---

accurate (*adv.*): carefully; meticulously
adiuvo, -are, adiuvi, adiutus: help
ago, -ere, egi, actus: act; manage
Burgundia, -ae *f.*: Burgundy
caedes, -is *f.*: slaughter, massacre
capio, -ere, cepi, captus: seize; capture
dux, ducis *m.*: leader; duke
episcopus, -i *m.*: bishop
everto, -ere, everti, eversus: overturn; destroy
gero, -ere, gessi, gestus: bear; wage war (+ *bellum*)
gravis, -e: heavy; severe
ineo, -ire, -ivi(ii), -itus: enter; begin
iniuria, -ae *f.*: injustice

Leodiensis, -e: of or from Liège
libero, -are, -avi, -atus: free
ostendeo, -ere, ostendi, - : show; make clear
pello, -ere, pepuli, pulsus: drive out; banish
persequor, -sequi, -secutus sum: take vengeance on
pertineo, -tinere, -tinui, -tentus: concerns, pertains to
pontifex, pontificis *m.*: pontiff, pope
solus, -a, -um: only; alone
tandem (*adv.*): finally
Tricaricensis, -e: (the Bishop) of Tricaro
verum (*conj.*): however

---

ob pulsum ... episcopum: "because of their bishop having been expelled (i.e. the expulsion of their bishop)"
iniuria: abl. of manner; the preposition *cum* is often left out with this word
quam accurate: "so carefully" (like *tam accurate*)
ut ... ostenderet: result clause
a Leodiensibus: abl. of agent, used as a substantive, "by the people of Liège"
capitur: subj. is still Onofrio, Bishop of Tricarico
Lodovico, Franciae rege: Louis XI, King of France (r. 1461-1483)
Leodienses: acc. obj. of *persecutus*
persecutus: agrees with *dux*

The second example of an attempt to increase papal power through influence: Paul deposed the Hussite King of Bohemia; he unsuccessfully tried to replace him with Mathias Corvinus

76 Preterea vero {239v} Paulus, cognita regis Boemiae perfidia, in hominem Laurentio Roverella episcopo Ferrariensi legato ita Ungaros et Germanos concitavit, ut brevi et stirpem Georgii funditus sustulerit, et nomen haereticorum fuerit deleturus, ni Poloni, id regnum ad se pertinere dicentes, Matthiam Ungariae regem tenuissent bello lacessitum, quominus regno Boemiae potiretur.

Boemia, -ae *f.*: Bohemia
brevi (*adv.*): in a short time
cognosco, -noscere, -novi, -nitus: know; learn
concito, -are, -avi, -atus: rouse
deleo, -ere, -evi, -etus: destroy
episcopus, -i *m.*: bishop
Ferrariensis, -e: of Ferrara, a city in northern Italy
funditus (*adv.*): utterly, completely
Germani, -orum *m.*: the Germans
haereticus, -i *m.*: heretic
lacesso, -ere, -ivi, -itus: provoke; harass
legatus, -i *m.*: envoy
ni (*adv.*): if … not

perfidia, -ae *f.*: faithlessness; heresy
pertineo, -tinere, -tinui, -tentus: concerns, pertains to
Poloni, -orum *m.*: the Poles
potior, -iri, -itus sum: obtain; become master of
preterea (CL *praeterea*) (*adv.*): in addition
quominus: that not, from
regnum, -i *n.*: kingdom
stirps, stirpis *f.*: stock; stem; family
teneo, -ere, tenui, tentus: hold, keep
tollo, -ere, sustuli, sublatus: lift; remove
Ungari, -orum *m.*: the Hungarians
Ungaria, -ae *f.*: Hungary
vero (*adv.*): in fact

---

regis Boemiae: George of Podebrady, King of Bohemia (r. 1457-1471)
perfidia: George was a Hussite
in hominem: that is, against King George
Laurentio … legato: abl. abs.
Laurentio Roverella episcopo Ferrariensi: Lorenzo Roverella, Bishop of Ferrara 1460-1474
stirpem Georgii funditus sustulerit: result clause; the expression suggests weeding, pulling out the whole stock from the root
fuerit deleturus: perf. subjunctive (with fut. pple.) in result clause
ni … tenuissent: protasis of past contrafactual cond.
Poloni … dicentes: George had named as his successor the King of Poland's son; thus the Poles fought to keep Corvinus from taking Bohemia
id regnum: that is, Bohemia
Matthiam Ungariae: Matthias Corvinus, King of Hungary (r. 1458-1490)
quominus … potiretur: prevention clause dependent on *tenuissent*

First example of an attempt to increase papal power through arms: Paul unsuccessfully besieged Tolfa before buying its loyalty

77 Duo tamen bella et quidem parva in Italia suscępit, quae, nulla re prius repetita bello sed insidiis primo incohata, postea deseruit*. Cum igitur Tolphae veteris dominos insidiis primo, mox armis (cum id non cessisset), duce Vianesio aggręssus esset, obsidęretque locum et oppugnaret, supervenientibus regiis copiis, quae a bello,

---

aggredior, aggredi, aggręssus sum (CL *aggressus sum*): approach; attack
arma, -orum *n.*: arms
cedo, -ere, cessi, cessus: yield
copia, -ae *f.*: abundance; troops (*pl.*)
desero, -ere, deserui, desertus: abandon
dominus, -i *m.*: lord
duo, -ae, -o: two
dux, ducis *m.*: leader
igitur: therefore
incoho, -are, -avi, -atus: begin
insidiae, -arum *f.*: ambush; plot
Italia, -ae *f.*: Italy
locus, -i *m.*: place

mox (*adv.*): soon, next
nullus, -a, -um: no; none
obsideo, -ere, obsedi, obsessus: besiege
oppugno, -are, -avi, -atus: attack
postea (*adv.*): afterwards
primo (*adv.*): at first, in the first place
prius (*adv.*): previously, first
regius, -a, -um: royal
repeto, -ere, -ivi, -itus: demand back
supervenio, -venire, -veni, -ventus: arrive
suscipio, -cipere, -cępi (CL *suscepi*), **-ceptus**: undertake
Tolpha, -ae *f.*: Tolfa, a town in central Italy
vetus, veteris: old

---

quae ... deseruit: that is, Paul could walk away from the wars without losing face because he was not openly demanding the return of something, but rather secretly pursuing his ends
nulla re ... repetita ... incohata: abl. abs.
bello: abl. of means
insidiis: abl. of means
deseruit*: Platina originally wrote and then later crossed out before printing: ... *turpiter deseruit, parvi siquidem animi erat, licet ambitione vasti haberetur; praeterea etiam avaritia laborabat. Quae homines a rebus gerendis, et quidem magnis, retrahunt* ("which he shamefully deserted since he was a man of little spirit, although he was thought to be of great spirit because of his ambition; moreover, he also suffered because of his greed. Such things keep men back from accomplishing things, and in particular great things")
Cum ... aggręssus esset, obsidęretque ... et oppugnaret: circumstantial *cum* clause
id: the town of Tolfa, important because of its alum mines
duce Vianesio: abl. abs.; Vianesio Albergati of Bologna, Paul's vice-chamberlain; Platina originally added *suo cum grege lenonum* ("with his flock of pimps")
regiis copiis: royal; that is, from the kingdom of Naples
quae a bello: antecedent of *quae* is *copiis*; this clause, interrupted by another rel. clause, lacks a verb; Platina presumably meant to add something like *reveniebant*

123

quod in Flamminea contra Bartholemeum Bergomatem gestum esse diximus, quo in exercitu Ursini militabant, repente effusa fuga obsidionem deserit, cum amplius sexaginta millibus passuum hostes abessent. Atque ita Tolpham post longam contentionem, qua etiam Ursinos sibi inimicos ac prope hostes fecerat, decem et septem

---

absum, abesse, afui, afuturus: be away, distant

amplius (*adv.*): greater; more

contentio, -onis *f.*: struggle

contra: against (+ *acc.*)

decem (*indecl.*): ten

desero, -ere, deserui, desertus: abandon

effusus, -a, -um: disorderly

exercitus, -us *m.*: army

Flamminea, -ae (CL *Flaminia*) *f.*: the region around the Via Flaminia, near Rimini in northern Italy

fuga, -ae *f.*: flight

gero, -ere, gessi, gestus: bear; wage (+ *bellum*)

hostis, -is *m./f.*: enemy (of the state)

inimicus, -a, -um: hostile to

longus, -a, -um: long

milito, -are, -avi, -atus: serve as soldier

mille, millia *n.*: thousand (CL abl. *milibus*)

obsidio, -onis *f.*: siege; blockade

passus, -us *m.*: step

prope (*adv.*): nearly

repente (*adv.*): suddenly

septem (*indecl.*): seven

sexaginta (*indecl.*): sixty

Tolpha, -ae *f.*: Tolfa, a fortress in central Italy

Ursini, -orum *m.*: the Orsini, an aristocratic Roman family

---

quod ... diximus: ch. 39-40; the Neapolitan forces, along with Milan, were helping Florence fight off Bartolomeo Colleoni and the Venetians

Bartholemeun Bergomatem: Bartolomeo Colleoni, an Italian *condottiero* who changed sides multiple times and fought for both the Sforza and the Venetians. Ultimately, he was appointed captain-general of the Republic of Venice for life in 1455

effusa fuga: abl. of means, "in a disorderly flight"

deserit: main verb

cum ... abessent: concessive *cum* clause

sexaginta millibus: abl. of comparison, more "than sixty thousand" (of) steps; i.e. sixty miles

Tolpham: acc. obj. of *emit*; Paul ultimately bought Tolfa in 1469

qua: abl. of means; antecedent is *contentionem*

sibi: dat. with *inimicos*

decem et septem millibus: abl. of price, 17,000

millibus nummum auri emit, familiae Ursinae potentiam veritus, quae dominis loci affinitate coniuncta erat.

Second example of an attempt to increase papal power through arms: Paul besieged Rimini but failed to take it due to his stinginess in paying soldiers and his indecisiveness

78 Hisdem quoque [394] artibus Robertum Malatestam Sigismundi mortui filium aggressus, cum etiam dolo suburbium Ariminense cępisset, urbemque aliquandiu oppugnasset, Laurentio Spalatrensi archiepiscopo tantum negocium procurante, superveniente

---

affinitas, -tatis *f.*: relationship by marriage
aggredior, aggredi, aggressus sum: attack
aliquandiu (CL *aliquamdiu*) (*adv.*): for some time
archiepiscopus, -i *m.*: archbishop
Ariminensis, -e: of Rimini
ars, artis *f.*: craft; method
aurum, -i *n.*: gold
capio, -ere, cępi (CL *cepi*), **captus**: seize
coniungo, -iungere, -iunxi, -iunctus: join
dolus, -i *m.*: deceit, trickery
dominus, -i *m.*: lord
emo, -ere, emi, emptus: buy
familia, -ae *f.*: family
idem, eadem, idem: same

locus, -i *m.*: place
mille, millia *n.*: thousand (CL abl. *milibus*)
negocium, -i (CL *negotium*) *n.*: business, activity
nummus, -i *m.*: coin
oppugno, -are, -avi, -atus: besiege
potentia, -ae *f.*: power
procuro, -are, -avi, -atus: manage
Spalat(r)ensis, -e: of Split, in modern Croatia
suburbium, -i *n.*: suburb
supervenio, -venire, -veni, -ventus: arrive
Ursinus, -a, -um: of the Orsini
vereor, -eri, -itus sum: fear

---

nummum: gen. pl., syncopated from *numm(or)um*
auri: gen. of material
familiae Ursinae: the Orsini family
dominis: dat. with *coniuncta*
loci: gen. sing., dependent on *dominis*
Hisdem: CL *isdem* (abl. pl.)
Robertum Malatestam: Roberto Malatesta (1441-1484) of Rimini, *condottiero* and illegitimate son of Sigismundo
Sigismundi: Sigismundo Pandolfo Malatesta (1417-1468), Lord of Rimini and *condottiero*
cum ... cępisset ... oppugnasset: circumstantial *cum* clause
Laurentio Spalat(r)ensi archiepiscopo: Lorenzo Zanni, Archbishop of Split 1452-1473

postea Foederico comite Urbinati cum regio ac Florentini populi exercitu, et obsidionem relinquere coactus est, et fuso turpiter ac fugato eius exercitu, pacem turpi etiam conditione initam non renuit. Affirmat Laurentius potiundi Arimini opportunitatem amissam esse, dum avare nimium stipendia militibus persolvit, dumque ignoratione rerum et tarditate ingenii, rem ipsam quae momento temporis colligitur, in bello potissimum, in longum ducit.

---

affirmo, -are, -avi, -atus: affirm
amitto, -ere, amisi, amissus: lose
avare: greedily; stingily
cogo, -ere, coegi, coactus: force, compel
colligo, -ere, collegi, collectus: bring together; compress
comes, comitis *m.*: companion; count
conditio, -onis (CL *condicio*) *f.*: agreement
exercitus, -us *m.*: army
Florentinus, -a, -um: Florentine, of Florence
fugo, -are, -avi, -atus: put to flight
fundo, -ere, fudi, fusus: pour; rout
ignoratio, -onis *f.*: ignorance
ineo, -ire, -ivi(ii), -itus: enter; undertake
ingenium, -i *n.*: nature, character
longus, -a, -um: long
miles, militis *m.*: soldier
momentum, -i *n.*: moment
nimium (*adv.*): excessively
obsidio, -onis *f.*: siege
opportunitas, -tatis *f.*: opportunity
pax, pacis *f.*: peace
persolvo, -solvere, -solvi, -solutus: pay off
populus, -i *m.*: people, nation
postea (*adv.*): afterwards
potior, -iri, -itus sum: obtain; capture
potissimum (*adv.*): especially
regius, -a, -um: royal
relinquo, -ere, reliqui, relictus: abandon
renuo, renuere, renui, - : to refuse
stipendium, -i *n.*: (military) wages
tarditas, -tatis *f.*: slowness
tempus, temporis *n.*: time
turpis, -e: disgraceful
turpiter (*adv.*): disgracefully
Urbinatis, -e: of Urbino

Foederico comite Urbinati: Federico da Montefeltro (1422-1482), *condottiero* and a major patron of humanists
cum regio ... exercitu: "with the royal army and that of the Florentine people"; the royal army is that of Naples
fuso ... fugato ... exercitu: abl. abs.
potiundi Arimini: gerundive phrase "of Rimini to be seized (i.e. of seizing Rimini)"
amissam esse: ind. statement; acc. subj. is *opportunitatem*
dum ... dumque: *dum* here with a circumstantial sense verging on causal
ignoratione ... et tarditate: abls. of cause
momento: abl. of time when
in longum ducit: "to prolong"; acc. obj. of *ducit* is *rem ipsam*

Paul had a hesitant nature, which he himself valued but which ultimately proved harmful

79 Natura enim in rebus agendis ita praeposterus Paulus erat, ut <non> nisi fatigatus, rem quantumvis claram et apertam incoharet, aut incohatam perficeret*. Quanquam ipse iactare solebat id sibi in multis usui fuisse, cum in pluribus, si verum fateri volumus, sibi ac Romanae Ecclesiae id admodum nocuisset.

Paul was aggressive in collecting money, and his actions sometimes verged on simony

80 In colligendis autem pecuniis ita diligens fuit, ut fere semper beneficia et episcopatus his committeret, qui officium aliquod [395]

---

admodum (*adv.*): certainly
ago, -ere, egi, actus: do
aliqui, -qua, -quod: some
apertus, -a, -um: open; obvious
beneficium, -i *n.*: favor; benefice (fief)
clarus, -a, -um: clear
colligo, -ere, collegi, collectus: collect
committo, -mittere, -misi, -missus: entrust
diligens, -entis: diligent
Ecclesia, -ae *f.*: Church
episcopatus, -us *m.*: bishopric
fateor, -eri, fassus sum: admit
fatigo, -are, -avi, -atus: weary; harass
fere (*adv.*): almost

iacto, -are, -avi, -atus: boast
incoho, -are, -avi, -atus: begin
noceo, -ere, -ui, -itus: harm (+ *dat.*)
officium, -i *n.*: duty; office
perficio, -ficere, -feci, -fectus: complete
plus, pluris: more
praeposterus, -a, -um: backwards; absurd
quanquam (CL *quamquam*): although
quantumvis (*adv.*): to as great a degree as you like
usus, -us *m.*: use; advantage
verum, -i *n.*: truth
volo, velle, volui, - : wish; be willing

Natura: abl. of cause "by nature"
perficeret*: Platina originally wrote and then later crossed out before printing: *perficeret, quod erat parvi animi signum et consilii non multi* ("this was a sign that he was a man of small mind and not much sense")
id: referring to his hesitant nature
in multis … in pluribus: "in many things … in more things"
usui: dat. of purpose, "of use"
cum … nocuisset: concessive *cum* clause
In colligendis … pecuniis: gerundive phrase, "in money to be collected (i.e. in collecting money)"
ut … commiteret: result clause
episcopatus: acc. pl.
qui … haberent: rel. clause of characteristic; antecedent is *his*

venale haberent, unde elici munus posset. Omnia enim officia suo tempore venalia erant, quam ob rem factum est, ut qui episcopatum aut beneficium vellet, officium aliquod emeret, quo lenocinio quod vellet consequeretur, superatis competitoribus omnibus, doctrina et probitate vitae quovis magistratu et honore dignis. Preterea vero cum episcopatus vacaret, quo plures annatae eodem tempore solverentur, digniores, ut ipse praedicabat, ad uberiores episcopatus movens,

---

aliqui, -qua, -quod: some
annata, -ae *f.*: annate, a tax on a benefice
beneficium, -i *n.*: favor; benefice
competitor, -oris *m.*: competitor
consequor, -sequi, -secutus sum: attain
dignus, -a, -um: worthy, worthy of (+ *abl.*)
doctrina, -ae *f.*: education
elicio, -ere, -ui, -itus: draw out, elicit
emo, -ere, emi, emptus: buy
episcopatus, -us *m.*: bishopric
fio, fieri, factus sum: happen
honor, -oris *m.*: honor; public office
lenocinium, -i *n.*: enticement
magistratus, -us *m.*: magistracy; office
moveo, -ere, movi, motus: move
munus, -eris *n.*: gift

officium, -i *n.*: duty; office
plus, pluris: more
praedico, -are, -avi, -atus: declare
preterea (CL *praeterea*) (*adv.*): in addition
probitas, -tatis *f.*: uprightness
quivis, quaevis, quodvis: any at all
solvo, -ere, solvi, solutus: pay off
supero, -are, -avi, -atus: overcome
tempus, -oris *n.*: time
uber, uberis: fertile, rich
unde (*adv.*): from where, whence
vaco, -are, -avi, -atus: be vacant
venalis, -e: for sale
vero (*adv.*): in fact
volo, velle, volui, - : wish, want

---

officium … venale: a venal office, a job whose holder had to pay to obtain it
unde … posset: subjunctive by attraction
elici: pres. pass. inf., complementary with *posset*
factum est: subject is the following *ut* clause
ut … emeret: substantive *ut* clause, subject of *factum est*
qui … vellet: rel. clause of characteristic; antecedent is assumed *is*, subject of *emeret*
quo … consequeretur: rel. clause of purpose, "in order that by this enticement he might attain"
superatis competitoribus: abl. abs.
omnibus … dignis: "all, although worthy"
doctrina et probitate: abls. of cause
quovis magistratu et honore: abl. with *dignis*
cum … vacaret: circumstantial *cum* clause
quo … solverentur: rel. clause of purpose, "in order that (by this) more annates might be paid"
digniores: compar. of *dignus*, here acc. pl. obj. of *movens*
uberiores episcopatus: acc. pl.

magnam pecuniarum vim undique colligebat. Redimendarum quoque {240R} pensionum usum non improbavit*.

Paul used his money liberally, caring for those in need and assuring necessary supplies for Rome

81 His autem pecuniis interdum etiam ad liberalitatem utebatur. Nam et cardinales pauperes maxime, et episcopos, et principes, ac nobiles domo extorres, virgines, viduas, aegrotos frequenter iuvabat. Curavit item ut Romae annona [396] cęteraque ad victum pertinentia vilius quam antea venderentur.

---

aegrotus, -a, -um: sick
annona, -ae *f.*: grain supply
antea (*adv.*): before
cardinalis, -is *m.*: cardinal
colligo, -ere, collegi, collectus: collect
curo, -are, -avi, -atus: take care of
cęterus, -a, -um (CL *ceterus*): the other
domus, -i *f.*: home
episcopus, -i *m.*: bishop
extorris, -is, -e: exiled
frequenter (*adv.*): frequently
improbo, -are, -avi, -atus: disapprove of
interdum (*adv.*): sometimes
item (*adv.*): likewise; also
iuvo, -are, iuvi, iutus: help
liberalitas, -tatis *f.*: generosity
nobilis, -e: noble

pauper, -eris: poor
pensio, -onis *f.*: pension; salary
pertineo, -tinere, -tinui, -tentus: concern, pertain to
princeps, -cipis *m.*: leader; prince
redimo, -ere, redemi, redemptus: buy back; redeem
Roma, -ae *f.*: Rome
undique (*adv.*): from everywhere
usus, -us *m.*: use
utor, uti, usus sum: use (+ *abl.*)
vendo, -ere, vendidi, venditus: sell
victus, -us *m.*: living; nourishment
viduus, -a, -um: widowed
vilis, -e: cheap
virgo, -ginis *f.*: young woman
vis, vis *f.*: strength; abundance (+ *gen.*)

Redimendarum ... pensionum: gerundive phrase, "of pensions to be redeemed (i.e. of redeeming pensions);" Platina used this sentence to replace the following: *... colligebat. Neque hoc contentus, seorsum etiam ab his quos pecuniosos intellexerat aliquid emungebat in usus cruciatae, ut ipse dicebat* ("And not content with this, he would separately also fleece away from those he understood to be rich something for use on the crusade, as he himself used to say")

ad liberalitatem: "for generosity"; Platina originally added *et largitionem* ("and bribery")

maxime: superl. adv. of *magnus*; here with sense of "especially"

Curavit ... venderentur: This entire phrase is lacking in V; Platina added it in the margin of A and F, where it replaced the phrase *Et in se aliquid principum auctoritate molientes pecunia strangulabat* ("and he would smother with money those plotting against him by authority of princes")

ut ... venderentur: substantive *ut* clause, obj. of *Curavit*

Romae: locative, or possibly gen. with *annona*

vilius: compar. adv. of *vilis*

Paul also used his money for building projects and popular entertainments

82 Aedificavit etiam splendide ac magnifice tum apud Sanctum Marcum, tum vero in Vaticano. Quod ad munificentiam pertinet, venationem quoque miro apparatu edidit duci Ferrariensi in campo Merulae. Huic autem praefuit eius ex sorore nepos S. Luciae cardinalis, quem una cum Baptista Zeno altero nepote cardinales ante creaverat.

Paul was nocturnal and difficult to deal with

83 Adire hominem die dormientem ac noctu vigilantem, [397] attrectantem gemmas et margaritas, difficile erat, nec nisi post

---

adeo, -ire, -ivi(ii), -itus: approach; have an audience with
aedifico, -are, -avi, -atus: build
apparatus, -us *m.*: preparation; splendor
attrecto, -are, -avi, -atus: touch; grope
campus, -i *m.*: field
cardinalis, -is *m.*: cardinal
creo, -are, -avi, -atus: create; appoint
dies, diei *m./f.*: day
difficilis, -e: difficult
dormio, -ire, -ivi, -itus: sleep
dux, ducis *m.*: leader; duke
edo, -ere, edidi, editus: produce; sponsor
Ferrariensis, -e: of Ferrara
gemma, -ae *f.*: gem
magnifice (*adv.*): magnificently
margarita, -ae *f.*: pearl

Merula, -ae *f.*: Merlo, a field near Magliana
mirus, -a, -um: wonderful
munificentia, -ae *f.*: munificence
nepos, -otis *m./f.*: nephew
noctu (*adv.*): at night
pertineo, -tinere, -tinui, -tentus: concerns, pertains to
praesum, -esse, -fui, -futurus: be in charge (+ *dat.*)
sanctus, -i *m.*: saint
splendide (*adv.*): splendidly
una (*adv.*): together
Vaticanus, -i *m.*: the Vatican
venatio, -onis *f.*: a hunt
vero (*adv.*): truly
vigilo, -are, -avi, -atus: remain awake

---

tum ... tum: "not only ... but also"
Sanctum Marcum: a church near modern Piazza Venezia; also the name of Paul's palace adjoining this church, now called Palazzo Venezia (see fig. 3, p. 72)
Vaticano: Vatican hill, the site of St. Peter's basilica
Quod ... pertinet: "(A thing) which ... pertains," a noun clause in apposition to the following clause
duci Ferrariensi: Borso D'Este, whom Paul made Duke of Ferrara in 1471
Huic: the hunt
nepos: Giovanni Michiel (1446-1503)
S. Luciae: Santa Lucia in Septisolio, a church near the Septizodium
Baptista Zeno: Giovanni Battista Zeno (d. 1501)
ante: they were made cardinals in 1468; the hunt was in 1471
Adire: subject of *difficile erat*
die: abl. of time within which
nec nisi: "nor (was it possible) except"

multas vigilias: quodsi tibi patuissent fores, audire hominem non audiri ab homine necesse erat, adeo copiosus in dicendo habebatur. Morosus erat et difficilis, tum domesticis, tum externis; et saepe quod promiserat mutata sententia invertebat. Volebat videri astutus rebus in omnibus; hanc ob rem perplexe nimium interdum loquebatur. Quare amicitias principum ac populorum non diu servavit, quod variarum partium haberetur.

adeo (*adv.*): so; to such a degree
amicitia, -ae *f.*: friendship
astutus, -a, -um: expert
audio, -ire, -ivi, -itus: hear; listen to
copiosus, -a, -um: abundant
difficilis, -e: difficult
diu (*adv.*): for a long time
domesticus, -i *m.*: household member
externus, -a, -um: external; those outside
foris, -is *f.*: door
interdum (*adv.*): sometimes
inverto, -ere, inverti, inversus: reverse
loquor, loqui, locutus sum: speak
morosus, -a, -um: hard to please
muto, -are, -avi, -atus: change

necesse (*undeclined*): necessary
nimium (*adv.*): excessively
pars, partis *f.*: part; faction
pateo, -ere, -ui, - : be open
perplexus, -a, -um: cryptic
populus, -i *m.*: people, nation
princeps, principis *m.*: leader; prince
promitto, -mittere, -misi, -missus: promise
quare (*adv.*): for this reason
quodsi: but if, and if
sententia, -ae *f.*: opinion
servo, -are, -avi, -atus: keep, preserve
varius, -a, -um: various
vigilia, -ae *f.*: vigil, time awake at night
volo, velle, volui, - : want, wish

quodsi ... patuissent ... erat: past contrafactual; apodosis often indic. in expressions of necessity
audire ... non audiri: Paul would do all the talking
dicendo: abl. gerund
tum ... tum: "both ... and"
quod promiserat: antecedent is assumed *id*, acc. obj. of *invertebat*
videri: "seem"; complementary inf. with *Volebat*
quod ... haberetur: clause of alleged reason, "on the grounds that he was considered to be (a member) of various factions"
variarum partium: gen. of description

Paul had peculiar tastes in food, which might have contributed to his death

84 Varia ciborum genera sibi apponi volebat, et peiora quaeque semper degustabat. Clamabat interdum, nisi quae expetebat ex sententia ei apposita fuissent. Bibacissimus quidem erat, sed vina admodum parva et diluta bibebat. Peponum esu, cancrorum, pastillorum, piscium, succidiae admodum delectabatur. Quibus ex rebus ortam crediderim apoplexiam illam, qua e vita sublatus est. Nam duos pepones et quidem praegrandes comederat eo die, quo sequenti nocte mortuus est.

---

admodum (*adv.*): exceedingly
apoplexia, -ae *f.*: apoplexy, stroke
appono, -ere, apposui, appositus: set before; serve up
bibax, -acis: given to drinking
bibo, -ere, bibi, bibitus: drink
cancer, cancri *m.*: crab
cibus, -i *m.*: food
clamo, -are, -avi, -atus: cry out
comedo, -ere, comedi, comestus: eat up; devour
degusto, -are, -avi, -atus: taste; sample
delecto, -are, -avi, -atus: delight
dies, diei *m./f.*: day
dilutus, -a, -um: diluted
duo, -ae, -o: two
esus, -us *m.*: eating

expeto, -ere, -ivi, -itus: demand; desire
genus, -eris *n.*: type
interdum (*adv.*): sometimes
nox, noctis *f.*: night
orior, -iri, ortus sum: arise
pastillus, -i *m.*: pastry
pepo, -onis *m.*: melon
piscis, -is *m.*: fish
praegrandis, -e: very large
quisque, quaeque, quodque: each
sententia, -ae *f.*: opinion
sequens, sequentis: following
succidia, -ae *f.*: leg of pork; bacon
tollo, -ere, sustuli, sublatus: lift; remove
varius, -a, -um: different; diverse
vinum, -i *n.*: wine
volo, velle, volui, - : want

---

sibi: dat. with *apponi*
apponi: pass. inf.
peiora quaeque: "each (of the) worst things"
nisi: the negation is taken closely with *apposita fuissent*
quae: antecedent is an assumed *ea* (n. pl.), subject of *apposita fuissent*
ex sententia: according to his wish
Peponum ... succidiae: a series of obj. genitives dependent on *esu*
esu: abl. of means
ortam (esse) ... apoplexiam: ind. statement
crediderim: potential subjunctive, the perf. is pres. time but completed aspect
qua: abl. of means; antecedent is *apoplexiam*
eo die: abl. of time when
quo sequenti nocte: two abls. of time when; same day "on which he died on the following night"

Paul was considered to be just and merciful

85 Iustus tamen est habitus et clemens*. Plęrosque autem latrones poena carceris ad sanitatem redigere conatus est: fures, parricidas, perfidos, periuros.

---

carcer, -eris *m.*: prison
clemens, clementis: merciful
conor, -ari, -atus sum: attempt
fur, furis *m./f.*: thief
iustus, -a, -um: just, fair
latro, -onis *m.*: brigand
parricida, -ae *m./f.*: murderer of near relative
perfidus, -a, -um: treacherous; heretic

periurus, -a, -um: perjurer, liar
plęrusque, -aque, -umque (CL *plerusque*): the majority, most
poena, -ae *f.*: penalty
redigo, -ere, redegi, redactus: drive back; return
sanitas, -tatis *f.*: sanity; reason

---

est habitus: "he was considered (to be)"

clemens*: Platina originally wrote and then later crossed out a different ending for the chapter: *clemens, si non est genus iniustitiae homines ob levem etiam causam in vinculis macerare. Nam cum addubitatum esset maiorne morte habenda esset poena diuturni carceris, parem esse censuere sacri canones. Cum, inquiunt, ultimo supplicio clericus capitali crimine convictus tradi non possit, perpetuo carceri adiudicandus est, quem duximus morti simillimum esse. In latrones, tamen, fures, parricidas, perfidos, peiuros clemens quos in carcerem tanquam in ergastula mittebat; qui postea tanquam fametici leones e cavea missi in optimum quenquam crassarentur* ("if it is not a kind of injustice to wear men down in chains for even a trivial cause. For although it has been doubted whether long imprisonment should be considered a greater penalty than death, the sacred canons have judged them to be equal. Since, they say, a cleric convicted of a capital crime may not be handed over for the ultimate punishment, he must be sentenced to perpetual incarceration, which we have judged to be most similar to death. He was merciful, nevertheless, to brigands, thieves, parricides, heretics, and perjurers, whom he would send into jail as if into a workhouse. They, afterwards, released like starving lions from a cage, raged against every decent man.")

Plęrosque ... latrones: acc. obj. of *redigere*

poena carceris: abl. of means and appositional gen., "with the punishment of prison"; Paul chose not to use the death penalty

Paul discouraged humanistic education, favoring only practical literacy

86 Humanitatis autem studia ita oderat et contemnebat [398] ut eius studiosos uno nomine haereticos appellaret. Hanc ob rem Romanos adhortabatur ne filios diutius in studiis litterarum versari paterentur; satis esse si legere et scribere didicissent.

---

adhortor, -ari, -atus sum: urge
appello, -are, -avi, -atus: call
contemno, -ere, contempsi, contemptus: despise
disco, -ere, didici, - : learn
diu (*adv.*): for a long time
haereticus, -i *m.*: heretic
humanitas, -tatis *f.*: culture, civilization
lego, -ere, legi, lectus: read

litterae, -arum *f.*: letters; literature
odi, odisse, -, - : to hate
patior, pati, passus sum: allow
satis (*adv.*): enough
scribo, -ere, scripsi, scriptus: write
studiosus, -a, -um: devoted to
studium, -i *n.*: eagerness; study
versor, -ari, -atus sum: spend time

Humanitatis ... studia: the humanities; humanistic education; Platina had originally written that Paul hated *Litteratos* ("the educated")

oderat: pluperf. form but imperf. meaning

eius studiosos: obj. gen., "devoted to it"; the *eius* should be *eorum*, referring to *studia*, but Platina is treating the humanities as conceptually singular

haereticos: a reference to Platina's own imprisonment, and esp. ch. 65 above

ne ... paterentur: ind. command; verb is imperf. subjunctive

diutius: compar. adv.

satis esse: ind. statement with no explicit verb setting it up; rather, it is suggested that this conveys the substance of his exhortation

si ... didicissent: subjunctive in a subordinate clause in ind. statement

Paul could be unkind to those asking favors, but he ultimately delivered more than he had promised

87 Durus interdum et inexorabilis, si quid ab eo peteres, habebatur; neque hoc contentus, convicia et probra in te coniiciebat*; plura tamen praestabat quam vultu facturum prae se ferret.

---

coniicio, -iicere, -ieci, -iectus: throw/pile together
contentus, -a, -um: content (+ *abl.*)
convicium, -i *n.*: noise; reprimand; abuse
durus, -a, -um: hard; harsh
fero, ferre, tuli, latus: bear; say
inexorabilis, -e: inexorable

interdum (*adv.*): sometimes
peto, -ere, -ivi, -itus: ask (for)
prae: before, in front of (+ *abl.*)
praesto, -are, -avi, -atus: fulfill; carry out
probrum, -i *n.*: disgrace; insult
vultus, -us *m.*: face, expression

---

si quid … peteres: cond. is mixed, with hypothetical protasis and factual apodosis, "if you were asking for … anything"; note *quid* (after *si, nisi, num* and *ne*, "*ali*" takes a holiday)

habebatur: "was considered (to be)"

coniiciebat*: Platina originally wrote and then later crossed out before printing: *coniiciebat; simultatum antiquarum memor iniurias ulciscebatur; plura* ("Mindful of old rivalries, he would avenge any injuries")

plura tamen … se ferret: in the manuscripts, Platina added this phrase in the margins

plura: acc. pl. neut. compar. of *multus*, here substantively "more (things)"

quam: "than"

vultu: abl. of means

facturum: ind. statement introduced by *ferret*; he actually does more than his expression suggests that he would when one is in his presence

Paul kept his underlings in check, which was appreciated by the Romans and the court

88 Uno tamen postremo laudari potest, quod domi monstra non aluerit, quodque domesticos suos et familiares in officio continuerit, ne ob fastum et insolentiam populo Romano et aulicis stomachum facerent.

---

alo, -ere, -ui, -itus: nourish, rear
aulicus, -i *m.*: courtier
contineo, -tinere, -tinui, -tentus: preserve; restrain
domesticus, -i *m.*: household member
familiaris, -is *m./f.*: household member
fastus, -us *m.*: arrogance

insolentia, -ae *f.*: insolence
laudo, -are, -avi, -atus: praise
monstrum, -i *n.*: monster
officium, -i *n.*: office; rightful place
populus, -i *m.*: people
postremus, -a, -um: final
stomachus, -i *m.*: annoyance, anger

---

quod ... aluerit: noun clause, "the fact that," in apposition to the substantive *Uno ... postremo*

domi: locative

quodque ... continuerit: a noun clause coordinated with the previous one, "and the fact that ... "

ne ... facerent: neg. purpose clause

Common Vocabulary

A a

ab, a: by, from (+ *abl.*)

ac: and, and also

ad: to, up to, towards (+ *acc.*), see also Introduction 7.B

alius, -a, -ud: other, another

alter, -a, -um: one (of two), another, other

ante: (*adv.*) before, previously; before, in front of (+ *acc.*)

apud: at, near, in the presence of, in the home of (+ *acc.*)

at: but

aut: or

autem: however; moreover

B b

bellum, -i *n.*: a war, combat

bellus, -a, -um: beautiful, excellent

bonus, -a, -um: good

C c

causa, -ae *f.*: a cause, reason; for the sake of (+ *gen.*)

cum: with (*prep.* + *abl.*); when (+ *indic.*); when, since, although (+ *subjunctive*)

credo, -ere, credidi, creditus: believe

D d

de: down from, about, concerning (+ *abl.*)

dico, -ere, dixi, dictus: to say

domus, -i *f.*: house, home

duco, -ere, duxi, ductus: lead

dum: while, until; see also Introduction 7.C

E e

ego, mei, mihi, me: I, me (*personal*); myself (*reflexive*)

enim: indeed, for

eo, ire, ivi(ii), itus: to go

et: and, even, also

etiam: also, even

ex, e: out of, from (+ *abl.*)

F f

facio, -ere, feci, factus: to make, do

femina, -ae *f.*: woman

filia, -ae *f.*: daughter

filius, -i *m.*: son

frater, fratris *m.*: brother; monk

H h

habeo, -ere, -ui, -itus: to have, hold; to consider

hic, haec, hoc: this; these (*pl.*)

homo, hominis *m.*: a human being; man; see also Introduction 7.E

I i

idem, eadem, idem: the same

ille, -a, -ud: that

in: in, on, at (+ *abl.*); into, about (+ *acc.*)

inter: between, among; during (+ *acc.*)

ipse, -a, -um: himself, herself, itself

is, ea, id: he, she, it

ita (*adv.*): thus, so

itaque: therefore, and so

iubeo, -ere, iussi, iussus: order, command

M m

magnus, -a, -um: large, great

mater, matris *f.*: mother

meus, mea, meum: my

mitto, -ere, misi, missus: to send

morior, mori, mortuus sum: to die

Common Vocabulary

N n

nam: for, indeed

natura, -ae *f.*: nature

ne: that not, lest (+ *subjunctive*)

nec (*adv.*): nor, and not

nisi: if not, except, unless

nomen, nominis *n.*: name

non (*adv.*): not, by no means, no

noster, nostra, nostrum: our

nunc (*adv.*): now

O o

ob: on account of, against (+ *acc.*)

omnis, -e: each, every

P p

parvus, -a, -um: small, little

pater, patris *m.*: father

Paulus, -i *m.*: Paul

pax, pacis *f.*: peace; harmony

pecunia, -ae *f.*: money

possum, posse, potui, - : to be able, be possible

post: (*adv.*) behind, afterwards; after (+ *acc.*)

puto, -are, -avi, -atus: think, reckon

Q q

quam: how; than (*comparative*)

-que: and (*enclitic*)

qui, quae, quod: who, which, what

quidem (*adv.*): certainly, at least

quod: because, as far as

quoque (*adv.*): likewise, also, too

R r

regina, -ae *f.*: queen

res, rei *f.*: a thing, event, matter

rex, regis *m.*: king

rogo, -are, -avi, -atus: to ask

S s

saepe (*adv.*): often

sed: but, however

semper (*adv.*): always

si: if

sine: without (+ *abl.*)

soror, -oris *f.*: sister

sub: under (+ *abl.*)

sum, esse, fui, futurus: to be, exist

suus, sua, suum: his own, her own, its own

T t

tamen (*adv.*): yet, nevertheless, still

tantus, -a, -um: so much, so great

tum (*adv.*): then, next

U u

unus, -a, -um: one

urbs, urbis *f.*: city

ut: as, when (+ *indic.*); so that, with the result that, that (+ *subj.*)

V v

-ve: or (*enclitic*)

vel: or

venio, -ire, veni, ventus: come

vir, viri *m.*: man

vita, -ae *f.*: life; career

voco, -are, -avi, -atus: to call, name

Made in the USA
San Bernardino, CA
29 December 2018